CAMBRIDGE LIBRARY COLLECTION

Books of enduring scholarly value

Medieval History

This series includes pioneering editions of medieval historical accounts by eye-witnesses and contemporaries, collections of source materials such as charters and letters, and works that applied new historiographical methods to the interpretation of the European middle ages. The nineteenth century saw an upsurge of interest in medieval manuscripts, texts and artefacts, and the enthusiastic efforts of scholars and antiquaries made a large body of material available in print for the first time. Although many of the analyses have been superseded, they provide fascinating evidence of the academic practices of their time, while a considerable number of texts have still not been re-edited and are still widely consulted.

Court Rolls of the Manor of Wakefield

The detailed records of the proceedings of the manorial court of Wakefield provide a unique insight into medieval life and commerce, the many legal disputes arising, and the mechanisms for resolving them. The manor court met every three weeks, as well as holding additional courts, or 'tourns', at various locations around the West Riding of Yorkshire. Recognising the historical significance of these exceptionally complete court records for one of the largest manors in England, in 1901 the Yorkshire Archaeological Society began publishing them as part of its Record Series. Up to 1945, five volumes appeared that span the years 1274–1331. Edited with an introduction and notes by John Lister (1847–1933) and published in 1917, Volume 3 contains the court rolls for the years 1312–13 and 1314–15 along with the surviving portion for 1285–86. The texts of the rolls are given in English translation.

Cambridge University Press has long been a pioneer in the reissuing of out-of-print titles from its own backlist, producing digital reprints of books that are still sought after by scholars and students but could not be reprinted economically using traditional technology. The Cambridge Library Collection extends this activity to a wider range of books which are still of importance to researchers and professionals, either for the source material they contain, or as landmarks in the history of their academic discipline.

Drawing from the world-renowned collections in the Cambridge University Library and other partner libraries, and guided by the advice of experts in each subject area, Cambridge University Press is using state-of-the-art scanning machines in its own Printing House to capture the content of each book selected for inclusion. The files are processed to give a consistently clear, crisp image, and the books finished to the high quality standard for which the Press is recognised around the world. The latest print-on-demand technology ensures that the books will remain available indefinitely, and that orders for single or multiple copies can quickly be supplied.

The Cambridge Library Collection brings back to life books of enduring scholarly value (including out-of-copyright works originally issued by other publishers) across a wide range of disciplines in the humanities and social sciences and in science and technology.

Court Rolls of the Manor of Wakefield

VOLUME 3: 1313 TO 1316, AND 1286

EDITED BY
JOHN LISTER

CAMBRIDGE
UNIVERSITY PRESS

CAMBRIDGE UNIVERSITY PRESS

Cambridge, New York, Melbourne, Madrid, Cape Town,
Singapore, São Paolo, Delhi, Mexico City

Published in the United States of America by Cambridge University Press, New York

www.cambridge.org
Information on this title: www.cambridge.org/9781108058636

© in this compilation Cambridge University Press 2013

This edition first published 1917
This digitally printed version 2013

ISBN 978-1-108-05863-6 Paperback

The Anniversary Reissue of Volumes from the Record Series of the Yorkshire Archaeological Society

To celebrate the 150th anniversary of the foundation of the leading society for the study of the archaeology and history of England's largest historic county, Cambridge University Press has reissued a selection of the most notable of the publications in the Record Series of the Yorkshire Archaeological Society. Founded in 1863, the Society soon established itself as the major publisher in its field, and has remained so ever since. The *Yorkshire Archaeological Journal* has been published annually since 1869, and in 1885 the Society launched the Record Series, a succession of volumes containing transcriptions of diverse original records relating to the history of Yorkshire, edited by numerous distinguished scholars. In 1932 a special division of the Record Series was created which, up to 1965, published a considerable number of early medieval charters relating to Yorkshire. The vast majority of these publications have never been superseded, remaining an important primary source for historical scholarship.

Current volumes in the Record Series are published for the Society by Boydell and Brewer. The Society also publishes parish register transcripts; since 1897, over 180 volumes have appeared in print. In 1974, the Society established a programme to publish calendars of over 650 court rolls of the manor of Wakefield, the originals of which, dating from 1274 to 1925, have been in the safekeeping of the Society's archives since 1943; by the end of 2012, fifteen volumes had appeared. In 2011, the importance of the Wakefield court rolls was formally acknowledged by the UK committee of UNESCO, which entered them on its National Register of the Memory of the World.

The Society possesses a library and archives which constitute a major resource for the study of the county; they are housed in its headquarters, a Georgian villa in Leeds. These facilities, initially provided solely for members, are now available to all researchers. Lists of the full range of the Society's scholarly resources and publications can be found on its website, www.yas.org.uk.

Court Rolls of the Manor of Wakefield, 1313–1316 and 1286
(Record Series volume 57)

The Wakefield manorial court rolls span more than six centuries from 1274 to 1925, making them one of the most comprehensive series now in existence, and the Yorkshire Archaeological Society has been engaged in their publication and preservation for more than a century. The manor of Wakefield was one of the largest in England, covering a huge area of the West Riding of Yorkshire, although it was divided into many sub-manors. The actual area over which the court had jurisdiction during the centuries for which the records survive was approximately 90 square miles. The records of the manor's property transactions, agricultural business and law enforcement are an important source for legal, social and economic historians. In 1898, several members of the Society provided a fund to employ Miss Ethel Stokes, a leading London record agent, to produce translations of the earliest surviving rolls.

This is the third of the five volumes in the Record Series devoted to these early rolls, the others being 29, 36, 78 and 101. Its title is somewhat misleading: in fact, it contains translations of the surviving rolls for 1312–13 and 1314–15 (and not the rolls for 1313–14 and 1315–16), together with the surviving portion of the roll for 1285–6 which, having been in the possession of Sir Thomas Phillipps, the Victorian self-styled 'vello-maniac', was purchased at auction by Sheffield City Library. This roll is now at Sheffield Archives, where it has the reference MD158. The other court rolls published here are owned by the Society and have the references MD225/1/38 and 40.

The editor of this volume, John Lister (1847–1933), prepared several publications for the Record Series, five of which are reissued in the Cambridge Library Collection. An obituary and bibliography of Lister, which can be found in the *Yorkshire Archaeological Journal*, 31 (1934), 423–6, records that he died 'at his ancestral home', Shibden Hall, Halifax, and that – like many of his colleagues in the Society – he was a member of the landed classes, and also a non-practising barrister. His obituary in *The Times* of 13 October 1933 reported that he was a founding member of the Labour Party in Halifax and had twice stood as a parliamentary candidate for the Independent Labour Party.

COURT ROLLS
OF THE MANOR OF WAKEFIELD.

VOL. III.

THE YORKSHIRE
ARCHÆOLOGICAL SOCIETY.

FOUNDED 1863. INCORPORATED 1893.

RECORD SERIES.
VOL. LVII.
FOR THE YEAR 1917.

COURT ROLLS
OF THE
MANOR OF WAKEFIELD.
VOL. III.
1313 to 1316, and 1286.

EDITED BY
JOHN LISTER, M.A.,
of B.N.C., Oxford, and Barrister of the Inner Temple.

PRINTED FOR THE SOCIETY.

1917.

PRINTED BY

J. WHITEHEAD AND SON, ALFRED STREET, BOAR LANE.

LEEDS.

INTRODUCTION.

It is more than fifteen years since the second volume of the *Wakefield Court Rolls* was published, though matter for this and quite another volume has been lying in MS. since 1901 in our Society's Library at Leeds. The two volumes already published were very ably edited, and Introductions written for them, by Mr. W. Paley Baildon. This being the case, so far as an Introduction is concerned to the present volume, it would seem that but a few pages are necessary.

The matter for this volume, however, is not quite entirely drawn from the Rolls preserved in the Manor Court Offices at Wakefield. Not a few of the Rolls, or portions of Rolls, that once were in the hands of the lords of the Wakefield manor, have gone astray, and have found other resting-places. Among these is a considerable section of the Roll for the year 1286. This appears to have come into the possession of the Wilson family of Broomhead, near Bradfield, and, afterwards, from thence into the Phillipps' Library.

When certain Wilson MSS. were sold out of the late Sir Thomas Phillipps' collection, the Sheffield Reference Library was able to purchase this portion of the 1286 Court Roll, as well as an Account Roll of the graveship of Holne[1] of the year 1316. The former consists, as its careful transcriber, Mr. Hermann Thomas [2] states, " of a number of membranes of fine vellum, sewn together head and foot," the writing being " in a clear, neat cursive hand," and " in an excellent state of preservation." The Court Roll—as the transcriber notes—" overlaps slightly in date those already published, but deals with different meetings of the various Courts from July 20th, 13 Edward I [1286] to September 29th of the same year." This MS., which we may call the " Sheffield MS.," is printed at the end of the present volume.

ANCIENT DEMESNE.

The tenants of the Manor of Wakefield " do not seem to have had the privileges of ancient demesne," writes Mr. Baildon, in his

---

[1] Holme.
[2] Keeper of the Records, Guildhall, London.

Introduction to the first volume, published by our Society. Herein, I venture to think, he must be mistaken, for (1) they could not be impleaded out of the Manor, and (2) they were free from toll for all things concerning their husbandry. These were privileges characteristic of tenure in " ancient demesne." So far as freedom from toll was concerned, King Henry VIII, in the first year of his reign, made a grant exempting the Manor of Wakefield, and the towns dependent thereon, from payment of toll, on the principle that, by ancient custom, the tenants of the old demesne lands of the crown had been, and ought to be, free from such payment.[1]

The privilege of being toll-free was confirmed on the accession of each king, which, as the author of the *History of Halifax* observes, shows that the tenants " durst not depend altogether on the custom," although it was such an ancient one.

DATE OF THE GRANT OF THE MANOR.

Regarding the charter containing the gift of certain churches to the Priory of Lewes, viz. Conisborough, Harthill, etc., which proves that the Manor of Wakefield was granted prior to the year 1121 to the Warrens by the King, the grant of the churches being confirmed by a charter dated in that year, it is strange that the names of the witnesses should have escaped the editor of Volume I.

Mr. Watson gives them in his *History of Halifax* as he took them from Archbishop Corbridge's Register at York, and these names Mr. Brown has kindly verified for me. They are Ralph de Waren, Hugh de Petroponte, Ralph de Playz, Robert de Frivele, Reginald de Waren, Adam de Puīg, Gwd. de Mencect, and William de Drossaio. So Watson gives them; but Mr. Brown reads Ralph and Reginald de Waren as Ralph and Reginald de Ware, and can not detect a missing final *n*, though there was probably a mark of contraction now undiscernible. There were two Warrens who respectively bore these Christian names living at this period, so that. I think, we may conclude, in spite of the omission of the final *n*, that these witnesses belonged to the family of William, the second Earl of Warren, who made the charter granting Conisborough, Halifax, and other churches to the monks of Lewes. The other variations in Mr. Brown's readings from those of Mr. Watson are trifling, *e.g.* Frivile, for Frivele, Puning for Puīg, Guydo de Mencect for Gwd. de Mencect. Mr. Baildon apparently hoped that the names of these witnesses might be some clue in deter-

---

[1] See Watson, *Hist. of Halifax*, p. 97.

mining the date of the grant of the Manor of Wakefield and its dependencies to the Warren family. I must confess that these names do not seem to make one much wiser.

SERJEANT OR BAILIFF.

I am inclined to think that, *pace* the Editor of Volume I, the word "serviens," which occurs in the margin of the Rolls, is better translated by "bailiff" than by "serjeant," and I have so translated it. In fact, John de Ravensfeld is often styled "bailiff" not "serjeant" in the Rolls.[1] "Serviens" and "Ballivus" seem to be words indifferently used. In fact, sometimes—as Mr. Baildon admits—it is open to translate "serviens" as merely "servant," and he gives the latter as an alternative in the case of William de Langfeld.[2] The duties of serjeants and bailiffs seem to have been very similar, and *servientes* appear, indeed, to have been, in most cases, the servants of the bailiffs.

On page 39 of this present volume we sometimes find "serviens" written in the margin, but the entry against it runs : "The Earl's bailiff [*ballivus*] charges, etc." It was the duty of the bailiff to make all attachments *per se* or by his deputies,[3] and in these Rolls against all such records the word "serviens," *i.e.* "bailiff," is set down in the margin. Sometimes we find, as in the case of William the Tayllur, that if "serviens" means serjeant, the latter was promoted to be a bailiff, but it is evident that this individual was indifferently described both as "serviens" and "ballivus." On page 71, Volume II, a fine is remitted to him "because he is a 'serviens,'" and yet we find that, at the same time, he was "ballivus," bailiff of the soke of Wakefield, page 73, and on page 68, he was pardoned an offence because "he is the bailiff—'*ballivus*'— of the liberty," and in later Rolls "ballivus," not "serviens" is written in the margin against all attachments, etc.

I can not, therefore, agree with the Editor of Volumes I and II in thinking that the "Serjeant seems to have been next in importance to the Steward."[4] I should rather say that the "Bailiff" held that honourable position.

---

[1] See vol. i, p. 150, where cattle are said to have been delivered up by means of "John de Ravensfeld, the Earl's bailiff."

[2] See p. 111.

[3] See "The Manner of holding Courts." Selden Society, vol. 4, "The Court Baron."

[4] *Introduction*, vol. ii, p. 12.

RASTRICK AND BRIGHOUSE.

I hope I shall not be hypercritical when I point out that on page vii of his Introduction to Volume II, the Editor of that volume has been guilty of a *lapsus calami* in speaking of courts at Rastrick and Brighouse as if they were distinct courts. It was one and the same court under different place-names.[1]

The Editor of the first and second volumes of our Wakefield Court Rolls[2] says "there is no 'custumal' of Wakefield Manor." This may be true, but there are " Extents," or copies of " Extents," existing which give the "customs" of the Manor in a very considerable measure. These, which have not been previously referred to in connection with the Rolls, it is, I think, well for any one interested in the subject to pay a little attention to. Of the value of such " Extents " or " Computi " let F. W. Maitland, in *Select Pleas in Manorial and other Seignorial Courts*, published by the Selden Society, bear his evidence.[3] He writes: " We are in good luck when we can compare a court roll with an extent; the one supplements the other; the extent tells us of the tenure and the status of the actors who appear on the court roll; the court roll shows us how great or how small is the influence which distinctions of tenure and of status have on the behaviour of suitors and litigants. The extent displays the manor at rest, the court roll the manor in motion; the one is statical, the other dynamical."

But are there any early Extents of the Wakefield Manor existing? Mr. Taylour has printed, in his *History of the Rectorial Manor of Wakefield*, an " Extent of Wakefield Soke, made on Christmas Day in the year of our Lord 1300," and he says, in reference to this document, that " the MS., from which the translation and the notes are transcribed, appears to be a copy." Whitaker gives, in *Loidis and Elmete*, an extract from this Extent, which is stated to be " from a roll formerly in the possession of the Rev. Brian Allott, of Bilham."

A Computus of the manor made in 1305 is an interesting document, and throws considerable light on the income derived from it by the lords who owned it.

This Computus was made by John de Doncaster, chief steward

---

[1] "Within the said lordship the King's Majestie hath Leetes kept yerelie in Halifax; and two other Leetes yerelie & three wekes Courtes beside Leetes in Wakefeld; two Leetes at Brighous; & two at Birton; and one other Courte monethlie in the Borough Town [*i.e.* Wakefeld] there." *From a Survey of the Manor of Wakefield made* 36, 37, Hen. viii.

[2] Vol. ii, p. xx.

[3] *Introduction*, p. xiv, vol. ii, Selden Society.

of the manor, who had the custody thereof, along with Master Richard de Haveringes, by virtue of a brief from the king, John de Warren, being under age at the death of his grandfather, John de Warren, Earl of Surrey, in 1304. Mr. Baildon remarks, in his Introduction to Volume II (p. 1), that " the Inquisition taken after the latter's death, if any, has·not been preserved." " This is most unfortunate," he adds, " as we might have had some interesting details of the Yorkshire property." This Computus of 1305, however, gives, at any rate, some details in reference thereto that are worth, in my opinion, recording.[1]

There is also, in the P.R.O., an Extent of the Manor of Sandal, made in 1309,[2] of which considerable use will be made in these pages.

Then we have portions of the same Extent of the manor made in 1309, which give full particulars relating to the graveships of Rastrick, Hipperholme, and Sowerby. The Extents of Rastrick, Hipperholme, and Sowerby are sixteenth century copies, made before 1585, of originals now apparently lost. These copies were transcribed by me many years ago in the Phillipps' Library at Cheltenham, where they then were reposing.[3]

Mr. Watson, in his *History of Halifax*, gives extracts from yet another Extent made at Christmas, 1314.[4] He, also, only had a copy before him, and he merely extracted therefrom certain particulars relating to Halifax parish. Then, lastly, in 1316, we have the Holne Computus, made by the Grave of that place, Adam Strakeys, and to the end of this is attached an interesting computus rendered by John de Amyas, regarding the market tolls of the town of Wakefield, the perquisites of the Court of the Burgesses there, and of the fulling mill, and of two water corn mills in the same town, together with the mills of Thurstanhawe [Thurstonland], Horbury, and Cartworth, all of which he farmed under the Earl. The roll is endorsed on the back, " *Computus Ballivi de Wakfeud et aliorum Ministrorum.*"

Of all the Computi and Extents of the Manor of Wakefield, by far the most interesting rental, in my opinion, is to be found in a " Contrariant Roll," dated 24th March, 15 Edward II [1322],

---

[1] *See* Appendix I.

[2] Duchy of Lancaster Surveys, ${}^{11}_{22}$.

[3] Published by the Halifax Antiquarian Society, Record Series, vol. ii, 1914.

Watson, *Hist. of Halifax*, p. 140.

on the occasion of the sequestration of the estates of Thomas, Earl of Lancaster, who was executed the next day, March 25th, on account of his being the leader of the barons in their rebellion against the king. This Roll gives a very complete list of the names of the principal free tenants and their rents, the number of cattle in the various vaccaries, the provisions and furniture stored in Sandal Castle, the horses and cattle there, armour and arms, etc. It also furnishes particulars of the rents of the free and neif tenants, and other particulars relating to the various graveships in the manor. It is a document that, I consider, is well worthy of being printed in full, some day, for our Society.

It is interesting to learn from these accounts what salary obtained in those days for a Chief Steward of a manor, the wages of foresters, and other officials.

THE EXTENTS OF 1309.

The Extent of Rastrick, and, presumably, those also of Hipperholme and Sowerby, were made at Wakefield on the Thursday next after the Feast of St. Matthew [September 21st], and that of Sandal on Tuesday after that of St. Faith [October 6th], 1309, before Ranulph de Folesham and his companions, the "auditors of Earl Warren's accounts."

FREE TENANTS.

The number of Free Tenants in Sandal was 10, of whom 8 held 31 oxgangs amongst them, ranging from 13 held by Master Robert of Ketelthorp to a minimum of 1 by some of the others. The oxgang is stated to have consisted of 14 [one case only], 12 or 10 acres, but 12 seems to have been the normal number in Sandal, while in Rastrick and Hipperholme it was, almost invariably, 14. In Sowerby it was 15, save in Warley in that graveship, where, the Extent tells us, it was 18, and in Soyland township, in the same graveship, it did not exceed 10. The difference, of course, was caused by the physical features of the district—the team of oxen in a flat country naturally ploughing far more acres in the course of a daywork than in a hilly one. The local "daywork" superficial measurement, even now—where it still survives—varies sometimes in townships adjacent to one another.

Turning to the Rastrick Extent, we find that there were 22 tenants—some of them joint tenants—who held oxgang land, and 44 who held acres [i.e. roydland], but, of these latter, 16 at least held lands under both tenures.

There were in Rastrick and Fixby 11 oxgangs the tenants of which had to "make the mill dam at Wakefield, as often as shall be necessary." This signifies that all the oxgang land in this graveship was of the nature of villein land, but does not mean that some of the tenants who held them were not free men; but they were so as holding other land of a freehold nature. We read in Lyttelton's *Tenures*, under the heading of "Villenage" [Lib. ii, c. 11]: "Some free tenauntes holde theyr tenementes, after the custom of certaine manours, by such services [as *e.g.* making the mill dam], and theyr tenure is called tenure in vyllenage, and yet they be no villaines. For no land holden in villenage or villaine landes, or any custome rising of the lande shal never make free man villain." Thus, for example, in the Extent of the year 1314, quoted by Watson, we find that John del Okes held in Rastrick freely a toft as well as one of these eleven oxgangs, which were charged with the repair of the Wakefield mill dam.

According to the 1314 Extent, there were only 3 freemen in the town of Rastrick, while there were 9 in the town of Fixby. The rents paid by some of these freemen, and also their holdings, seem to have been small, especially in the case of Alexander del Okes, of Brighouse, who held one perch and paid 1*d.* a year. Perhaps, such as he held land also in other graveships.

In the Hipperholme Extent of 1309, there is a long list of freemen holding native, *i.e.* villein, land, 48 in all, and 54 tenants described as "natives." None of the 48 in this case held any of the oxgang land.

There were only two free tenants in Sandal who rented no oxgang land, and they only held 1¾ acres between them. One of the holders of oxgang land also rented a toft containing half an acre at a rent of 8*d.* a year. A perch or rod, in these days—as the Extent tells us—consisted of 20 feet, 6⅔ yards, but, in some places, we know it was 7 yards; and a "rood," *i.e.* a rod or perch of walling, even in our days in the neighbourhood of Halifax, is still of this measurement. In fact, the mile in Yorkshire used to be as long as is the Irish mile at present, the rod of seven yards being the unit on which it was based.

SERVICES AND RENTS OF FREEHOLD TENANTS.

These in the Sandal Extent are set down as homage, rents, customary payments for the keep of swine [called "Thistletakes"], ploughing the lord's demesne lands, if the tenant possessed a plough and team, reaping and suit of court, and, in one exceptional instance, making the mill dam at Wakefield. This villein service seems to have been put upon· Master Robert de Kettelthorpe in respect of 12 oxgangs of land which had only been granted to him for the term of his life, and was not due for the rest of his land, which he " held freely."

FREEHOLD RENTS.

The Editor of Volume II of our Rolls remarks in his Introduction that " freehold quit-rents were very common on north-country manors, and although they do not appear very prominently on these Rolls, there are a few instances."

The Extents show that they were universal in the Manor of Wakefield. The free tenants in Sandal paid various yearly rents for their oxgangs, in some cases 2s. per oxgang, in others 1s. 1½d., in others 1s. 8d. Doubtless, as now, the quality of the land was a factor in fixing the rent.

In Sandal, the land let by " acre-tale " also varies in rent, being sometimes 4d., sometimes 4½d. per acre. In Rastrick and Hipperholme it is usually 4d. an acre, occasionally 3d.

THISTLETAKE RENTS.

The free tenants had also, throughout the manor, to pay at the feast of St. Andrew the " consuetudo porcorum "—the customary payment for keeping swine. In the Rastrick Extent we are told that " there are in the same place certain customs of pigs called ' thistle-takes,' two pigs at the Feast of St. Martin yearly, as is contained in the Rolls of Accounts for the time of King Henry." All the jurors who swore the Extent of 1309 were amerced because they had concealed the fact that this custom of claiming two pigs or their value held good there. This " thistletake " rent was exclusive of the charges made for pannage in the woods, for the Rastrick Extent goes on to say: " It is to be known also that the tenants of the graveship of Rastrick shall agist their swine in the Hipperholme wood, if they have any, and shall give pannage, viz. for each pig of their own breeding, 2d., and for each pigling, 1d., and for each pig bought, 3d." This last payment of 3d. is explained in the Hipperholme Extent to be due on pigs bought to sell again, " whether they shall be feeding on acorns or not." The term " thistletake " was usually shortened into " tak," when it occurs in the Extents.

The custom of swine was payable, the Sandal Extent tells us, as well by free as by neif tenants, and also the services of ploughing and reaping had to be rendered by both classes of tenants. In Sandal, the rents of the free tenants amounted to 39s. 9d. The ploughing services, five in number, rendered by the free tenants, were valued at 2d. each net, and the reaping services, six in number, 1½d. net. The tenants in Hipperholme paid every Easter 4d. if they had a full plough [team], and 1d. for reaping at Michaelmas. Similar payments have already been noted in regard to the Rastrick graveship. Mr. Baildon, in his Introduction to Volume II of our Rolls, does not seem to have realised that the ploughing and reaping, or the commuted payments for these services, fell on free tenants as well as on villein ones, as the Extents testify.

PLOUGHING THE LORD'S DEMESNE AND REAPING HIS CORN.

One day's ploughing was required of the free tenants, provided they possessed a plough and team of oxen, and they were to have one meal, costing 1½d., and the service of ploughing was valued at 2d. beyond the cost of the meal. A free tenant had to find a man for one day to reap the lord's corn, and a meal was provided costing ¾d., and the value of the service beyond the cost of the meal was, in this case, assessed at 1½d.

It is interesting to note that the service of ploughing was not at this time commuted at Sandal into a money payment, while in more distant graveships, such as Rastrick and others, it had been commuted into a money payment. Thus, in the Rastrick Extent, there is this " Memorandum ": " That every tenant holding lands in Stainland and Barkisland, who has a plough, shall give to the Earl yearly for one ploughing, 4d., and if he have half a plough he will give 2d., and if four neighbours have only one plough they will give to the lord for the ploughing boon 4d. in common." The same terms are in the Extent stated to apply to Fixby, but nothing is said as to their application to Rastrick. The reaping boon was also, like the ploughing service, commuted in places distant from the lord's demesne. Two houses in Rastrick were to give for reaping 3d. each, and " every house whence smoke issues " in Fixby " had to give for reaping 1d.," and there " were four houses there," each of which had to " give for reaping 4d." In Hipperholme the tenants of the under-lords, viz. Sir Hugh de Eland, John de Stansfeld, and Richard de Hipperholme, had to give the same sums as those above-mentioned for ploughing, and, if they had fires on their hearths, towards the custom of reaping 1*d*. Nothing is said about the other free tenants in Hipperholme in regard to these boons, but, doubtless, they were liable to these services, though as they held immediately of the lords of Wakefield, while the others held indirectly, it was not thought necessary to mention the matter in this particular Extent

It would appear that there was a considerable amount of sub-letting in the Manor of Wakefield. For instance, under Sandal, in the Computus of 1322, we find that all the freehold rents there are stated as being received from tenants of five individuals, viz. of Robert Atte-well, Thomas Coke, William del Okes, and John Skinner [*pelliparius*]. As the sum of the rents corresponds very nearly with that given in the 1309 Computus as payable by all the ten free tenants in that graveship, it would seem that five of the latter were under-tenants. In Quarnby there was a mesne lord, John de Quarnby, lord of the manor of that ilk, and in Toot-hill there was also a small sub-manor, of which, in 1322, Thomas de Tothill was the lord. Their tenants were accountable for the quit rents due to the chief lord of Wakefield. The free tenants of Rastrick—no names given—in 1322 paid for half a year's rent, 13*s*. 9*d*. The tenants of Thomas de Thornton and of Henry Frankish in Stainland, for the same period, 8*s*. 8*d*., and 32*s*. was paid by the tenants of Hugh de Tothill, Henry de Northwode, Richard del Rokes, Adam de Steyncliffe [Stancliff], John de Shipedene, and those of Sir John de Thornhill, knt., who were the principal free-holders there, and others in Hipperholme. So was it in other grave-ships and townships. A receipt of 2*s*. 1*d*. issuing from a toft and three acres of land formerly assigned, by a deed of Earl Warren, for the sustenance of lepers, and let to one German Filcok, is an interesting item. German was a trader who had booths in Wakefield market.

THE VILLEIN TENANTS.

The copyhold tenants in Sandal were 79, most of whom held oxgangs, but others were rented by their tale of acres. Their copy-hold oxgangs consisted of 16, 15, 14, 12, and 10 acres, but the normal number seems to be 14. There were 33½ oxgangs in Sandal held by 26 copyhold or customary tenants, and about 403 acres—not oxgang land—held by 53 tenants. Two other neif tenants of the graveship of Sandal paid rent only for houses and curtilages, and one appears to have been rented only on his swine. The

Extent tells us that " all the neifs shall be tallaged at the Lord's will, and shall give heriots, pay marchet, and lecherwite. They have to make the mill dam, and shall make suit at the lord's mill and pay 1 vessel in 16 for the grinding of their corn. They shall give for every pig of their own rearing in the time of pannage, 2d., and for every pigling [*hoggettus*], 1d. And if they buy pigs after the Nativity of St. John, they shall give 3d., and for piglings, 2d."[1]

In Rastrick there are—the Extent says—" eleven oxgangs of land, each of which contains in itself 14 acres, which ought to make the mill dam of Wakefield, with other customs of the Soke of Wakefield, and as often as shall be necessary." " Marchet " is thus referred to in the Rastrick Extent: " If any of the aforesaid neifs shall give his daughter in marriage, he shall pay fine according to the Earl's will, and also for making his son a clerk. And if the Lord the Earl desire tallage or aid from his men and his tenants, they shall give aid." The Hipperholme Extent also enjoins the payment of lecherwite, which the Rastrick one, accidentally, I suppose, omits. The Hipperholme and Rastrick tenants were all to grind their corn at Rastrick mill. The former, however, we know from other sources, had the opportunity of resorting to Shibden mill, which was dependent at first on that of Rastrick. The Sowerby tenants made use of the lord's mills at Warley, Soyland, and Saltonstall.

RENTS OF COPYHOLD LAND.

The rents of the copyholders seem to vary with the number of acres contained in the oxgangs of which the holdings consisted. Thus Peter the Shepherd, in Sandal, paid 5s. 3d. yearly for a 14-acre oxgang, while Agnes de Ossete and John son of Malle, for a 12-acre oxgang, paid 4s., and John Cokewald, for a 15-acre one, 4s., and so on. But some oxgangs, though consisting of the same number of acres, vary in their rents.

When the land was held by " acre-tale " the rent per acre was usually, if not invariably, 4d.

THISTLETAKE.

The " custom of pigs " was similar in its application to copyhold tenants as to the freeholders. The same demands were made upon both classes of tenants, and, in the summing-up of the Sandal Extent, the total receipts for the year, under this heading, " *tam de liberis quam de nativis*," are totalled up to 23s. 3d.

---

[1] *hoggetti.* A hogget seems to have signified a young pig, two years old.

PLOUGHING AND REAPING.

These services correspond in the case of the neifs with those rendered by the free tenants, and do not seem to have been more irksome. If they had a plough [team] they had to plough one day in the year, having a meal value $1\frac{1}{2}d.$, the value of the day's work being priced at $2d.$ if no meal was found. Also they had to reap, or each tenant had to find a reaper, one day in the year, who received a meal value $\frac{3}{4}d.$; the day's work, without food found, being valued at $1\frac{1}{2}d.$ These are the same figures as we have noted in the case of the freemen. In Rastrick and Hipperholme, where, owing probably to the distance of those graveships from the demesne lands, the services were commuted, the neifs, like the free tenants, paid $4d.$ for a whole plough team towards the "custom of ploughing," and $1d.$ for "the custom of reaping," chargeable upon every house that kept a fire on its hearth.

MAKING OF THE MILL DAM.

This service was the one distinctive service that marked off copyhold tenure from freehold. While even the free tenants had to plough and reap, at least one day a year, they had not at any rate to render this service of repairing and maintaining the mill dam at Wakefield.

Mr. Watson, in his *History of Halifax*, gives from the Extent of the Manor of Wakefield made in 1314, which he had the opportunity of seeing, "a list of the lands which were then bound to the repair of the mill dam." I think I may be excused for reproducing this. It runs as follows:

> *Sandal-cum-Crigllestone.*—$34\frac{1}{2}$ oxgangs, and 400 acres.
> *Ossett-cum-Gawthorpe and Earlsheaton.*—$37\frac{1}{2}$ oxgangs, and 34 acres and a toft.
> *Stanley-cum-Wrenthorpe.*—$13\frac{1}{4}$ oxgangs, and 319 a. 1 r. 1 p.
> *Alverthorpe.*—1 oxgang, and $32\frac{1}{2}$ acres.
> *Thornes.*—$2\frac{1}{2}$ oxgangs, and 32 acres.
> *Rastrick and Hipperholme.*—8 oxgangs, and $90\frac{1}{2}$ acres.
> *Wakefield.*—95 a. 3 r.[1]

In Volume II, p. 108, is an instance of the payment by a Stanley copyhold tenant of $4s.$ to a man whom he had hired for work on the mill dam. Of course, in the great majority of cases, the labour on the dam was done by proxy. This service was, I believe, entirely

---

[1] See Watson, *History of Halifax*, p. 124.

commuted in 1663, or thereabouts. On pages 169, 175, 178 of this volume there is an interesting case connected with a multure dish at Cartworth mill. The miller, in this instance, though successful at first in asserting his innocence, was eventually convicted.

ROYD LAND.

Royd Land, corrupted in its spelling about the sixteenth century from "rode-land," was, of course, land that had been ridded of trees, enclosed, and brought into cultivation. In the Extents it is subdivided into old rode-land and new rode-land, and there seem to have been some differences in regard to the conditions of the tenures. At a Court, held at Wakefield, 1st April, 1307, an Inquisition found that certain land in Alverthorpe was " villein land, because it owes aid to the lord, and [the holder] has to be grave." Asked if it is part of the villein bovates [otherwise oxgangs] they say it is not, " but it is called ' rode-land,' because it was cleared from growing wood." In another case, relating to Sandal, Agnes de Ossete is recorded as surrendering two bovates, " and a bovate called ' rode-land.' "

We find that tenants of " new land," as distinguished from the old royd-land, paid higher rents than the latter were accustomed to pay. In the Sowerby Extent, while the former paid 6d. an acre, the latter were rented at 4d. These figures seem almost invariable, though sometimes the old rode-land is only priced at 3d. per acre. All the land held by acre-tale in the various graveships seems to have been of the nature of " rode-land," as one would naturally expect it to have been.

There are very many other interesting points to note in the Court Rolls and in the Extents, but I fear that this Introduction has already grown to an inordinate length. In the Appendix will be found an interesting account, taken in 1316, from the Holne [Holmfirth] computus of the receipts and expenditure of John de Amias, the farmer, of the town, markets, and mills of Wakefield, and also one relating to Cartworth Mill of the same date. Mr. S. J. Chadwick, in his account of Kirklees Priory, gives an interesting note regarding the John de Amyas, who farmed the town of Wakefield, and other members of his family.[1]

The text of this volume has been prepared by Miss Stokes— transcribed by her many years ago with great care and accuracy. I have checked her work with the original Rolls myself.

[1] See *Yorks. Arch. Journal*, vol. xxii, p. 422.

The grateful thanks of the Society are due again to the Earl and Countess of Yarborough, Lord and Lady of the Manor. I have, moreover, to record my obligations to Messrs. Stewart and Chalker, Stewards of the Manor, for their readiness to permit me the privilege of, at all times, examining the Rolls, and to Mr. Gascoigne and Mr. Milner for their help and assistance in searching them.

The Rev. Carus Vale Collier, M.A., F.S.A., has very kindly compiled the Index — no trivial labour. Miss Stokes, moreover, who has copied and translated the Rolls at Wakefield so carefully, should not by any means be overlooked in our tribute of grateful recognitions.

Notes relating to the subject matter will be found at the end of the volume.

J. LISTER.

Wakefield Court Rolls.

[*mem.* 1.]

PLEAS and PERQUISITES of the Soke of Wakefeld, from Michaelmas, [6] Edw. II [1313], to the Michaelmas following;
in the time of John de [Dane]cas[tr]e, Steward.

COURT at Wakefeld on Friday, the Feast of St. Faith the Virgin,
[Oct. 6], in the year abovesaid.

ESSOINS.—Thomas de Langefeld, by Thomas de Northland.
Surety: John Patrik. He afterwards came.

John, s. of John de Soland, by Thomas the Clerk.

John de Podesay, attorney of Lady Margaret de Nevill, by
John the Smith [*faber*] of Walton. Surety: Robert Heyrode.

Robert Patrik, by John Patrik. Surety: William the Heyr.

Matthew de Bosco, by Thomas de Wytteley. Surety: William
del Okes.

Elias de Birton, by German Kay. Surety: William de Castilford.

John de Querneby, by John del Clay.

Dom. Reginald Flemmang, by Adam de Linne.

Thomas de Seyvill, by William de Castilford.

Thomas de Heton, by Robert Brok. Surety: John de Thornhill.

Richard de Birstall, by William Eril. Surety: William Wyldebore.

The suit [*loquela*] between Richard Hodde, plaintiff, and Elias
son of Ivo and Robert de Saltonstall *re* a plea of debt is respited
until the Turn of Halifax.

Adam de Lynne is plaintiff against John de Warren, Rector of
the church of Dewsbiry, Alan de Furneys and William the Bailiff
[*servientem*] of Dewsbiry *re* a plea of unjust detention of cattle. The
defendants were distrained in two horses, but did not appear,
therefore a further distress is to be levied.

Robert de Staynton, attorney of Godefrey de Staynton and of
Robert de Mora, executors of William de Staynton, essoin against
William Wytebelt, by William de Norton.

A

BAILIFF.—John, s. of Henry de Fekesby, 6*d.* for sundry defaults. William Grenehode and the said John [6*d.*] agree.

John de Mora makes his law against John Cussing, who is amerced 4*d.* for false claim.

Robert de Thurstanland and Ivo the Smith [*faber*] [6*d.*] agree, on condition of Ivo paying Robert 10*s.* sterling. Surety : Robert the clerk of Horbiry.

William the Goldsmith and Henry Erl [6*d.*] agree by license.

ALVIRTHORP.—Roger de Mara, 6*d.* for not prosecuting suit against Richard Withundes.

Anabilla Wlf, 3*d.* for license to agree with William, s. of Thomas, on a charge of slander.

BAILIFF.—Alexander de Wodehouse, 6*d.* for non-appearance of John de Querneby, whom he attached.

[? STANL]AY.—Ellen, wife of Richard Isabell, 3*d.* for not prosecuting suit against Emma Walhoc.

William de Bello-monte, 6*d.* for defaults.

Thomas de Dro[? n]sefeld, fined for the same, but pardoned at the instance of Dom. Henry de Percy, and because he fined afterwards.

Nicholas de Cayly, 6*d.* for the same.

Thomas de Schefeld to be distrained for the same.

John del Quithill, 6*d.* for contempt.

SANDALE.—Henry Fox gives 12*d.* for license to take 1½ acres in Crigleston from John, s. of William de Plegwyk.

Thomas, s. of Roger, 6*d.* to take 1½ perches there from Robert, s. of Richard Beausir.

William, s. of William de Wodethorp, 4*s.* as a heriot on 1½ bovates in Sandale, after the death of John del Wro, his brother, whose heir he is.

William de Sandale, 10*s.* for license to take 1½ bovates in Sandale from . . . . . de Wodethorp.

. . . . . [?]AY.—Gilbert de Kendale, 2*s.* for license to marry Matilda, d. of Philip de Horbiry, and to live with his goods on the land Matilda holds in custody for John, her son, until said John is of age.

HIPERUM.—William de Haylay and John, s. of John de Haldeworth, give 6*d.* for license to take 4 acres in Hyperum, left unoccupied by John de Haldeworth 10 years ago.

New rent.—William de Sunderland gives 6*d.* to take an acre of new land between Stanclifrode and . . . . . . , at 6*d.* yearly.

[HOLNE ?].—Thomas [? C]ouper, 12*d.* to take [2] acres of new land in Thwong ; rent, 4*d.* an acre.

Jordan the Milner, 12*d.* for two acres there ; rent, 4*d.* an acre.

. . . . .—Henry the Syour, 12*d.* for 2 acres in Fouleston, at 4*d.* an acre.

Hugh del Hole, 6*d.* for an acre of waste land in Alstanlay ; rent, 4*d.*

Alan de Alstanlay, 2*d.* for a perch of the same ; rent, 1*d.*
[*mem.* 1 *dors.*]

HIPERUM ; new rent.—John de Holway gives 2*s.* for license to take an acre of waste land in Holkanleghis, at 3*d.* rent.

ALVIRTHORP.—William Grenehod, 6*d.* to take an acre of land in Neuton fields from Adam Gerbod for 9 years.

WAKEFELD.—Henry de Wald sues John Peger for taking his corn from the scales [?] [*scaloppa*] of the mill, and throwing it down in the mill. John acknowledges it, and is to pay damages ; fine, 2*s.* Surety : Robert Peger.

ALVIRTHORP.—Adam Gerbot, 3*d.* for false claim against German Swerd.

OSSETE.—William Hyrnyng sues Robert Sonneman for ¼ bovate of land in Gaukethorp, part of his inheritance from Richard Hirning, his father, into which Robert had entry through Ralph Hyrning, plaintiff's brother, who had no right therein, as is shewn by the rolls of Peter du Lounde, at the Court held at Wakefeld on Friday after the Feast of St. Dyonisius, 23 Edw. I. Defendant cannot deny, so William is to recover ; fine, 12*d.*

ALVIRTHORP.—William, s. of William, serving-man of Gerbot of Alvirthorp, has license for God's sake, because he is poor, to heriot a certain piece of a curtilage, after his father's death.

THORNES.—An inquisition finds that Robert Peger slandered Agnes Wlf, by saying she loosed her horses feeding on the common, with a view of their escaping into the Earl's meadow, for which she is amerced 40*d.*; he is to pay damages, fine 6*d.*

STANLEY.—Henry de Ayketon, and Ellen and Isabella, daughters of Symon de Everingham, give 12*d.* as a heriot on 6 acres of meadow and a toft, etc., in Stanley, after the death of Eva de Ayketon, mother of the said Henry, and aunt of Ellen and Isabella.

OSSETE ; new rent.—Thomas Hog and Adam, s. of William s. of Jordan, give 12*d.* to take a thicket [*spinetum*] in Ossete, to include in their paddock [*parcus*] between the . . . . . rode and Richardpyghel, from Richard, s. of Bate, and John Maunsel ; new rent, ½*d.*

STANLEY.—Robert, s. of Ralph de Stanley, gives 6*d.* to take ½ acre of meadow in Stanley for 6 years [*from whom not stated*].

ATTORNEY.—Margaret de Nevylle appoints Hugh the Nodder her attorney to do suit of court, by the King s writ and by his letters patent.

Attachments.

STANLEY.—Nicholas de Bateley, 6*d.*; Robert Leper, 4*d.*; Simon de Monte, 2*d.*; John Cockespore, 1*d.*, all for pannage ; John Page, serving-man of Richard del Bothem, 3*d.* for shaking down acorns ; John de St. Swithin, 3*d.* for dead wood ; Julian the Diker, 2*d.* for beasts carried outside the paling [*sic, but quære*] ; Beatrice Gunne, 3*d.*; Robert del Spen's widow, 3*d.*; the wife of Benedict del Stanley, 3*d.*, all for same ; Peter the Pinder, 6*d.* for escapes.

ALVIRTHORP.—John Broun, 6*d.*; Adam Wlf, 2*d.*; Henry Wlf, 3*d.*, and Adam Gerbot, 4*d.* for escapes.

OSSETE.—Richard Snart, 6*d.*; Henry Alcok's wife, 2*d.*; Alice, wife of the Carpenter, 2*d.*; Swayn de Ossete, 4*d.*; Richard Pasmer, 5*d.*; John, s. of Richard, 2*d.*; Roger the Colier's wife, 2*d.* for wood, etc.

WAKEFELD.—Robert the Mareschall, 6*d.*; John Peger, 3*d.*; Julian the Roper, 2*d.*; Juliana Yolmer, 2*d.*; Johanna Leget, 2*d.*; the daughter of Robert the Goldsmith, senior, 3*d.*; Ellen, d. of Robert de Vrennegate, 2*d.*; Alice Coly, 2*d.*; the son of Robert s. of Ralph, 3*d.*; William the Goldsmith, 2*d.*; John Clement's handmaid, 2*d.*; the daughters of Roger Wassche and Adam de Castelforthe, 2*d.* each, of Elias, s. of Peter, and Walter Ape, 3*d.* each ; John Leche's daughter, 2*d.*; the handmaids of William Bull and Henry Bull, 2*d.* each ; John Kay, 4*d.*; Thomas the Roller, 3*d.*; Robert Liftfast's handmaid, 2*d.*; Robert the Couper's wife, 2*d.*; the son of Hugh the Chapman, 2*d.*; John Clement, 3*d.*; Robert the Yunger, 2*d.*; the daughter of Robert the Walker, 2*d.*; Alice the Roller, 2*d.*; the daughter of Matilda Franceys, 2*d.*; Robert Broun and John Dun's daughters, 2*d.* each ; Idonia Pollard, 2*d.*; Isabel Roper, 2*d.*; Adam, s. of Laurence, 4*d.*; John Tassche, 2*d.*; and John de Amyas, 2*d.* for escapes, dry wood, etc.

THORNES.—Alice Graffard, 2*d.*; Philip de Mora, 6*d.* for escapes.

SANDALE.—John Monkes, 6*d.*; Adam de la Grene, 3*d.* for escapes.

Sum total of this Court : 51*s.* 5*d.*, *i.e.* Bailiff, 4*s.* 4*d.*

Hiperum,	3*s.* 6*d.*	Ossete,	3*s.* 11*d.*
Wakefeld,	9*s.* 1*d.*	Stanneley,	4*s.* 9*d.*
Holne,	3*s.* 8*d.*	Horbiry,	2*s.*

Alverthorp, 2s. 9d.   Thornes, 14d.
Sandale,   16s. 3d.
Total annual rents, 3s. 2½d.

[*mem.* 2.]

TOURN held at Wakefeld on Friday, the Morrow of St. Wilfrid
the Archbishop [12th Oct.], 6 Edw. II.

12 JURORS.—John Patrick, Walter de Gunston, Richard de
Burstall, John de Wyrunthorp, Thomas de Seyvill, William Ingreys
[of] Chevet, John de Mora, John Rased, Thomas Aleyn, Robert de
Fetherston and German Swerd, who say that

BAILIFF.—The township of Sothill shewed contempt to the
jury, refusing to come when summoned.

John the Walker of Emmeley and Henry de Heton, 6d. each for
not coming.

Thomas, s. of Peter de Walton, drew blood from Agnes, d. of
Margery de Walton.

Thomas Bull and John Brown assaulted Henry Schepe at night,
whilst he was standing in his own house ; and Henry raised the hue ;
they are to be attached ; 12d.

John Hode had blocked up a pathway at the end of the town
of Wakefeld, in Kergate, between Hesperode and Schiterike ; 12d.

John Dun raised the hue on Henry de Ayketon for carrying off
his corn in the night ; Henry to be attached.

William the Goldsmith raised the hue on Henry Erl, who is
amerced 6d.; and another 6d. for raising the hue without cause on the
said William, when he rescued the corn Henry was carrying off.

Nicholas Nodger raised the hue on Robert Heward and Alan
Tumbald, for entering his garden without his consent, with a view
of doing mischief there ; they are to be attached.

Mariota, widow of William the Taillur, on Robert the Taillur,
wno is fined 6d.

Amabilla, formerly wife of Robert Dernlove, raised the hue on
Henry Dernlove, who is fined 12d.

The wife of Walter the Cook drew blood from John Peger's wife ;
6d.

Alice, formerly wife of Ralph the Theker, 6d. for raising the hue
on Agnes Suerd at night.

Elizabet Fisc, for raising the hue on Magota, d. of Geoffrey, 6d.

Philip Damson drew blood from Michael the Carpenter in his
own house ; to be attached.

Mariota Bele, 6d. for raising the hue on Adam Waynman.

Magota, d. of Geoffrey, raised the hue on Robert Liftfast for striking her ; he is fined 6d.

William Suerdsliper, to be attached for wandering about the town at night, armed.

Adam the Painter of Crigelston to be attached for deflecting a little syke at the head of the town of Crigelston, to the injury of all the neighbours.

Thomas Herkyn's wife, 12d.; Agnes, wife of Robert the Clerk of Dewesbiri, 2s. for brewing, etc.

Amabilla, wife of John, s. of John the Skinner, drew blood from Agnes de la Grene ; 12d.

Agnes, wife of William Molman, 6d. for selling ale before it was ? casked [cascet'].

Thomas, s. of Robert s. of John de Horbiry, drew blood from Hugh Modisoule ; 12d.

The wife of John, s. of Hugh, 12d. for brewing weak beer.

In prison.—Richard, s. of John de Bretton, wounded Robert del Hay in the head with a sword, in which he was helped by Robert, his brother. Robert del Hay died of his wounds, and his murderers fled. They were to be taken. They are taken and are in prison.

Thomas the Fisher is a constant offender in the Earl of Warenne's parks, especially as regards a deer he killed in the old park in John Walton's time.

Henry Tyting drew blood from ? Sybil the Webster ; 12d.

ALVIRTHORP.—Robert Gerbot's wife for brewing weak beer, 6d.

Elizabeth Longeschankes for brewing against the assize, 6d.

In prison.—William Dodeman wounded Richard, his brother, so that his life was dispaired of ; he is taken and in prison.

ALVIRTHORP.—John Tope's wife for brewing "insufficient" ale, 6d.

Sum total of this Tourn : 19s. 6d., i.e. bailiff, 18s.
Alvirthorp, 18d.

COURT held at Halifax on Sunday after the Feast of St. Luke the Evangelist [Oct. 18], in the year abovesaid.

SOURBY.—Richard Hodde sues Elias, s. of Ivo, and Robert de Saltonstall for debt, and does not prosecute the suit. His fine is pardoned because he is blind and old.

Robert del Brigges de Soland gives 3s. as a heriot on half a bovate in Soland, after the death of Adam, s. of the widow, his brother.

John the Milner of Sourby, accused of cutting a swarm of bees from an oak in Luddingdene, is found guilty by an inquisition. He is to pay the value of the bees, 10d., and fine, 40d. Sureties : Robert de Saltonstal and Richard del Feld.

New rents.—Roger Rotele gives 12d. to take an acre of new land at Snape in Sourby ; rent, 6d.

Robert de Saltonstal gives 18d. for an acre there, at 6d.

Robert, s. of John de Sourbi, 4d.; Agnes de Holgate, 2d.; Thomas, s. of John de Miggelay, 2d.; the wife of Richard, s. of Stephen, 1d.; the wife of John del Hole, 1d.; the wife of John, s. of John, 2d., the wife of Henry, s. of Robert, 2d.; the daughters of Amabilla del Bothom, John the Harper and of Henry, s. of Nalle, 1d. each ; John de Miggeley's son, 1d.; Richard Attetounend of Sourby, 1d.; Henry, s. of Bete, 3d.; Alice del Mere, 3d.; Ellen Gose, 1d.; John Sourmilch, 1d.; Ivo, s. of William, 1d.; Philip, serving-man of Hanne, s. of William, 3d.; William de Lithesels, 1d., and Hancoke de Soland, 2d. for nuts.

John, s. of Hugh the Frere, 4d. and 6d., Adam, his brother, 2d., John de Holgate, junior, 2d.; John Culpun's daughter, 2d.; Elyas de Waddisworth's son, 3d.; John, s. of Radulph, 2d.; Amery de Stodeley, 3d.; the daughter of Magge ad Pontem, 2d.; Dobbe del Castilstede, 4d.; John, s. of Amery, 2d.; Richard de Azerlaye, 2d.; John del Westwod, 1d.; John, s. of Dobbe, 2d.; Hugh, s. of Walter, . . . ; Thomas de Royelset, . . . ; Richard the Smith, . . . ; the servants of Thomas de Lithesels and Hugh de Lithesels, ... for escapes and nuts.

New rents.—John de Gledeholt gives 2s. to take 2 acres of new land in Warloley, at 6d. an acre.

Henry de Saltonstal, 6d. for ½ acre ; rent, 3d.

SOURBY ; grave.—Henry de Saltonstal, grave of Sourby last year, is continued for this year.

MAINPRISE.—Richard, s. of Hugh s. of Reginald de Warloley, charged and indicted for sundry trespasses in the Earl's free chases, finds the following mainprisers for keeping the peace, etc.: Hugh, s. of Reginald, Henry de Holgate, John del Gledeholt, Adam-at-Townend of Miggeley, Henry de Saltonstall, and Elias, s. of Ivo.

MILLS.—Wardens of Soland Mill this year, to answer to the Earl for the profits under a suitable penalty : Robert de Saltonstall, Roger Rotel, Hugh de Lihthasles, Henry de Luddingdene, Thomas de Soland and Richard del Feld. Ratified elsewhere.

Wardens of Warloley Mill, as above : Hugh, s. of Reginald, John, s. of Jordan, Thomas de Rothelset, Richard the Smith, Richard de Saltonstall and Henry de Saltonstall. Ratified elsewhere.

Elias, s. of Ivo de Warloley, gives 12d. to take 3½ roods in Sourby from Roger Rotel.

[The edge is worn at the bottom, and no trace of the " total " left.]

[*mem. 2 dors.*]

TOURN there the same day.

12 JURORS [*sic*].—Richard de Waddisworth, Matthew de Bosco, John de Stansfeld, John Fox of Stansfeld, Adam del Schaye, German de ? Vrenwod, Richard the Taillur de Waddisworth, Adam-at-Townend of Miggeley, Richard de Saltonstal, John de Cockecroft, John de Miggeley, Thomas de Belhous and Gilbert ? Prestinethorp [Prestineth] of Halifax, who say that

SOURBY.—John, s. of Robert de Miggeley, drew blood from Adam Cappe ; 12d.

Cecilia Webster raised the hue on Alice de la Mere for assaulting her ; Alice fined 6d.

Peter Swerd drew blood from Thomas, s. of Isabel de Brimleye ; 12d.

Juliana, wife of Adam de Birkinschagh, drew blood from Margery, d. of Thomas s. of Vilbert ; 6d.

Richard Alman, from Roger, his serving-man ; 12d.

Eva, d. of Roger Spivi, from the handmaid of the clerk of Halifax ; 6d.

Richard Alman's wife, 6d.; Amabilla, wife of Henry de Sourby, 6d.; Mogota de Ripon, 6d.; Sarah, wife of Bate the Lister, 6d., and Amicia del Loue, 6d. for brewing against the assize.

Henry del Loue drew blood from Robert, s. of John Hodde ; 12d.

John Pikeston, from Robert, s. of William de Saltonstall ; 12d.

Sum total of this Tourn : 9s.—all from graveship of Sourby.

COURT at Brighouses on Monday after the Feast of St. Luke the Evangelist [Oct. 18], 6 Edw. II.

HIPERUM.—Thomas, s. of Thomas, 6d. for unlawfully withholding tithe-sheaves from William of the Bothes.

Henry de Coppeley was elected grave of Hyperum for a bovate of villein land [*terra nativa*] that he held in the said graveship; he came and said he is a free man, and did not wish to be grave on account of the said land, which he surrendered. And John del Clif, the Earl's villein [*nativus*], fined 40*d*. to take the said bovate.

William the Milner of Brighouses, 12*d*. for false presentment.

Roger de Clifton, charged with having a stray swarm of bees, says the forester gave them into his charge, to keep for the benefit of the lord; Roger the Forester confirms this, and they are now committed to Roger to keep during the year, for half the profits.

Simon de Schipdene sues Robert, s. of Christiana of the same, for ½ rood of land in Northourum, which was exchanged between their respective ancestors. Defendant says Simon sued him for the same 5 years ago, when the land was adjudged to himself, and calls the rolls to witness.

John the Milner gives 6*d*. to take ½ acre of land in Northourum from John de Birstall for 18 years.

RASTRIK.—Roger de Aula and Hugh Lump of Lynneley and Robert, his son [6*d*.], agree.

HIPERUM.—An inquisition finds that Cecilia, formerly wife of Roger de Brighouses, junior, carried off a waif swarm of bees, worth 15*d*.; she is to pay the 15*d*., and 12*d*. fine.

William del Bothes, 6*d*. for breaking an agreement with Richard, s. of Thomas de Hiperum.

Robert de Weteker's daughter; Jordan del Hou and Agnes Crymbel, 3*d*. each; William de Lynneley's daughter, John de Lynneley's son, Adam de Lynneley's son and Ote de Lynneley's son, 2*d*. each for nuts.

John del Botherode, 3*d*.; Roger the Forester, 3*d*.; William of the Bothes, 6*d*.; the grave of Halifax, 4*d*.; Henry del Rode, 3*d*. for escapes.

Henry de Coppeley gives 12*d*. to take back from John del Clif a bovate of land surrendered above.

MILLS.—Wardens of Rastrik Mill: Roger del Bryghous, senior, Roger de Clyfton, John de Schepeley, Peter de Southclyf, Thomas, s. of Thomas, William del Bothes, John de la Botherode, Matthew de Tothill, Henry, s. of John, William del Wodehous, John de Rastryk sold to William the Milner for 20 marks, under the above sureties.

Wardens of the Mill of Schypedene : William de Sunderland, Symon del Dene, Walter de Aderychgate and John de Sunderland.

Sum total of this Court : 12s. 7d., i.e. Hiperum, 12s. 1d.
Rastrik,   6d.

TOURN there the same day.

[JURORS.]—Master Thomas de Dalton, John de Hertesheved, John, s. of Adam de Lockewod, John del Rode, Thomas de Whitewod, Henry de Coldley, ... r . . . ll, John, s. of William de Steynland, John the Flemeng of Dalton Thomas del Wode of Fekesby, Locokes de Nettilton, and William the . . . . . of Hyperum, who say

. . . . . . del Okes drew blood with her nails from Alice, wife of Matthew de Totehill ; 6d.

. . . . . . s. of Diota, drew blood from Agnes, his sister ; 12d.

Matilda, d. of Alice de Northourum, villein [nativa] was deflowered ; she fines 12d. for the mercy and for marchet.

Agnes, wife of Roger de Brighouses, senior, 6d.; Alice, wife of William the Milner, 6d.; Johanna, wife of William of the Bothes, 12d., and Margaret, wife of John Speht, 6d. for brewing, etc.

The township of Barkesland, 40d. for contempt of the twelve.

Total of this Tourn : 8s. 4d.—all from Hiperum.

HOLNE.—Margery de Thwong sues Agnes, wife of John s. of Hugh de Thwong, for land. Surety : William Strekeyse.

BAILIFF.—Emma the Yonger sues Mariota Bele for trespass. Surety : William Nelot.

OSSETE.—Richard del Dene sues Alice, wife of Adam Broun, for land. Surety : Richard Broun.

John Mauncell sues Thomas . . . . . . for trespass. Surety : William Hyrning.

[Three lines, at least, are torn away at the bottom.]

[mem. 3.]

COURT at Birton on Wednesday,[1] the Feast of St. Luke the Evangelist [Oct. 18], 6 Edw. II.

HOLNE.—Robert del Scoles has license to agree in a plea of trespass with Adam, s. of Elyas, because he is poor.

[1] This membrane is misplaced in order of chronology.

Richard, s. of Gilbert de Gaunt, gives 12d. for license to heriot 3 acres with buildings in Alstanneley, after his father's death. As he is an infant under age, he is given into the guardianship of Matilda, his mother, with the said land. She finds sureties for his proper maintenance, and for the holding of the tenements without waste, etc.: Richard, s. of Michael, and Adam, s. of Hugh de Alstanneley.

Emma, formerly wife of Richard, s. of Locok de Heppeworth, gives 40d. for license to marry in the Earl's fee.

John, s. of Emma de Holne, gives 6d. to take an acre in Holne from John, s. of John de Holne.

William de Buttirley, 6d. to take part of a toft in Foghleston from Adam Denyas.

The said William surrenders 13¼ acres in Fouleston, and afterwards takes them again for his life, with remainder to Adam, his son, and his heirs, who fines 6s. 8d. for the recognition.

Thomas, s. of William de Buttirley, gives 12d. to take part of a toft, and a rood of land in Fouleston, from his father.

Adam Strekeise and Richard del Bothe, agree ; and Richard amerced 6d. for false claim against Adam.

Adam Strekeise gives 13s. 4d. to take 2½ bovates with buildings in Thwonges from Richard del Bothe.

Henry the Sawyer [Sarrator] of Fouleston gives 6d. to take a rood in Fouleston from Thomas de Buttirley.

New rents.—Richard de Cartworth gives 12d. to take an acre of the land formerly rented of John the Couper ; and another 12d. for ½ acre of new land in Cartworth ; rent, 3d.

Adam Benne of Fouleston, 12d. to take 1¾ acres of waste land there, at 4d. an acre.

Matthew, s. of Gilbert de Alstanley, 2s. to take 4 acres of new land in Alstanneley, at 4d. an acre.

Alan del Dam of Wlvedale, 3d. to take ½ acre of new land in Wlvedale common ; rent, 2d.

Agnes, d. of John s. of Hugh de Holne, pardoned for false claim against John, s. of Thomas, concerning a little pot [pocenetto], because she is poor.

Margery de Thwonges sues Agnes, formerly wife of John s. of Hugh de Holne, for her dower in 4 messuages and 7 acres in Thwonges, after the death of Nicholas, s. of Hugh, her late husband, to which land she says Agnes has no right. Agnes says Margery had her dower therein 15 years ago ; both parties request an inquisition, which is taken by the oath of Adam, s. of Adam de W[o]lvedale, Thomas, s. of Gilbert de Alstanneley, Thomas, s. of Richard de la Rode, Matthew de Mora, Adam the Bray, John de Holne, Peter Bulloc, Thomas Brid, Thomas de Billeclifes, John Kenward, Nicholas Kenward and Gilbert de Alstanneley, who say that both Agnes's husband, during his lifetime, and afterwards Agnes, broke agreements with Margery with regard to her said dower ; which she is therefore to recover ; Agnes fined 3d. for unjust detention.

Robert Chobard of Birchewrth gives 40d. for license to take 14 acres with buildings in Littelwod from Richard del Dene [which the said Richard had till the coming of age of William, s. and heir of John de Craven], for 7 years.

John the Couper of Wlvedale, 3s. 4d. for beating Johanna the Webster deliberately, against the prohibition of the Earl's Bailiff.

New rents.—Adam the Couper, 3d. to take ½ acre of new land in Wlvedale common ; rent, 2d. per annum.

William the Turnour of Holne, 6d. for an acre of new land in Holne ; rent, 4d.

John, s. of Locok de Wlvedale, 3s. to take ¾ bovate in Holne from William Strekeyse.

Thomas, s. of Simon de Heppeworth, and Alice, his sister, 2s. to take 7 acres in Heppeworth with buildings for 12 years from Henry Wade.

Richard, s. of Hebbe, surrendered 12½ acres with buildings in Fouleston, and afterwards takes them again for his life with remainder to Nichola, his daughter, and her issue, and, in default of such issue, to his own right heirs. Nichola fines 5s. for the recognition.

New rent.—Adam, s. of Hugh de Alstanneley, gives 6d. to take an acre of new land in Alstanneley ; rent, 4d.

Peter Pede gives 18d. to take 1¾ acres in Cartwrth from Adam de la Grene.

Thomas, s. of Simon de Heppeworth, 6d. to take ½ acre in Heppeworth from William, s. of Thomas Kenward, who fines 6d. to take another ½ acre from Thomas in exchange.

Attachments.

HOLNE.—Emma Fabbe, 3d.; Agnes, d. of Jordan, 3d.; Peter Bulloc, 4d.; John, s. of Geoffrey, 12d.; John, s. of Magge, 4d.; Juliana de Cartwrth, 12d.; William de Cartwrth, 6d.; Adam de Dalton, 2d.; John, s. of Matilda, 2d.; Richard de Cartewrth,

2d.; Thomas Fayrbef, 6d.; John the Couper, 3d.; Richard del Bothe, 4d.; William Strekeyse, 4d.; Jordan the Milner, 2d.; Robert, s. of Ralph, 3d.; Adam the Bray, 3d.; William, s. of Thomas del Rode, 12d.; Elyas, s. of Henry, 3d.; Henry, s. of Richard, 2d.; John, s. of Thomas, 2d.; the son of William, s. of Wilkes, 2d.; Alice, d. of Alice, 2d., and Adam, s. of Nicholas, 4d. for gathering nuts.

Sellers of Wood in Holnfryhtes : Hugh del Hole, Richard, s. of Michael, John de Heppeworth, Adam de la Grene and John de Ryeley.

Sum total of this Court : 62s. 1d., and new rents, 3s. 2d.; all from the graveship of Holne.

TOURN there the same day.

12 JURORS.—John Withir, Richard de Thornie, William de Riley, Robert de Wlwro, John de Braitwait, John, s. of Adam de Heppewrth, Adam del Scoles, Hugh del Holes, Adam de la Grene, Adam de Wlvedale, Richard de Birton, and John de Stokis, who say that

Adam, s. of the Grave, drew blood from Adam de la Grene ; 12d. John de la Grene, from Adam, s. of the Grave ; 12d.

The wife of Robert del Scoles, 6d. for brewing against the assize.

BAILIFF.—Christiana de Schelveley, Emma the Bagger, and Amabilla, wife of Robert the Bagger, 2s. each for brewing bad ale and selling by false measure.

Adam Tresal pursued Margery, d. of Geoffrey, with a view of robbing her of a jug of ale ; and she was in the house of Matilda de Pomerio, and shut the door ; and Adam broke open the door, entered and searched the house for her and the said ale, but did not find either. He is to be attached.

HOLNE.—Juliana de Cartewrth, Peter Bullock's wife, Cecilia del Witeston, the wife of Hugh de la Hole, and Adam, s. of Jordan, 6d. each for brewing against the assize.

[*One line, at any rate, is destroyed at the bottom of the membrane.*]
[*mem. 3 dors.*]

SOURBY ; mills.—The mills of Soland and Warloley, whose dams are carried away by the overflow of the superfluous water, are farmed this year for 66s. 8d. to Richard de Saltoun-stal. Sureties : Thomas de Waddeswrth, clerk, John the Milner of Sourby, and John del Gledeholt.

HOLNE ; mill.—Cartworth Mill, carried away by the over-
flowing of the water, together with the house and dam, is demised
for the year, after the repair of the premises, to John de Amyas,
for £17 6s. 8d. Sureties: Richard, s. of Michael, Richard del
Bothe, William, s. of William de Heppeworth, Henry Wade,
Richard Child and Jordan the Milner.

Graves.—Stanlay : Robert de Milkelfeld elected.

Horbery : Thomas Elin, grave last year, continued.

Sandale : Robert, s. of Adam, the same.

Ossete : Adam, s. of William s. of Jordan, elected.

Alverthorp : Robert Gerbot elected.

[mem. 4.]

COURT held at Wakefeud on Friday, the Vigil of SS. Simon
and Jude [Oct. 28], 6 Edw. II.

ESSOINS.—Thomas de Seyville, by German Swerd. Surety :
William de Castilforth.

Elyas de Byrton, by William Erl. Surety : William del Okys.

Peter Swerd, by William de Castilforth. Surety : Richard de
Byrstall.

Thomas de Thorneton, by Hugh de Thorneton. Surety :
Richard the Saussemer.

Thomas de Heton, by Robert his servant. Surety : Robert de
Wyrunth[orp].

Robert del Grene of Osset, by Thomas the Clerk. Surety :
John de Mora.

John de Schypedene, by Thomas de Wytteley. Surety : John
de Lepton.

Nicholas de Caylli, by Henry his son. Surety : Richard de
Byrstall.

Edmund the Normaund, by William, servant of Margery.
Surety : John de Mora.

BAILIFF.—Agnes, wife of Robert the Clerk of Deusbiry, 3d.
for brewing, etc.

John de Querneby, 2s.; Matthew de Bosco, 2s.; John de Thornhill,
4s.; William de Bello Monte, 2s.; Dom. Reginald le Flemmyng, 4s.;
Thomas de Langefeld, 40d.; John, s. of John de Soland, 2s., and
Thomas de Dronsefeld, 2s. for respite of suit of court.

Robert, s. of Richard Beusire, 4d. for not prosecuting his suit
against William Cort. He also sues the said William for trespass.
Surety : William the Goldsmith.

Adam de Staynclif gives 12*d.* for respite of suit till Michaelmas.

RASTRIK.—William del Lee and Robert de Rysseworth, 6*d.* each for not prosecuting their suits against one another.

HYPERUM.—John, s. of Walter of Northourum, is elected grave of Hyperum; but pays half a mark that his term of office may be deferred.

The land that was the land of Alexander, s. of Walter de Sonderland, is seized because he is dead.

HOLNE ; grave.—Adam, s. of Nicholas Keneward, elected grave of Holne.

BAILIFF.—Emma the Yong, 3*d.* for not prosecuting her suit against Mariota Bele.

John de Eland made default at this court ; he is in the Earl's service.

Richard de Crosseland gives 2*s.* for respite of suit of court till Michaelmas.

ALVIRTHORP.—Walter del Hill, 6*d.* to take ½ perch of land in a garden in Alvirthorp, from Adam Gerbot.

OSSETE.—John Mauncell, 6*d.* for false claim against Thomas Pees, and 6*d.* for contempt.

STANLEY.—Thomas Bull and John Bull quitclaim to Richard Ysabell and Ellen his wife all their right in 6½ acres in the graveship of Ouchethorp, which Thomas formerly sold to Richard before the present steward ; and Richard Isabel fined 18*d.* for the recognition.

William Albray gives 2*s.* as a heriot for a toft and 4 acres in Stanley, after the death of Eva Albray, his mother.

SOURBY.—William the Smith [*faber*] of Sourby gives 6*d.* to take ½ acre of new land at the Snape, in Sourby ; rent, 3*d.*

HYPERUM ; grave. — Simon Attedene is elected grave, and sworn in the place of John, s. of Walter, elected above, who is respited this year.

BAILIFF.—Thomas But and John Broun, for assaulting by night Henry Chepe.

Henry de Ayketon, for carrying off by night the corn of John Dun.

Robert Horward and Alan Thrumball, for entering the garden of Nicholas Stodger without his consent with the object of evil doing.

[Orders for attachments.]

Philip Dampson, for assaulting Nicholas Carpenter by night in his own house.

William Swerdsliper, because he wanders by night in the town carrying arms, for which he has been indicted at the Turn.

Adam the Painter of Crigleston, for one sike turned aside from its course at the Town-end of Crigleston to the damage of the neighbours.

Thomas the Fisher of Warnefeld, because he is a common evil-doer in the Earl's free chaces, and for having slain a doe in the Old Park in the time of John de Wanton, whereof he was indicted at the Turn.

Adam Trostell, for assaulting Margery, d. of Geoffrey, with the object of taking from her a jug of ale.

Robert, s. of Robert for violently drawing blood from Matilda the Ragged, indicted at the same Turn.

Symon the Clerk of Thurstanland, for a footpath ploughed up there.

Attachments.

The handmaid of Henry Bul, 1d.; William the Theker, 2d.; William Richard, 2d.; the handmaids of William Bul, 3d.; Robert Capoun, 2d., and Nicholas Hog, 1d.; the daughter of Ralph s. of Malle, 2d.; John de Skulbroke's handmaid, 2d.; Hugh Bylle's daughter, 1d.; the handmaid of German the Gardiner, 2d.; William de Sandale, 2d., and Richard the Clerk, 2d. for dry wood.

. . . . . .—Hugh Findiren, 6d.; surety, Peter Pinder; John Peger, 6d., and Henry Campion, ... 1d. for vert, etc.

WAKEFELD.—Robert the Roller, 3s. for three logs carried away by the flood.

THORNES; grave. — William, s. of Roger de Snaypthorp, elected grave of Thornes.

William Lacer, 2d. for not prosecuting Robert Peger and Thomas Lilman.

[BAILIFF.]—Thomas de Heton gives 4s. for respite of suit of court till Michaelmas.

[mem. 4 dors.]

WAKEFEUD; bailiff.—John de Amias took from the lord the office of dyeing [tinctura] in the town of Wakefeld, and in any other place in the soke of that town, for 5 years, paying 8s. 8d. rent yearly.

Attachments.

The handmaids of William Wyles, 4d., and of John Pollard, 2d.; the serving-man of Henry, s. of Ellen, 2d.; Robert Goldsmith's son, 2d.; Jordan the Mawer, 2d.; Peter Spynk, 4d.; Robert

Liftfast, 2*d*.; Robert Hodde, 6*d*.; Robert Hood of Wakefeud, 4*d*.; John Broun, 3*d*.; Adam de Castelford, 3*d*.; Robert, s. of Ralph Ters, 3*d*.; Joan, d. of Sybil, 3*d*. for vert, acorns, etc.

THORNES. — Margery Hawe, 2*d*.; Thomas Viron's daughter, 2*d*.; Joan Costel, 3*d*. for dry wood, etc.

HORBIRY.—Gilbert de Horbiry, 2s. for vert.

SANDALE.—Adam Sprigonel, 3*d*.; Margery de Monte, 3*d*.; Robert de la Grene, 3*d*.; William de Notton, 4*d*., surety, Thomas Monkes; Hugh Tubbyng's son, 2*d*. for escapes and dry wood.

STANNELEY.—John Poket, for vert and dry wood, 6*d*.

ALVIRTHORP.—John Tup, 6*d*.; Alice Gerbod, 2*d*.; Alice, wife of Roger, 3*d*.; John Swan, 2*d*.; Adam Wlf, 2*d*.; Walter del Hill, 2*d*. for dry wood and vert.

OSSETE.—Adam, serving-man of Robert de Ossete, 6*d*.; John Maunsel, 12*d*.; William de Heton, 2*d*. for vert, acorns, palings broken, etc.

Sum total of this Court : 67s. 10*d*., and new rent, 3*d*.

i.e. Thornes,	9*d*.	Stannelay,	5s. 1*d*.
Horbiry,	2s.	Bailiff,	37s. 10*d*.
Sourby,	6*d*.	(and new rent, 3*d*.)	
Osset,	2s. 8*d*.	Alvirthorp,	23*d*.
Sandale,	15*d*.	Wakefeud,	8s. 2*d*.
Hiperum,	6s. 8*d*.	Rastrik,	12*d*.

SOUREBY.—William de Sunderland sues John, s. of Michael de Lum, for trespass. Surety : Henry de Saltonstall.

STANNELEY.—Henry the Dyker sues William del Spen for trespass. Surety : Henry Gunne.

SOURBY.—William del Storthes and Alice, his wife, sue William the Harpur of Deusbiry for trespass. Surety : John de Migeley.

ALVIRTHORP.—John Attebarre sues William, s. of Walter de Neuton, for debt. Surety : William de Castelford.

HOLNE.—Robert Spynk sues William, s. of Wilkes, and Robert de Wade for trespass. Surety : John de Leek.

SOURBY.—John the Taylur sues Alan, servant of John de Horbiry, for trespass. Surety : William de Lockewod.

John Pollard, junior, sues William de Lihthasles, for debt. Surety : Will. de Castelforth.

BAILIFF.—Henry Erl sues Thomas, s. of Ralph, and William, s. of Robert de Crygleston, for trespass. Surety : John Patrykes.

B

[*mem.* 5.]

COURT at Wakefeld on Friday, the Morrow of St. Edmund the Archbishop [Nov. 16], 6 Edw. II.

ESSOINS.—John de Schepedene, by Thomas the Clerk. Surety: John de Mora.

John de Lepton, by Thomas de Witteley. Surety: Thomas de Thornton.

Peter Suerd, by William de Castilford.

Nicholas Cailly, by Henry, his son. Surety: Henry de Suilington.

Edmund the Normaund, by John Patrickes. Surety: William del Okes.

Thomas de Bellehouses, by William de Saltonstall.

BAILIFF.—William the Harpur of Deuwesbiri, in the mercy for impleading William del Storthes and Alice, his wife, in the consistory, on a plea of debt contrary to the King's statute   Afterwards pardoned, because he brought the suit to this court.

Robert de Risscheworth [12*d*.] and John de Quernby agree.

Godefrey de Steynton and Robert de Mora, the executors of the will of William de Steynton, request license to withdraw their suit against William Witebeltes for debt, because he has no property with which to satisfy any claims, and because the two horses, by which he had been distrained, were sold for the king's debt. This is granted.

SOURBY.—John de Leyland, plaintiff, and Henry de Holgate, Robert de Soureby, and Richard de Saltonstall [3*s*.], agree.

HYPERUM.—Symon del Dene appears against Robert, s. of Christiana de Northourum, who was at the last court, but makes default at this ; fined 6*d*.; distraint to be made.

OSSET.—Richard, s. of Bate, 3*d*. for not coming.

HOLNE.—Robert, s. of Robert, 12*d*. for shedding the blood of Matilda the Ragged.

SOUREBY.—John, s. of Michael de Lum, 6*d*. for not appearing to answer William de Sunderland.

HOLNE.—Robert Spink [12*d*.] and William, s. of Wilkes, and Robert Wade, agree.

OSSETE.—Henry, s. of Richard de Erlesheton, 6*d*. for license to marry Margery, his daughter.

BAILIFF.—William del Storthes and Alice, his wife, sue William the Harpur of Deuesbiry for impleading them in the Consistory, and afterwards making default, in consequence of which the officer granted them their expenses. William cannot deny; an order is therefore given for plaintiffs to recover expenses, taxed at 5s. William the Harpur fined 2s. Surety: Thomas Pes.

HIPERUM.—John, s. of Alexander de Sunderland, gives 2s. as a heriot on ¾ bovate of land in Northourum on the death of his father.

SANDALE.—Robert, s. of Robert the Carpenter of Crigelston, gives 6d to take an acre with buildings in Crigelston from William de Sandale of Wakefeld.

Robert, s. of John s. of Alan de Crigelston, surrenders 3 roods with buildings in Crigelston, and afterwards takes them again for his life, with remainder to Robert, s. of Robert the Carpenter, who pays 6d. for the recognition.

THORNES.—Thomas Viron gives 12d. for license to take 2¾ acres in Snaypethorp for 20 years, from Alice, Alice and Christiana, daughters of Philip de Alvirthorp.

STANLEY.—John, s. of Richard del Bothum, gives 12d. to take 5 acres in Stanley from Henry [? Swilington], for 9 years.

HIPERUM.—Matilda and Alice, daughters of John de Sunderland, give 5s. for license to marry. Sureties: John de Sunderland and William de Sunderland.

William de Sunderland sues Thomas de Waddesworth for land. Surety: William de Lockewod.

BAILIFF.—Agnes, formerly wife of Robert the Clerk of Deusbiry, and Ellen, wife of Richard Dyer, 6d. each for brewing, etc.

HOLNE.—Adam, s. of Jordan, sues Emma del Storthes for trespass. Surety: William Wether.

John del Grene sues John, s. of Matilda, for trespass. Surety: Richard del Rode.

STANLEY.—Richard Poket sues Robert Leper for trespass.

ALVIRTHORP.—Henry the grave [?] of Sourby sues John de . . . . .

John Dade sues Henry Nonne . . . . . .

. . . . . .—Adam de Wodesom sues . . . . . . de Amyas.

[*The membrane ends in rags, but this is apparently the last line of writing. There is no trace of a total.*]

[*mem.* 5 *dors.*]

COURT at Wakefeud on Friday, the Feast of the Conception of the Blessed Mary [Dec. 8], 6 Edw. II.

ESSOINS.—Elyas de Byrton, by William de Castilforth. Surety: Richard Saussemere.

Thomas de Seyuill, by William de Seyuill. Surety: Robert del Grene.

Thomas de Thorneton, by Hugh de Thorneton.

THORNES.—Robert de Thornes to be distrained by all his cattle to answer Richard the Clerk, Peter de Acom, and Nicholas de Bateley.

BAILIFF.—John de Mora, plaintiff, against John de Heton, by William de Notton. Surety: William del Okys.

William Corte, defendant against Robert, s. of Richard Beausire, by John Patrikes. Surety: Henry de Wakefeud.

Richard, s. of Robert de Radeclyf, junior, defendant, against John the Clerk of Hertesheved, by John de Wakefeud. Surety: Henry Erl.

SOURBY.—John, s. of John Pollard, and William de Lighteheseles [6d.] agree.

John, s. of Michael de Lum, 6d. for not coming to answer William de Sunderland.

BAILIFF.—Henry Erl sues William, s. of Robert de Crigelston, on an agreement, under which William bought 3 pieces [placeas] of underwood in different places in Crigelston, with the understanding he could cut what wood he liked between Easter and Whitsuntide [3 Edw. II], but should then leave what was standing to grow till the following Michaelmas; for which he paid 40s. He broke the condition by cutting the wood before the term specified; damages, 100s. William cannot deny; is fined 6d., and to pay damages.

Peter Swerd gives 12d. for respite of suit till Michaelmas.

Adam de Wodesom sues John de Amyas for driving 2 cows of his from Walton to Wakefeld, and detaining them; damages, 6s. 8d. John acknowledges the seizure, saying he farmed the said town of Wakefeud, with the mill, and its appurtenances; and that he leased the new mill under Thorstanhagh, with Sandale mill, to one Henry Calf, for 9 marks for last year; and Adam was surety for 6 marks of the rent, 2 of which were in arrears. Adam denies any arrears. [The entry is unfinished.]

ALVIRTHORP.—Robert de Fery gives 6d. to take 1½ roods in Alvirthorp from Richard Wythundes.

Robert Attehue, 12d. to take 2¼ acres from John de Flansou for 20 years.

HOLNE.—Peter de Wildeborlee and Mary his wife, 18d. to take 2½ acres in Alstanley from Thomas, s. of Gilbert.

John del Grene, 6d. to take an acre in Scoles from Adam his brother, for 8 years.

HYPERUM; new rent.—William de Northourum, 2s. for license to take an acre of new land in Northourumclyf; rent, 6d.

HOLNE.—Richard del Bothe gives 3s. to take ½ bovate in Holne, with buildings, from William Benet.

. . . . . .—[? Richard] del Dene fined . . d. for wrongful detention of dower from Alice, formerly wife of Richard Broun.

[SANDALE] ; new rent.—John de Cokewald and . . . . . . his wife, give 6d. to take a piece of herbage in the dam belonging to the mill under Sandal Castle ; rent, 18d.

[ALVIRTHORP.]—. . . . . . Grenhode gives 6d. to take a piece of meadow in the Morecroft from Robert Gerbot for 20 years, after the 6 years William de Wakefeld has in a moiety thereof, by demise of John Torald, and 4 years in the other moiety, by demise of Robert Gerbot.

HOLNE ; new rents.—Adam the Bray gives 21d. for license to take 1¼ acres of new land in Cartworth ; rent, 7½d.

Mariota, wife of Peter del Wildborlee, 6d. to take an acre of new land in Alstanneley ; rent, 4d.

WAKEFELD.—William de Heitefeld, parker in the old park, 12d. for license to take 2 acres in the graveship of Wakefeld between Wyndochill and the great gate of the old park, from John Cussinges of Wakefeld, in marriage with Johanna, wife of said William, to hold to them and their issue, with remainder, in default of issue, to the right heirs of John Cussinges.

STANNELEY.—Henry de Benninges, forester in Stanneley wood, 6d. to take 1½ roods in Stanneley from Richard Poket.

WAKEFELD.—Master William de Finchedene, 2s. to take a piece of waste land in Wakefeld, outside the eastern end of the graveyard of the church of that town, 50 feet by 24 feet ; rent, 12d.

. . . . . .—Richard Poket, 6d. . . . . . .

[At least three lines are torn away at the end of the membrane, fines being entered in the margin for 12d., 12d., and . . d.]

[mem. 6.]

HORBIRY.—John, s. of Robert Pollard, and Alice his wife, sue Adam, s. of William de Horbiry ; fined 4d. for not prosecuting the suit.

ALVIRTHORP.—John Attebarre, 6d. for withdrawing his suit against William, s. of Walter de Neuton.

HORBIRY.—John, s. of Robert Pollard, and Alice his wife, give 2s. for an attaint of 24 jurors on a jury of 12 as to a bovate of land with buildings in Horbiry, against Adam, s. of William de Horbiry.

ALVIRTHORP.—Richard, s. of Broun, 6d. for not coming.

OSSET.—John Maunsel, 6d. for false claim against Thomas Pes.

HOLNE.—John, s. of Matilda, 6*d.* for not coming.

ALVIRTHORP.—Henry, the grave of Sourby, and John de Flansowe [3*d.*] agree.

Robert Gerbot is elected grave of Alvirthorp.

SOURBY.—William de Stodeley, 3*d.*; Thomas de Stodeley, 2*d.*; William, s. of Wymark, 2*d.*; Agnes de Ponte, 2*d.*; Hugh de Northland's wife, 3*d.*; Hugh, his son, 2*d.*; Eva de Godeley, 3*d.*; William, her son, 2*d.*; Michael de Routonstall, 2*d.*; John de Holgate, 2*d.*; John, s. of Hugh Frere, 2*d.*; Richard de Saltonstal, 2*d.*; John, s. of Dobbe, 2*d.*; William del Estwod, 2*d.*; Adam de Routonstal, 2*d.*; John the Milner, 2*d.*; Richard, s. of Cecilia, 2*d.*; Alice and Cecilia, daughters of Oto, 2*d.* each ; the wife of Thomas de Lihthasles, 2*d.*; Hugh de Lihthasles, 2*d.*; the wife of Adam de Lihthasles, 1*d.*; Dande de Sourby, 2*d.*; Adam Migge, 1*d.*; Alice de Mara, 2*d.*; Richard, s. of Dobbe, 2*d.*; Richard, s. of Adam, 2*d.*; Alan de Miggeley, 1*d.*; Margery de Bosco, 2*d.*; Oto the Smith, 1*d.*, for escapes.

HOLNE.—Roger del Rodes, 3*d.*; Adam de Paldene, 6*d.*; Richard, s. of Michael, 6*d.*, for escapes ; William de Heppeworth, for nuts, 3*d.*; William, s. of Hugh de Langside, his pigs and hogs, 11*d.*

WAKEFELD.—John de Wragby's handmaid, 3*d.*; the daughter of Ralph, s. of Malle, 2*d.*; John de Skulbroke's daughter, 4*d.*; the handmaids of Richard de Otteley and John de Grenegate, 1*d.* each ; John, s. of Magge the Collier [*Carbonar*], 4*d.*, surety, John Torald ; Robert Alayn, 4*d.*; Adam Torkatro, 2*d.*; Adam de Wodesom, 6*d.*, surety, William, servant of Margery,—for vert, pannage, and escapes.

SANDALE.—Adam de la Grene, 3*d.*; Emma, wife of Hugh, 3*d.*; John Feldfare, 3*d.*; William de la Grene, 2*d.*; Adam Wylimot, 2*d.*; Alcok de Wodethorp, 2*d.*; Adam del Okes, 3*d.*; Sybil del Nubigging, 2*d.*; Margery de Ketilthorp, 2*d.*, for escapes.

WAKEFELD.—Letitia Milner, 6*d.*, surety, John Pollard ; William de Hethensale, 6*d.*; William Wyles' wife, 18*d.*, for escapes, etc.

Nicholas Nodger and Adam de Castelford, 4*d.* and 2*d.* for going beyond the paling.

Roger de Silkeston, 2*d.*; Simon Fox, 6*d.*; Alice Coly, 2*d.*; Johanna Leget, Idonea Pollard, Robert Broun's wife, John Dun's daughter, Alice, niece of the priest, Robert de Fethirston, and John Tasse, 2*d.* each ; Henry Erl, 3*d.*, for dry wood and escapes.

STANNELEY.—Beatrice Gunne, 2*d.*; Alice, wife of Robert del Spen, Alice, wife of Walter, William del Spen, John de St. Swithin,

John Cokspor, William, s. of Robert the Hagger, John de Rigeway, [surety, Philip Syour], 2*d*. each, for dry wood.

Thomas de Thorp, for attempting to break the paling, 4*d*.; Roger the Carter, 2*d*.; Philip the Sawyer, 2*d*.; Richard Spinkes, 2*d*.; Roger Bele, 2*d*.; Matilda the Schepehird of Methelei, 3*d*.; Robert Pesci, 2*d*.; Robert, s. of Geoffrey, 4*d*.; Walter Odam, 4*d*., and Hugh Tagges, 4*d*., for vert.

ALVIRTHORP.—Henry Nunne's son, 3*d*., surety, Henry Nunne ; Richard, s. of Broun, 6*d*.; John de Flansou's wife, 6*d*.; Alice de Alvirthorp, 2*d*., for escapes, etc.

THORNES.—Roger Viroun, 3*d*.; William, s. of Agnes, 3*d*., for wood.

OSSETE.—William Hirning, 2*d*.; his wife, 6*d*.; Amabilla, his sister, 6*d*.; Jordan Elyot, 6*d*.; Elizabeth de Chikkinley, 2*d*., and Jordan Skot, 6*d*., for vert, breaking palings, etc.

Sum total of this Court in fines and amercements, 51*s*. 4*d*.; and new rent, 4*s*. 11½*d*.

i.e. Holne,	11*s*. 8*d*.	(and new rent, 23*d*.)
Hyperum,	2*s*.	(and new rent, 6*d*.)
Stanneley,	5*s*. 9*d*.	Alvirthorp, 4*s*. 8*d*.
Wakefeld,	10*s*. 6*d*.	(and new rent, 12*d*.)
Horbiry,	2*s*. 4*d*.	Bailiff, 2*s*. 3*d*.
Sourby,	6*s*.	Osset, 3*s*. 4*d*.
Thornes,	6*d*.	Sandale, 2*s*. 4*d*.
		(and new rent, 18*d*.)

[*mem.* 6 *dors.*]

COURT held at Wakefeud on Friday, the Morrow of St. Thomas the Apostle [Dec. 21], 6 Edw. II.

ESSOINS.—Hugh the Nodder, attorney of Margaret de Nevill, by Adam de Wodesom. Surety: Robert de Heyrode.

Thomas de Thorneton, by Hugh de Thorneton. Surety: Richard de Salsa-mara.

Nicholas de Caylee, by Henry de Metheley. Surety: Henry de Wakefeud.

Edmund the Normaunt, by John Patrikes. Surety: Henry Erl.

John de Lepton, by John de Wakefeud.

John de Schipdene, by Henry de Wakefeud. Surety: William de Castelford.

BAILIFF.—Elias de Birton, by William the Goldsmith. Surety: Thomas the Clerk of Wakefeud.

Robert, s. of Richard Beausir, and William Cort have a love-day.

Henry Erl sues Thomas, s. of Ralph de Crigleston, for damaging and destroying his growing underwood in three places in Crigleston ; damages, 100s. Defendant cannot deny. To pay damages, which are to be taxed, and 12d. fine.

Thomas, s. of Adam Forester, and Richard de Birstal, 6d. each for default.

SOURBY.—William de Sunderland and John, s. of Michael del Lum [6d.], agree.

HORBIRY.—John the Tailor of Wakefeld sues Alan, servant of John de Horbiry, for taking a horse from his enclosure in Wakefeld ; damages, 6s. 8d.; Alan fined 6d.

HOLNE.—Emma del Storthes [6d.] and Adam, s. of Jordan, agree.

John de la Grene and John, s. of Matilda [6d.], agree.

THORNES.—William the Lacer, plaintiff, and Robert Peger and Thomas Lilleman [6d.] agree.

HIPERUM.—Henry del Ridding de Illingworth, 2d.; Hugh Little, 2d.; Thomas the grave of Ovendene, 3d.; Henry the Smith of Schipdene, 4d.; Robert, s. of Alcoke de Northourum, 3d.; Peter del Barm, 3d.; Alcok Waynwriht, 12d.; Richard, s. of Thomas s. of Alot, 4d.; Adam the Shepherd of Rastrik, 4d.; and Richard, s. of William de Illingworth, 6d., surety, William Squier,—for escapes and vert.

ALVIRTHORP.—Richard, s. of Broun, 2d.; Thomas Hancokes, 4d.; John Bunny, 2d.; John the Smith, 2d., for dry wood.

STANNELEY.—Richard, s. of Robert, 3d.; Richard Longschankes, 3d.; John Cort, 2d.; Broun de Wirunthorp, 2d.; Richard Spinkes, 6d.; Roger Carter's serving-man, 6d., surety, Robert the Yung,—for wood cut, etc.

WAKEFEUD.—Hugh Chapman's daughter, Thomas Molle's handmaid, William the Theker's son, John Richaud's daughter, for dry wood, Robert Tropinel's son, and William Bul's handmaid, 2d. each for vert.

BAILIFF.—Henry Fox sues . . . . . . and James, sons of John Monkes, for trespass. Surety : William the Goldsmith, and they are attached.

The said Henry sues John de Raygate for trespass. Surety, the same goldsmith. He is attached.

HOLNE.—Robert, s. of Ralph de Cartworth, sues Adam de Dalton for land. Surety : Adam Keneward.

STANLEY.—Henry de Walda sues Walter Gunne for trespass. Surety: Thomas de Wytteley. Walter is attached by Robert Gunne.

Sum total of this Court: 11s. 9d., i.e. Bailiff, 2s.

Sourby,	6d.	Horbiry,	6d.
Holne,	12d.	Thornes,	6d.
Hiperum,	3s. 7d.	Alvirthorp,	10d.
Stanlay,	22d.	Wakefeld,	12d.

[mem. 7.]

COURT at Wakefeld on Friday after the Feast of St. Hilary [Jan. 13], 6 Edw. II.

ESSOINS.—Nicholas de Cailly, by Henry de Metheley. Surety: William the Goldsmith. . . . . 2.

John de Schepedene, by Thomas de Qwitteley. Surety: Richard de Salsa-mara. . . . . 2.

William de Rastrikes, by William de Hingandrode. Surety: Robert de Heyerode. . . . . 1.

Richard de Birstal, by German Cay. Surety: William de Castelford. . . . . 1.

BAILIFF.—John the clerk of Herteshed sues Richard son of Robert de Radeclifes, jun., for taking cattle, by John Patrikes. A day is given.

[KING'S] BENCH.—The suit between Adam de Linne and Master John de Warrenne, parson of Deusbery, Alan de Fourneys and William, bailif of Deusbery, removed into the Bench by the King's writ.

BAILIFF.—Robert, s. of Richard Beusire, and his surety amerced 12d. for not being present to prosecute suit against William Cort, on a plea of trespass.

Henry the Diker, 4d. for false claim against William del Spen.

Adam, s. of Adam Sprigonel, defendant, essoins against Mergery del Hill, by Adam Sprigonel. Surety: Adam Hod.

The [Inquest of] Attaint in regard to the 12 nonjurors in the cause between John, s. of Robert Pollard, and Alice his wife, plaintiffs, and Adam, s. of William of Horbery, re one messuage and one bovate of land in Horbery, is respited until the next Court on account of the jurors of the Attaint having made default. And the 12 jurors came and the Attaint [i.e. the jury thereof] did not come. Therefore the graves of Horbery, Ossett, Alverthorpe, Stanley, and Thornes are enjoined by writ to cause a view of the aforesaid tenements to be made before the next Court, and to see that they have here 12 recognitors from any [*quolibet*] of the graveships.

HOLNE.—Robert, s. of Ralph de Cartworth, sues Adam de Dalton for 5½ acres and half a toft with buildings in Cartworth, demised by Adam to plaintiff for 3 years. They afterwards agree, Adam paying 6*d.*

STANLEY.—Walter Gunne, 6*d.* for allowing 60 beasts in his charge to graze on Henry de Walda's grass.

OSSET.—Mergery, Johanna, Emmota, Alice, and Alice [*sic*], daughters of Henry, s. of Richard de Erlsheton, give 6*d.* as a heriot on a bovate of land in Erlsheton, after their father's death.

Agnes, d. of Jordan de Gaukethorp, gives 12*d.* as a heriot on 1½ bovates and 4 acres in Gaukethorp.

ALVIRTHORP.—Adam, s. of Walter, 6*d.* to take 3 roods in Neuton fields from William de . . . . . . for 12 years.

Emma, Idonea, Avicia, and Alice, daughters of William Hoskel, give 6*d.* as a heriot on 6½ acres in Alvirthorp, after their father's death.

Henry Wlf, 6*d.* to take a rood in Alvirthorp from John de Flansawe.

THORNES.—Philip del Hill, 6*d.* to take 3 acres in Snaypthorp fields from Margery Hawe.

John, s. of Magges, 6*d.* to take 6 acres from the same.

STANLEY.—Robert Gunne, 6*d.* to take ½ acre in Stanley from Gerard Quintyn.

John, s. of Robert the Mercer [*mercenarius*], 6*d.* to take an acre of meadow in Wirnthorp from Richard Longchankes, for 14 years.

The wives of Adam Spinkes and Nicholas de Bateley, 6*d.* each for weak ale, and for not sending for the wardens of assize.

BAILIFF.—An inquisition finds that Henry Chep, John Dun, Nicholas Nodger and Philip Damson raised the hue without cause on . . . . ; each fined 12*d.*

The same inquisition finds William Suerdsliper is not guilty of wandering about the town at night armed, for which he was indicted at the Tourn.

Attachments.

WAKEFELD.—Thomas, s. of Josua, 3*d.*; William Lentyn, 3*d.*; Adam the Waytes, 3*d.*; Alice Coly, 2*d.*; Amabilla, handmaid of Alison, 2*d.*; Johanna Leget, 2*d.*; Alice, d. of Alexander, 2*d.*; the handmaid of William, s. of Margery, ... ; John, s. of William, 2*d.*; Henry . . . . rd's handmaid, 2*d.*; the daughter of Robert the Goldsmith, senior, 2*d.*; Robert Walker's handmaid ; John Leche, 2*d.*; Robert Hodd, 3*d.*; Robert Liftfast, 2*d.*, and Richard Man's wife, 2*d.*, for dry wood.

STANLAY.—[*There are six entries, in none of which a whole name is legible ; and one name has been torn away from the Wakefield list.*]

WAKFELD.—John Pollard, 2*s.* for a waif hog, sent from Hiperum, with which the grave of Wakefeld is chargeable.

[*mem. 7 dors.*]

STANLAY.—William Tagge, 2*d.*; Isolda Roo, 4*d.*; Robert the Wyt of Metheley, 3*d.*; Walter del Spen's wife, 2*d.*, for dry wood.

WAKFELD.—The sons [or daughters ?] of John Salman, John Sotheron and Hugh Bille, 3*d.* each ; the handmaids of Henry de Scolbrok and Richard, brother of Henry, 3*d.* each, for dry wood.

STANLEY.—The wife of Thomas, s. of Stephen, Broun's wife, Margery, d. of Adam, Richard Ruddok, and Thomas, s. of Adam, 3*d.* each ; John Costel's wife, 1*d.*, for the same.

THORNES.—John del Hagh, 8*d.*, and Alice del Hill, 2*d.*, for wood.

OSSETTE.—Hugh del Wro, Richard the Pynder, Richard Suartes and Jordan Elyot, 2*d.* for escapes, etc.

THORNES.—John Graffard, 2*d.* for turning [a path] [*quia deviavit*].

ALVERTHORP.—John Cussing gives 12*d.* to take one acre in Newton Field from Henry the Stunt.

WAKEFELD.—Wytaccok's daughter, 3*d.*; John Richaud's daughter, 3*d.*; the handmaids of Thomas Molle, 3*d.*, and of William Bul, 2*d.*; William de Sandale's son, 2*d.*, for dry wood.

STANLEY.—Martin de Wirnthorp's son, 2*d.*; John Cort's son, 2*d.*; Nicholas de Bateley, 3*d.*, and Thomas Hancok's maid, 3*d.*, for dry wood.

WAKEFELD.—William Richaud's daughter, 3*d.* for the same.

OSSET.—Robert Sonman and Agnes, handmaid of Susan, 2*d.* each for escapes.

John Maunsel, 6*d.* for vert.

ALVIRTHORP.—Robert Gerbot, 6*d.* for a cartload of wood.

OSSET.—William Graffart, 12*d.* for vert.

WAKEFELD.—Henry Erl, 3*d.*, and Robert Marescall, 2*d.*, for escapes.

STANLEY.—Richard Longschankes, 6*d.* for vert.

ALVERTHORP.—John Cussing gives 12*d.* to take 1⅛ acres in Neuton fields from Henry the Nunne.

HIPERUM.—John de Westwod sues William Stirk of Warlolay for trespass. Surety : Robert, s. of Roger de Sourby.

ALVERTHORP.—Richard, s. of Philip, sues John, s. of Broun, for trespass. Surety : Thomas, s. of Philip.

OSSET.—John Moloč sues Richard Passemir for trespass. Surety : Adam, s. of William.

ALVERTHORP.—Henry, s. of Richard s. of Broun, sues Richard de Collay for trespass. Surety : Henry Wlf.

Sum total of this Court : 31s. 5d., *i.e.* Bailiff, 6s. 4d.

Holne,	6d.	Stanlay,	7s. 1d.
Osset,	4s.	Alvirthorp,	3s.
Thornes,	2s.	Wakefeld,	8s. 6d.

[*mem.* 8.]

COURT held at Wakefeld on Friday after the Feast of St. Agatha the Virgin [Feb. 5], 6 Edw. II.

ESSOINS.—Elyas de Birton, by William Cussing. Surety : William de Castelford.

Hugh Nordar, attorney of Lady Margaret de Nevile, by Richard de Brerlay. Surety : Robert de Heyrode.

William de Rastrikes, by William de Castelford. Surety : John de Mora.

John de Lepton, by Thomas de Witteley. Surety : John de Mora.

Thomas de Thorneton, by Hugh de Thorneton. Surety : Richard de Salsa-mara.

Eadmund the Normaunt, by John Patrikes. Surety : William del Okes.

BAILIFF.—John de Mora amerced 6d. for withdrawing his suit against John de Heton.

HIPERUM.—William de Sunderland, 6d. for withdrawing his suit against Thomas de Waddesword, clerk, William quitclaiming all his right in 5 acres in Blacker to the said Thomas.

BAILIFF.—John de Hertesheved, clerk, surrenders to Richard, s. of Robert de Radeclif, junior, by his charter, all the lands and tenements in Hertesheved he had of the feoffment of Richard de Radeclif, senior ; and Richard, junior, does fealty. John de Hertesheved withdraws his suit, and is amerced 12d.

SANDALE.—Henry Fox, plaintiff, and William and James, sons of John Monk, have a love-day ; also Henry Fox and John de Raigate.

HIPERUM.—John de Westwod sues William Stirkes of Warlolay for cutting down and carrying away a tree in Warlolay belonging to plaintiff, worth 3s.; damages, 20s. William makes no defence ; and he is convicted ; fine, 12d.

THORNES.—John Dade gives 12*d.* to take ½ bovate in Thornes from John Pimerich for 9 years.

HIPERUM ; new rent.—William de Sunderland gives 2*s.* to take two acres of new land in Hiperum, at 6*d.* an acre.

SANDALE.—Idonia, wife of John Kokewald, gives 6*d.* to take an acre in the bounds of Sandale (½ acre being . . . . . . under Burghes, and 1 rood on Kilngrenes), from John, s. of John the Skinner.

HOLNE.—Richard del Bothe gives 6*d.* to take a rood in Over-thwonges, left unoccupied by Richard Dun.

STANLAY.—John, s. of Richard del Bothum, gives 6*d.* to take an acre in Stavenmere, from Richard, his father, the same that Richard bought from Eva de Ayketon.

HOLNE —John de Haroppe gives 40*d.* to take 9 acres in Alstanlay with buildings from Alice de Haroppe, his mother.

SOURBI ; new rent.—Adam de Midelton has license to take ½ acre of stone waste land in Soland ; rent, 3*d.*

John Pimerich sues Angnes Pimerich for land, appointing John Dade his attorney.

WAKEFELD ; new rent.—Peter de Acom gives 6*d.* to take a piece of the waste in Wakefield Market, to enlarge his booth, 15 feet by 1 foot ; rent, ½*d.*

HOLNE ; new rents.—John, s. of Michael de Holne, gives 6*d.* to take an acre of new land in Holne ; rent, 4*d.*

Henry de Heppeworth gives 2*d.* to take a rood there ; rent, 1*d.*

Alice, d. of Nelle, gives 2*d.* to take a rood of new land in W[o]lvedale ; rent, 1*d.*

Richard Bullok, 2*s.* for an acre of new land in Cartworth ; rent, 6*d.*

John de Rolkelay, 9*d.* for 1½ acres of new land in Wlvedale ; rent, 6*d.*

John the Hewer, 8*s.* for 4 acres of new land in Cartworth . . . . . .

John de Gairgrave, 6*s.* 8*d.* for a waif cow that came from Hiperum . . . . . .

William de Lockewod, 18*d.* for a waif hog stopped in the grave-ship of Osset.

Thomas the Litster of Wakefeld, who was a stallager, fined 40*d.* for alienating his tenement in Wakefeld . . . . .

Attachments.

HIPERUM.—William de Hailay, 2*d.*; John de Quitil de North-ourom, 3*d.*; Thomas Attenorthend, . . *d.*; Thomas, s. of Thomas, 2*d.*; John the Pinder, of Hiperum, 2*d.*; Henry the Pinder, 1*d.*;

William, s. of Addecokes, 1*d.*; Henry de Bentlay, 2*d.*; Thomas Bokerel, 1*d.*; Alice, d. of Henry the grave, 1*d.*; William Hare, 1*d.*; John, s. of Beton, 2*d.*; Henry Finche, 2*d.*; Alexander de Brighous, 2*d.*; John de Hilton, 2*d.*; Henry the Harpur, . . *d.*; John Soud [?], for vert.

. . . . .—Henry the Nauthird, 3*d.*; Robert the Yonger, 6*d.*; the handmaid of Walter Sko . . . . [*apparently two or three lines are torn away here at the bottom*].

SOURBY.—Nelle, s. of Ivo, 12*d.* for pigs that did not pay agistment.

Richard, s. of Swayn, 4*d.* for escapes and pigs.

Richard de Saltonstall and Ivo de Saltonstall, for pigs, agistment unpaid, 3*s.* and 10*d.*

Hugh, s. of Reginald, for disobeying the lord's prohibition, 40*d.*

The said Hugh, 5*d.*; Richard de Saltonstall, 3*d.*; Ivo de Saltonstall, 1*d.*, and Henry de Godelay, 6*d.*, for pigs, nuts, etc.

WAKEFELD.—Robert Beskes, 3*d.*; Robert Capon, 3*d.*; Margery, d. of Ivo, 2*d.*; the handmaids of Margery, d. of Geppe, 2*d.*; of John de Grenegate, 6*d.*, of John the Harpur, 2*d.*, of Hugh Bille, 2*d.*; Robert Tropynel, 2*d.*, for dry wood.

. . . . . .—John Bunny, 3*d.*; the wife of John, s. of Alan, 2*d.*; [?] John, s. of Margery, 6*d.* . . . . for dry wood.
[*Several entries apparently torn away here at the end of the membrane.*]
[*mem. 8 dors.*]

STANLAY.—Robert, s. of Walter, 6*d.*, for dry wood ; Richard del Ker, 6*d.*; John Fegald, 2*d.*; Robert Gunne, 12*d.*, and William Tagge, 2*d.*, for escapes.

OSSETE.—Adam, serving-man of Dobbe, William Cool, and the handmaid of Adam Loveladi, 2*d.* each for escapes, and the latter for going beyond the palisade.

THORNES.—Richard the Smith of Snaypethorp, 3*d.*; Roger Viron, 12*d.*, and Ivo the Smith, 6*d.*, for dry wood.

Sum total of this Court : 57*s.* 11*d.*; and new rent, 4*s.* 3½*d.*

i.e.				
Bailiff,	18*d.*	Thornes,	2*s.*	9*d.*
Hiperum,	6*s.* 6*d.* (and new rent, 6*d.*)			
Holne,	15*s.* 5*d.* (and new rent, 3*s.* 6*d.*)			
Sandale,	6*d.*	Stanlay,	2*s.*	10*d.*
Sourby,	9*s.* 9*d.* (and new rent, 3*d.*)			
Wakefeld,	15*s.* (and new rent, ½*d.*)			
Osset,	2*s.*	Alvirthorp,	20*d.*	

SANDALE.—Robert, s. of Petronilla, sues Thomas, s. of Robert de Milnethorp, for land. Surety: the grave of Sandale.

BAILIFF.—Thomas de Totill sues John, s. of Henry de Fekesby, for trespass. Surety: Alexander de Wodehous.

OSSET.—Richard del Dene sues Richard Broun on a plea of warranty of land. Surety: Adam de Dene.

COURT held at Wakefeld on Friday, the Morrow of St. Peter-in-Cathedra [Feb. 22], 6 Edw. II.

ESSOINS.—Edmund the Normaund, by John Patrickes. Surety: William, s. of Margery.

John de Lepton, by Thomas de Witteley. Surety: Richard de Birstall.

Elias de Birton (who afterwards came), by William de Castelford. Surety: John de Mora.

John de Schepedene, by John Pollard. Surety: Robert de Heyrode.

Nicholas de Cailli, by Henry de Methley. Surety: Richard de Birstall.

John de Thorneton, by Hugh de Thorneton. Surety: John de Mora.

BAILIFF.—Margery del Hill, 6d. for not prosecuting suit against Adam, s. of Adam de Sprigonell, in a plea of trespass.

Adam de Wodessom and John de Amyas [6d.] agree.

. . . . . .—Matilda, formerly wife of William Ilhore, . . d. for not prosecuting suit against Robert the clerk of Sandale.

. . . . . .—Henry Fox, plaintiff, against William and James, sons of John Munkes and John de Reygate, agree. [*The entry of fines paid by defendants is torn away from the margin.*]

BAILIFF.—The said Henry, plaintiff, against Thomas, s. of Peter de Walton [40d.], agree.

ALVIRTHORP.—John Dade, 3d. for false claim against Henry Nunne.

Richard, s. of Philip, and John Brun [2s.], agree.

OSSET.—John Moloce and Richard Passemer [12d.] agree.

THORNES.—John Pimeriche, by John Dade, his attorney, sues Agnes Pimeriche for ⅓ of a bovate in Thornes which defendant withholds under the name of dower; because after the death of William Pimeriche, her husband, and plaintiff's father, she received her full dower in a house and a curtilage. An inquisition is taken by the oaths of Philip de Mora, Robert de Lopsheved, Thomas Lilman,

William del Rodes, Richard Peger, Roger, s. of Alexander, John, s. of Magges, John de Haya, John, s. of Richard, Richard Proudfot, John Swan, and Richard, s. of [?] Philip ; who find for the defendant. Plaintiff fined 12*d*.

. . . . for false claim against Richard de Colley, for a sow torn by his dog.

. . . . to take a piece of waste ground in Wakefeld Market . . . . . . to enlarge his booth.

. . . . . . formerly wife of Elias ad Fontem [Attewell] de Wlve-dale gives 2s. for license to marry Thomas, s. of Simon de Heppe-worth [?].

HYPERUM.—. . . . . d. of Alexander de Sondirland, and Sarah, d. of John del Botherode, give 6*d*. each for license to marry.

RASTRIK.—Alice, sister of the said Sarah, 6*d*. for the same.

John, s. of John de Boutherode, 40*d*. to take a bovate of land in Rastrick, from Henr. [?] . . . . decease of the said John, his father.

ALVIRTHORP.—John Dade sues Henry Nunne, Adam Gerbot, and William, serving-man of Margery, on an agreement.

THORNES.—John, s. of Margery of Sneypthorp, gives 6*d*. to take 4 acres left unoccupied in Sneypthorp, for 6 years.

WAKEFELD.—John Dade gives 12*d*. to take an acre in the grave-ship of Wakefeld, viz. on Codenilcroft, from John Teuetes, to have half an acre at once, and the other half after the expiry of 7 years which John de Geirgrave has therein.

[*mem. 9.*]

THORNES.—John Postill's wife, 1*d*.; John de Haya, 8*d*.; Alice del Hill, 2*d*., for wood.

HORBIRY.—Hugh del Wro, for vert, 2*d*.

OSSETE.—Richard the Pinder, Richard Suartes, Jurdan Eliot, John Graffard, Robert Sunman, Agnes, serving-maid of Susan, 2*d*. each for escapes, etc.

John Maunsel, 6*d*. for vert.

ALVIRTHORP.—Robert Gerbot, for a cartload of wood, 6*d*.

OSSETE.—William Graffard, for vert, 12*d*.

WAKEFELD.—Robert Marescall, for an escape, 2*d*.

STANLEY.—Richard Longeschankes, for vert, 6*d*.

WAKEFELD.—Thomas, s. of Jose, 3*d*.; William Lentyn, 3*d*.; Adam the Weite, 3*d*.; Alice Coly, 4*d*.; Amabilla, handmaid of Alison, 2*d*.; Johanna Legette, 4*d*.; Alice, d. of Alexander, 6*d*.; the handmaid of William Margery, 2*d*.; John, s. of William, 2*d*.; Idonia Pollard,

2*d*.; the son of Robert the Goldsmith, senior, 2*d*.; Robert the Walker's handmaid, 2*d*.; John Leche, 2*d*.; Robert Hodde, 3*d*.; Robert Liftfast, 4*d*.; Richard Man's wife, 2*d*.; John Nolottes, 3*d*.; John Peger, 2*d*.; son of William Richaud, 3*d*., for dry wood.

Adam de Castilford, Richard de Ledis, William the Syour, and Henry Schepe, 3*d*. each for going beyond the palings.

Robert, s. of Jose, 3*d*.; Matilda Fraunceys' dau., 3*d*.; Idonea Pollard, 3*d*.; the handmaid of William Margerie, 2*d*., for dry wood.

The handmaid of John, s. of the same William Margery, 6*d*. for going into the park at night.

Ellen Cort, 2*d*. for dry wood.

Roger and William de Mara, 12*d*. each for going beyond the paling.

Henry de Aiketon, 6*d*. for vert beyond the paling.

Alice the . . . . . . ? [*presbitecysa*], 3*d*.; Henry Drake, 2*d*.; John Leche, 3*d*.; John Peger, 2*d*.; Magota Mouse, 3*d*.; Robert Capoun, 3*d*.; Elias, s. of Peter, 3*d*.; the son of Walter Ape, 2*d*. for dry wood.

Robert Tropinell and Thomas Molle, 3*d*. and 4*d*. for going beyond the palings.

Peter Spink's handmaid, 3*d*.; John de Rigewey's wife, 4*d*., surety, John Torald ; William, s. of Nicholas, 4*d*.; the daughters of Hugh Scapman and of John Richaud, 3*d*. each ; Gilbert Tynkeler's son, 3*d*.; the servant of Walter Scote, 3*d*.; the daughters of Beatrice de Aula and William Richard, 3*d*. each ; John Wilcocke's servant, 3*d*.; the sons of William the Lacer and Elias, s. of Peter, 3*d*. each; the servants of Nicholas Hogge and John Peger, 3*d*. each ; Henry the Bagger, 3*d*., and the daughter of Roger, s. of Kitte, 3*d*., for dry wood.

STANLEY.—John Flachard ; William, s. of Thomas de Wodehall ; Idonea de Wodehall ; Johanna, wife of Roger the Turnur, and Nicholas de Bateley, 3*d*. each for dry wood.

ALVIRTHORP.—William, s. of Walter ; the servants of John de Scolebrok and of Avice de Grengate ; Richard the Cobbler [*sutor*] ; Philip, s. of Emmote the Schacer ; William Damsel ; John the Bowere ; Peter the Lorimer ; and John the Mire's daughter, 3*d*. each for dry wood.

STANLEY.—Beatrice Gunne, 3*d*.; Robert del Spen's wife, 2*d*.; William del Spen's wife, 2*d*.; Walter del Spen's wife, 2*d*.; Walter Gunne, 3*d*.; John Attekirke, 2*d*.; William Tagges, 2*d*.; Isolda Ro, 4*d*., and Robert the Wite of Metheley, 3*d*., for dry wood.

WAKEFELD.—The sons of John Salman, John Sotherin, and Hugh Bille, 3*d*. each ; the handmaids of Henry de Scolebrokes and of Richard, s. of Henry, 3*d*. each, for dry wood.

C

STANLEY.—The wives of Broun and Thomas, s. of Stephen ; Margery, d. of Adam ; Richard Ruddockes and Thomas, s. of Adam, 3*d.* each for the same.

WAKEFELD.—Adam White's [*albi*] daughter, 3*d.*; John Richaud's son, 3*d.*; Thomas Molle's handmaid, 3*d.*; William Bull's handmaid, 2*d.*, and the son of William de Sandale, 2*d.*, for the same.

STANLEY.—Martin de Wirunthorp's, 2*d.*; John Cort's son, 2*d.*; Nicholas de Bateley, 3*d.*; Thomas Hannecok's handmaid, 3*d.*, for dry wood.

Beatrice Gunne, 3*d.*, and Julian Diker, 2*d.*, for going beyond the paling.

Walter Gunne, for vert, 6*d.*

WAKEFELD.—Robert Capon's daughter ; Peter Spink's wife ; the servants of William Wlmer and Walter Scotte ; William de Sandale's daughter ; William Richaud, and John Richaud's son, 3*d.* each for dry wood.

ALVIRTHORP.—Adam Gerbot and John Tup, 3*d.* each for the same.

STANLEY.—Adam the Heuwer, 3*d.*; John Bullockes, 2*d.*; Philip Isabell, 2*d.*; John Isabell, 2*d.*; Richard, s. of Robert, 2*d.*, and Gilbert Spritt, 3*d.*, for dry wood and escapes.

HOLNE.—William Weyer, 3*d.*; Henry, s. of Hugh de Tong, 2*d.*; Adam de la Grene, 3*d.*; Nicholas de Littelwode, 3*d.*, and Richard Child, 3*d.*

SANDALE.—Adam Sprigonell, 3*d.*; Robert Isoud, Adam Sprigonel, junior, William de la Grene and Margery del Hill, 3*d.* each, for escapes.

OSSETE.—John de Northwode ; Agnes, d. of Richard s. of John ; John, serving-man of Richard ; and Richard Suart's son, 2*d.* each for dry wood.

ALVIRTHORP.—John de Flansowe's wife, 7*d.* for vert, etc.

Alice, wife of Roger, 2*d.* for dry wood.

WAKEFELD.—The s. of John de Fery, senior, 2*d.* for the same.

ALVIRTHORP.—Alice de Flansowe, 3*d.* for the same.

WAKEFELD.—John de Grengate, John de Wrageby, John Sotheren, and Richard, brother of Henry, . . *d.* [*amounts worn away*] for dry wood.

THORNES.—Ivo the Smith, . . . ; John de Haya, . . . ; Roger Vyron's handmaid, 6*d.*; Thomas Vyron's daughter, 6*d.*; Alice Graffard, 6*d.*; Alice del Hill, 4*d.*, and John Costel, 2*d.*, for dry wood.

ALVIRTHORP.—Richard Broun's handmaid, 6*d.*; Alice Gerbot, 2*d.*, for the same..

WAKEFELD.—John de Scolebrokes, 3*d.*; Ralph, s. of Henry, 2*d.*; Alice Dayville, 2*d.*, for the same.

ALVIRTHORP.—Adam Gerbot, 3*d.*; Henry Wlf, 2*d.*, and Amabilla Wlfes, 2*d.*, for the same.

OSSETE.—William the Carpenter's wife, 2*d.* for the same.

WAKEFELD.—Hugh Bille's son ; Robert de Fery ; the handmaids of John the Harpur and of Robert Marescal ; Henry Dernelove and John Dade, 2*d.* each for the same.

OSSETE.—John Maunsel, . . *d.* for the same.

WAKEFELD.—Robert the Tailor [*Cissor*], [?] 2*d.* for the same.

ALVIRTHORP.—John Rate and Alice, d. of Robert de Alvirthorp, . . *d.* for the same.

[*Here the margin, containing the names of graveships, is torn away.*]

Margery del Hill sues Adam Sprigonel, junior, for trespass. Surety : Nelle de Donecastre.

John Attebarre sues Thomas Bunny for trespass. Surety : Peter de Acom. Thomas brings a cross-suit for breach of agreement. Surety : Richard Bunny.

. . . . . . sues John del Rode of Hecmundwik for debt. Surety : Richard del Rode.

William, s. of Roger de Sneypthorp, sues Robert, s. of Ivo, Hugh Viron and John Barett for trespass. Surety : Elias Bulmer.

Thomas de Tothill sues John, s. of Henry de Fekesby, for trespass. Surety : John, s. of Alexander.

Adam Strekeys sues Richard del Bothe on an agreement. Surety : Adam the Waynwriht.

[?] THORNES.—Margery, formerly wife of John Malin, sues Robert Pymme for dower. Surety : Thomas, s. of German.

. . . . . . Thomas Pees sues Robert Pees, his brother, for trespass. Surety : Matthew de Schellay.

[?] BAILIFF.—Robert Pees sues Matthew de Schellay for trespass. Surety : William de Lokkewod.

Thomas de Tothill sues John, s. of Henry, for trespass. Surety : John, s. of Alexander.

Sum total of this Court : 72*s.* 8*d.*; and new rent, 1½*d.*

i.e.			
Bailiff,	11*s.* 8*d.*	Sandale,	15*d.*
Alvirthorp,	6*s.* 7*d.*	Ossete,	4*s.* 6*d.*
Thornes,	5*s.* 3*d.*	Wakefeld,	27*s.* 5*d.*
Holn,	3*s.* 2*d.*	(and new rent, 1½*d.*)	
Rastrik,	4*s.* 4*d.*	Hiperum,	6*d.*

. . . .

[*mem.* 9 *dors.*]

COURT at Wakefeld on Friday after the Feast of St. Gregory the Pope [March 12], 6 Edw. II.

ESSOINS.—Hugh the Nodder, attorney of Margaret de Neville, by German Kay. Surety: Robert de Heyerode.

John de Schipedene, by Thomas de Qwittlay. Surety: Richard de Salsa-mara.

William de Rastrikes, by Thomas de Tothill. Surety: William Wildebor.

Robert del Grene of Osset, by John Dade. Surety: John de Lepton.

Elias de Birton, by William de Castelford. Surety: Richard de Birstall.

Nicholas de Cailly, by Henry de Metheley. Surety: Richard de Birstall.

RASTRIK.—Alcokes, grave of Rastrik, 12*d.* for concealing two plaints.

BAILIFF; recognisance.—Richard de Radeclif, junior, s. of Robert de Radeclif, appears before the full court and by his cirograph grants to John de Herteshed, clerk, half of all his lands and tenements in the bounds of Herteshed, to hold for a term of twenty-four years.

ALVIRTHORP.—Thomas Bunny, 6*d.* for resisting distraint by John Attebarre, the grave.

John Attebarre, 4*d.* for breach of agreement with Thomas Bunny.

BAILIFF.—Thomas de Tothill and John, s. of Henry de Fekesby, have a love-day.

William de la Rode sues John de la Rode of Hecmondwik for 3*s.* 9*d.*, balance of a sum of 37*s.* due for 2 acres of land in Hekmondwik, sold by plaintiff to defendant, 4 Edw. II. Defendant wages his law. Surety: John de Wodesom.

ALVIRTHORP.—John de Grenegate gives 12*d.* to take ½ acre in Alvirthorp fields (one rood lying under Neuton[clyf] [?], the other in le Morecroftes) from John Torald.

John, s. of Robert, 6*d.* to take a rood under Neutonclif from Adam Gerbod.

Nalle, widow of William Hoskel, sues Richard Wythundes for trespass. Surety: John de Flansau.

. . . . .—Thomas Martin, John, s. of Robert Slenges, Robert Nelotes and Robert, s. of John Roller, 40*d.* each for fishing at night in forbidden waters and taking water-wolves.

Robert Capon, 2*d.*; Walter Ape, 2*d.*; Ralph Bate, 2*d.*; . . . . . .
Molle, . . *d.*; [*two names illegible*] ; Matilda de Sourby, . . *d.*;
[*two names illegible*] ; Agnes, d. of Roger s. of Richard, 3*d.*; the
servant of Walter Scottes, 2*d.*; Robert the Couper, . . *d.*; Beatrice
de Aula, 1*d.*; Ralph, s. of Mille, 2*d.*; William the Lacer, 3*d.*; Thomas
Bole, 6*d.*; William Leuton, 2*d.*; Thomas Jose, 2*d.*; Adam, his brother, 2*d.*; Adam de Castelford, 3*d.*; Roger Wasche, 2*d.*; Walter
Pollard, 3*d.*; John . . . . . . , 6*d.*; Henry Drake, 6*d.*; Richard
Bullok, 12*d.*; John Wlmer, 12*d.*; John Peger, 12*d.*, Henry Faukon-
berg, 12*d.*, and John Withoundes, 2*d.*, for wood, vert, and taking
hay from the Earl's barn.

HIPERUM.—Henry Horum, 1*d.*; Gilbert Bridde, 3*d.*; Alexander
de Brighous, 2*d.*; Henry the Milner, 2*d.*; John de Scheplay, 2*d.*;
Henry Finche, 1*d.*; Thomas del Clifes, 2*d.*; Henry del Rode, 2*d.*;
William, s. of Adam, 1*d.*; John the Milner, 3*d.*; Peter del Barm, 1*d.*;
John de Quitill, 4*d.*; [*two names illegible*], 2*d.* and 3*d.*, for wood.

STANLEY.—Robert, s. of Geppe de Stanley, 6*d.*; the wives of
Robert del Spen and John Attekirk, 2*d.* each ; Richard del Bothum,
6*d.*; John Page, 6*d.*; Henry Tytinges, 2*d.*, John, s. of ʻAlice, 2*d.*;
Robert, s. of Walter, 6*d.*; Ibbota [?], sister of Gelle, 3*d.*; John, s.
of Philip Dod, 3*d.*; John Kokkespor, 2*d.*; Robert Chapman, 3*d.*;
Walter Odam, 4*d.*; Richard del Ker, 4*d.*; Gilbert the Theker, 2*d.*;
Walter Bateman, 2*d.*; Emma Wal . . . , 3*d.*; Robert de Milkelfeld,
2*d.*; [*four names illegible*], for dry wood.
[*mem.* 10.]

STANLEY.—Robert, s. of Geoffrey, 6*d.*; the daughter of Emma
Dulli, 3*d.*; Emma Dulli, 2*d.*; Adam Spinkes, 2*d.*; Johanna, wife of
Roger the Tornur, 3*d.*; John Hancokes, 2*d.*; the wife of Thomas s.
of Stephen, 2*d.*; Robert the Tailor of Erdeslaue, 12*d.*, surety, Robert
de Wyrunthorp,—for escapes and dry wood.

THORNES.—Ivo the Smith, 3*d.* for his dog.

ALVIRTHORP.—Adam Gerbot, 3*d.* for an escape.

OSSETE.—John the Walker, 3*d.*; Richard the Pynder, 2*d.*; the
wife of Adam the grave of Ossete, 6*d.*; Agnes, sister of the grave, 3*d.*;
John the Carpenter's daughter, 3*d.*; John de Northwod's wife, 2*d.*;
William Cool's son, 2*d.*; Richard Chapman's handmaid, 2*d.*, for
dry wood.

Sum total of this Court :—40*s.* 5*d.*, *i.e.* Rastrik,   12*d.*

	Alvirthorp,	2*s.* 7*d.*	Wakefeld,	23*s.* 6*d.*
	Hiperum,	2*s.* 5*d.*	Stanley,	8*s.* 9*d.*
	Thornes,	3*d.*	Ossett,	23*d.*

COURT at Wakefeld on Friday after the Feast of
St. Ambrose [April 4], 6 Edw. II.

ESSOINS.—Hugh the Nodder, attorney of Margaret de Nevill,
by German Cay. Surety: William de Casteforth.

Robert, s. of Geoffrey de Stanley, by William de Castelforth.
Surety: Richard de Salsamara.

John de Lepton, by Thomas de Wyttley.

John de la More, by John Pollard. Surety: Robert del Grene.

John de Schypedene, by John de Halifax.

Edmund the Normaund, by William, servant of Margery.
Surety: William Wildebor.

Robert de Heyrode, attorney of Dom. Thomas de Burgh, by
John Patrykes.

Thomas de Thorneton, by Hugh de Thorneton. Surety: Richard the Saussemer.

BAILIFF ; relief.—William, s. of Henry Erl de Wakefeld, and his
heir, comes into the full court and offers the lord the services he
owes for two royds [assartis] in Crigleston, and 7s. 6d. rent, which he
holds by charter, and 30s. 3d. rent, by another charter, which
tenements and rents he holds of the lord in chief by the service of
3s. 10½d. and half a pound of pepper yearly ; and he does fealty.
An ox to the Steward.

Thomas de Tothill and John, s. of Henry de Fekesbi, have
a love-day at the prayer of the parties [prece partium] in a plea
of warranty of land.

OSSETE.—Richard del Dene, 3d. for false claim against Richard
Broun.

. . . . . .—Margery del Hill, . . d. for false claim against Adam
Sprigonel, junior, in a plea of trespass.

. . . . . .—John del Rode of Hecmonwike makes his law against
William del Rode, who is fined 4d.

BAILIFF.—Thomas, s. of Peter Lewyn, essoins against John
Patrikes, by John Bullok, 6d.; void [vacet].

THORNES.—Margery, formerly wife of John Malin, appears
against Robert Pimerich in a plea for dower.   Robert does not come,
and the land in dispute is to be taken into the lord's hand by the
grave, assisted by 4 lawful men [legalibus hominibus].

BAILIFF.—Robert Pees essoins, by John Patrikes. Surety:
Henry, s. of German.

[mem. 10 dors.]

[OSSETE.]—The township of Ossete presents that Robert Pees took and imprisoned William, s. of William de Balne, the Earl's villein [*nativus*], keeping him in his house till he was delivered by William Wildbor and William de Heton, who mainprised him. Robert is to be attached for contempt.

. . . . . .—Roger the Minour, 6*d.* for withdrawing his suit against William Calf. Surety : John Mollan.

Beatrice, d. of Thomas de Fekesby, 6*d.* for not prosecuting her suit against William Wiles of Eland, John de Lyghtrige, and Thomas del Rode.

BAILIFF [*serviens*].—The Earl's bailiff charges John, s. of Henry de Fekesby, with bringing the Earl of Lancaster's bailiffs into Earl Warenne's fee to distrain on Thomas de Tothill. John wages his law.

SANDALE.—Robert, s. of Petronilla, and Thomas, s. of Robert de Milnethorp, agree, Robert taking one-sixth and Thomas five-sixths of the royd land in dispute between them. Robert fines 6*d.*

HIPERUM ; new rent.—William de Sunderland gives 6*d.* to take ½ acre of new land in the Holcans and the Bothes, in the graveship of Hiperum, paying 3*d.* rent.

ALVIRTHORP.—John, s. of Robert, gives 6*d.* to take a " broddole " in the graveship of Alvirthorp from Walter del Hill, for 12 years, after two crops [*vestures*] that Thomas, s. of Laurence, has in the same close by demise of the same Walter.

. . . . . .—William the Turnour, 6*d.*; Richard del Grene, 6*d.*; John del Grene, 6*d.*, and Matthew, s. of Thomas, 4*d.*, for vert, etc.

SOURBY.—John the Milner, 12*d.*; Roger, s. of Amabilla, 12*d.*; Robert Sabson, 3*d.*; Ellen Goos, 2*d.*; William, s. of Michael, 2*d.*; John, s. of William del Both, 2*d.*; Eva de Godeley, 3*d.*; William, her son, 2*d.*; the wife of William de Saltonstall, 40*d.*, and Henry Forester, 12*d.*; William, grave of Warlolley, 6*s.* 8*d.*; John, s. of Jordan, 13*s.* 4*d.*; Richard the Smith, 10*s.*; Adam, s. of Ivo, 6*s.* 8*d.*; Hugh, s. of Reginald, 6*s.* 8*d.*; Thomas de Rothelsete, 10*s.*; Robert, s. of Nabbe, 13*s.* 4*d.*, for dry wood, vert, etc.

STANLEY.—Henry, s. of John Poket, 6*d.*; Simon Tyting, 12*d.*, for thorns.

SANDALE.—Thomas Monkes, 6*d.*; John Mounk, Adam the Chapman of Wlfveley, Robert, s. of Hugh, John, s. of Ralph, John the Harpur, Walter del Bothe's handmaid, and Alice Gerbotes, 2*d.* each, for dry wood.

STANLEY.—John Corte's daughter ; the handmaid of Philip, s. of Agnes, and Martin Dede's daughter, 3*d.* each for timber felled.

WAKEFELD.—Robert de Chedel, 3*d.*; Walter Scot's handmaid, 4*d.*, and William de Sandale's son, 2*d.*, for dry wood.

ALVIRTHORP.—Robert Tupper, 3*d.* for wood felled.

WAKEFELD.—Richard the Clerk, 3*d.* for the same.

ALVIRTHORP.—Alice, d. of Broun, 3*d.*; John Suan's wife, 2*d.*, and Agnes, d. of Saynt, 2*d.*, for the same.

STANLAY.—Mille, wife of Richard Bullokes, 3*d.*; John Bullokes, 2*d.*, and the wife of Richard Longskank, 3*d.*, for the same.

WAKEFELD.—Hugh Chapman's son, 2*d.*; Margery, d. of Richard Junne, 3*d.*; William the Theker, Agnes, d. of Roger, William de Sandale's son, Robert the Couper's son, and the handmaid of Philip s. of Emma, 2*d.* each ; William Nelot, John Dun, Robert Snerd, 6*d.* each, for wood, etc.

Robert Walker, 6*d.* for putting a " fish-lepp " in the mill-pond.

OSSETE.—William, s. of Gotte, 6*d.* for dry wood.

ALVIRTHORP.—Richard Brounson's handmaid, 2*d.* for the same.

OSSETE.—Richard Suart, 6*d.*; Richard Passemer, 3*d.*, and Evota, wife of Serlo, 3*d.*, for dry wood and escapes.

ALVIRTHORP.—Richard, s. of Broun, 6*d.*; John Broun, 6*d.*; William of the Holyns, 2*d.*, and Adam Wlf, 2*d.*, for the same.

THORNES.—William, s. of Agnes, 6*d.*; Agnes, wife of Roger, 2*d.*, for dry wood.

WAKEFELD.—Robert Capoun, 3*d.* for the same.

Sum total of this Court : 102*s.* 11*d.*; and new rent, 3*d.*

i.e. Bailiff,	10*s.* 9*d.*	Sandale,	2*s.* 4*d.*
Ossettes,	21*d.*	Thornes,	12*d.*
Hiperum,	6*d.* (and new rent, 3*d.*)		
Alvirthorp,	3*s.* 2*d.*	Holne	22*d.*
Saureby,	74*s.* 2*d.*	Stanley,	2*s.* 11*d.*
Wakefeld,	4*s.* 6*d.*		

. . . . . .—. . . . . . sues Richard the Carpenter for trespass. Surety : Thomas Viron. Richard is attached by John, s. of Alan.

. . . . . . sues John Carpenter of Paynelhoton . . . . . .

. . . . . . sues . . . . . . Gerbotes for debt. Surety : William de Castilford.

[Alice de Birkingschaue] sues Alice Gerbot for trespass.

. . . . . . le . . gher sues John Pokettes for trespass. Surety : Robert Gum.

. . . . . . , wife of Elias, sues Adam Keneward for land.

...... sues Edmund the Normaund on an agreement.

William, s. of Peter de Thorp, sues Henry, s. of Wymark del Brok, for .... Surety: Henry de Northclyf.

[?] Richard del Ker sues Robert Gunne for seizure of cattle. Surety: Richard Steel.

[*mem.* 11.]

COURT held at Wakefeld, Friday after the Feast of
St. George [April 23], 6 Edw. II.

ESSOINS.—Elias de Birton, by William de Castilford. Surety: Richard Sausemer.

Richard de Birstall, by Richard Prestes. Surety: Robert de Heyrod.

Nicholas de Cailly, by Henry de Metheley. Surety: William Wildebor.

SANDALE.—A waif mare, hitherto in the keeping of the grave of Sandale, sold to Robert de Alta Ripa [and] Thomas de Holgate for 4s.

BAILIFF.—Thomas Pees [12d.] and Robert Pees agree.

Robert Pees [6d.] and Matthew de Schelveley agree. Surety: Richard, s. of John de Ossete.

THORNES.—William, s. of Roger de Snaipthorp, and Hugh Viron [6d.] agree. Surety: Roger Trailment.

ALVERTHORP.—William Grenehode sues Adam Gerbot for 7s., which is acknowledged; fine, 6d.

HOLNE.—Emma, wife of Elias, 6d. for not prosecuting her suit against Adam Strekeeyse.

BAILIFF.—Edmund the Normaund, 2s. for contempt of court. Sureties: William de Lockeuod and William Goldsmith.

HORBIRY.—Hugh Fox of Horbiry gives 2s. as a heriot on half a bovate and ½ acre in Horbiry, after the death of John Fox, his father.

ALVIRTHORP.—Adam, s. of Laurence, gives 6d. to take 3½ acres in Alvirthorp from Quenilda de Alvirthorp, for 12 years.

Thomas, s. of Laurence, 6d. to take ½ acre in Morecroftes from John Torald.

SANDALE.—Constance, d. of Roger de Castelford, 2s. to take a bovate, all but 2 acres, in Sandale, from her father.

Matilda, d. of Robert Clerk of Sandale, 6d. to take a garden with the meadow adjoining, and three acres of land, in Sandale, from her father.

STANLAY.—Robert Goes of Ouchethorp surrenders 16 acres of land in Ouchethorp, and one acre of meadow, and afterwards pays 12d. to take them again for his life, with remainder to Hugh de Balne, forester and Johanna, his wife. Hugh and Johanna pay 2s. for the recognition.

THORNES.—Margery, formerly wife of John Malyn, appears against Robert Pymerich [as on former occasions], in a plea of dower. The half bovate of land in question was taken into the lord's hand by William, s. of Roger, grave, of Thornes, Robert de Luppsheved, Richard Peger, John, s. of Richard, and Richard Proudfot. Defendant continues to make default. It is therefore adjudged that Margery, by default of defendant, shall recover her dower, by the view of the persons aforesaid and of the whole graveship. Robert fined 6d. for detention and defaults.

HORBERY.—The attaint of 24 (for which John, s. of Robert Pollard of Wakefeld, and Alice his wife, fined, against Adam, s. of William de Horbery), on the verdict of 12 jurors, who returned that after the death of Simon, father of the plaintiff Alice, a messuage and bovate of land in Horbery were left unoccupied for 4 years on the hands of Dom. John de Horbery, whereby Alice lost her rights therein, is taken by the oath of Henry le Wyte, Adam Heperourum [?], Hugh . . . . . . , John Silkelyng, Adam de Goukthorp, Robert Sonman, Richard del Dene, Richard Armerawe . . . . Hirnyng, Richard Passemer', John Maunsel, Richard, s. of Broun de Alvirthorp, John, s. of . . . . . . , ... Colley, John Swan, Henry del Bothom, Richard Withoundes, Richard, s. of Philip, and Robert, s. of Symon [?], who find for the defendant. John and Alice to go to prison for their recrimination. [*In the margin is* 12d.]

. . . . . .—. . . . . . Harpur sues William, s. of Robert de Heygherod, for trespass. Surety : Robert le Harpur.

. . . . . . sues the township of Schellay for trespass. Surety : William the Goldsmith.

. . . . . . sues John Dade for land. Surety : Henry Ganton. [*mem.* 11 *dors.*]

ALVIRTHORP.—Richard, s. of Philip de Alvirthorp, 6d. for an escape in the new park.

William, s. of Thomas, for an escape, 2d.

Robert de Flansau, 12d. for a cartload of wood.

OSSETT.—William Graffard, 12d.; Thomas the Pynder, 12d.; John, s. of Richard s. of John, 6d.; Adam, serving-man of Robert, 6d.; Richard Suart, 6d.; Margery, d. of the grave, 2d.; Richard, s.

of John, 2*d.*; the wife of Matthew de Ossete, 2*d.*; John the Wayn-wricht's son, 3*d.*; William Gotson, 6*d.*, for vert.

THORNES.—Thomas Viron's son, 2*d.* for dry wood.

WAKEFELD.—John de Sculbrokes, 2*d.* for the same.

Richard the Clerk, 6*d.* for a cartload of wood.

HORBERY.—Agnes Dipsy, for vert in the Hallerode, 6*d.*

Robert in the Wro, 2*d.* for dry wood.

STANLEY.—Hugh Findyrn and Margery Cocer, 3*d.* each for vert, etc.

Sum total of this Court:—*27s. 5d.*, *i.e.*

		Bailiff,	3*s.* 6*d.*
Holne,	6*d.*	Alvirthorp,	3*s.* 2*d.*
Ossete,	4*s.* 9*d.*	Sandale,	6*s.* 6*d.*
Thornes,	14*d.*	Wakefeld,	8*d.*
Stanlay,	3*s.* 6*d.*	Horbiry,	3*s.* 8*d.*

SOURBY.—Alice the Mercer sues Wymarka, d. of Seye, for trespass. She is distrained by a woollen cloth.

John de Sonderland sues Michael de Routonstal for trespass. Surety: Henry de Saltonstall.

Amabilla, d. of Elias de Warloley, sues Hugh, s. of Roger [?], for land. Surety: Elyas, s. of Hugh.

HYPERUM.—Richard the Hopper sues Henry the Marrewe for land. Surety: Symon del Dene.

SOURBY.—Robert the Sklatter sues Adam Cappe for trespass. Surety: Richard Alman, who likewise sues the said Adam.

RASTRIK.—Henry de Tothill sues William de Tothill on an agree-ment. Surety: Thomas de Hasti.

HYPERUM.—John de Schepley sues William de Tothill for tres-pass.

COURT held at Halifax on Monday before the Feast of
St. Dunstan [the deposition, May 19], 6 Edw. II.

SOURBY.—Alice the Mercer, 2*d.* for false claim against Wymarka, d. of Seye.

HYPERUM.—John de Sonderland, 6*d.* for false claim against Michael de Routonstall.

SOURBY.—Elyas, s. of Elyas the Milner, 12*d.* to take 3½ acres in Sourby from John the Milner, for 12 years.

Robert, s. of Roger, 12*d.* to take 2 acres in Sourby to himself and his heirs, and 1½ acres, for 11 years, from Henry del Loue.

Henry del Loue, 6*d.* to take an acre in Sourby from Richard Azerley.

John de Cogcroftes, 5s. to take the whole of the moiety of the land, with three houses, which Adam the Crouder held in Sourby, excepting one enclosure of new land.

Elyas, s. of Ivo, 3d. for wrongfully withholding ½ quarter of oats from Matilda the Webster.

Robert the Couper of Warleley gives 6d. to take ½ acre in Warleley from John the Webster of Warleley.

Robert, s. of John Hodde, gives 2s. to take 2½ acres with buildings in Soureby of John Pikeston, for 11 years.

Robert de Saltonstal, 6d. for wrongfully detaining from Matilda, formerly wife of Thomas de Counale, her dower in 4 acres and a toft in Sourby.

The said Matilda sues the said Robert for her dower in 6 acres in Bentlayrode ; defendant says her husband Thomas had no rights in the said land, except as guardian of his son John, who took the said land from the lord ; and he calls the rolls to witness. They are to be examined.

Amabilla, d. of Elyas de Werlouleye, sues Hugh, s of Reginald, for a bovate of land in Werlouleye, after the death of John, s of Elias, her brother, who died without issue, whose next heir the said Amabilla is ; Hugh says he had entry into the land from the present Steward, because it was lying waste, and calls the rolls to witness.

The township of Sourby presents that the goods and chattels of Philip the Waleys, fugitive, were collected to the value of 100s. and more, and given over to John de . . . . . . , E . . . . . . Mora, who were . . . . . . of the said Philip. And the township of Soland, after the flight of the said Philip, was distrained for wrong- fully withholding the said [goods] and chattels, etc., by eleven beasts, which were sold by the said John de Miggely, and by William, s of Ivo de Soland, and Thomas the Geldhird for 55s., which the said three men received. And the whole township of Soland is charged with the default of the said John and the others, with regard to the felon's goods.

Sourby.—Elyas, s. of Ivo, 4d.; William Horsenave, 2d.; John de Holgate, junior, 3d.; Adam, s. of Hugh, 3d.; William del Estwod, 3d.; Hugh, s. of Nalle, 3d.; Alota; wife of Hugh, 2d.; Alan de Miggeley, [?] 2d.; Richard atte Townend [ad caput ville], 2d.; William, s. of Michael, 2d., for escapes in the Frith, the Baytinges, and in Saltonstal.

John, s. of Robert Cheswelleye, 2d.; Richard, s. of Robert de Cheswelleye, 3d.; Ivo, s. of William, 2d.; John Sourmilk, 1d.; Oto the Smith, 1d.; Hugh, s. of Eva, 1d., and Jordan del Hirst, 2d., for the same.

Amabilla, d. of Elyas de Warleley, and Hugh, s. of Reginald, agree on condition that Amabilla quitclaims to Hugh all her right in the bovate for which she sued, and Hugh fines 40d. for the recognition.

Sum total of this Court : 17s. 11d., i.e. Sourby,   17s. 5d.

Hyperum,   6d.

[mem. 12.]

TOURN there the same day.

12 JURORS.—John del Hassenhirste, William del Estwod, Adam del [?] Schaye, Richard the Taillur of Waddesworth, John de Cogcrofte, John, s. of John de Soland, John de Langley, Henry de Hollegate, Henry, s. of Wilcocke, William de Counale, William de Skircotes, and Bate the Litster [tinctor] of Halifax, who say :—

SOURBY.—Eva, wife of Richard de Saltonstal, drew blood from Adam the Wild in defending herself in her own house. Adam is therefore fined 12d. for assaulting her.

Henry Forester drew blood from Richard, s. of Hugh, 12d.

Ellota de Bradeley, 4d. for brewing bad ale.

BAILIFF.—Thomas, s. of Christiana Skot of Extwysel, which Thomas is called Cockehakel, is a common thief, and stole 3 cows from Dom. Matthew the chaplain ; one from Alice, wife of Adam, and a steer from Robert, s. of Jordan. He is to be taken.

John del Risseleye, adulterer with the wife of Thomas de Langefeld, by the will of the said wife, received a quantity of the said Thomas's goods ; they were carried to the house of the said John by one Alice, d. of the Genour, having been delivered to her by the said wife. They are to be attached.

SOURBY.—Hugh de Lyghthesels made an encroachment of about 20 feet by 10 feet [as is testified by divers of the neighbours] on the lord's unoccupied land. He is to be attached. The township of Soland concealed this encroachment.

Sum total of this Tourn : 2s. 4d.—all from Sourby.

COURT at Brighouses on Tuesday before the Feast of St. Dunstan [May 19], 6 Edw. II.

RASTRICK.—Henry, s. of Peter, fails to prosecute his suit against Alice, d. of Thomas s. of Simon ; he is pardoned at the instance of Beatrice de Tothill.

HYPERUM.—Robert, s. of Christiana, 6*d*. for not coming to answer Symon del Dene.

William, s. of Peter, 6*d*. for not prosecuting his suit against Henry, s. of Wymarkes del Brokes.

Symon the Toller gives 12*d*. to take 4 acres in Hyperum from Dom. Richard, chaplain, for 12 years.

Henry de Coppley, John, s. of Walter de Northourum, and Wauter de Adderiggate, 3*d*. each for not coming.

Richard, s. of Henry the Hopper, sues Henry Marrue for a bovate of land with buildings in Prestley, as his inheritance after the death of Alice his mother, to whom the inheritance descended after the death of Elyas de la Grene, brother of Alice, who died without issue, seised of the said land. Defendant says the land lay unoccupied after Alice's death for 2 years and more, and that Peter de Lounde, then Steward, forced defendant, the Earl's villein [*nativus*], to take the land, by default of the heirs of said Alice. An inquisition is taken by the oaths of William del Bothes, Thomas, s. of Thomas, Alexander the Waynwrith, Henry de la Rode, Thomas the Webster, Thomas del Clif, Richard, s. of Jordan de Northourum, Bate del Bothe, Roger de Brighouses, Richard, s. of Walter de North ourum, John del Clyf and Henry the Pynder, who confirm the defendant. Plaintiff fined 6*d*. for false claim.

He also sues Thomas, s. of Jordan de Rokes, for 8 acres on a similar claim ; the jury say the land lay unoccupied for 8 years and upwards, and Peter de Lounde gave it as above, fined 6*d*. for false claim.

Henry, s. of William de Halifax, gives 6*d*. to take ½ acre in North-ourum from Richard, s. of . . . . . .

RASTRICK.—William de Tothill surrenders ½ bovate . . . . . . and afterwards takes it again, with remainder to . . . . . . , s. of Richard de Tothill.

HYPERUM.—Symon del Dene sues Robert, s. of Christiana de Northourum, for ½ a rood of land . . . . . . An inquisition is taken by the above jurors, who say the land belongs to the bovate the plaintiff holds. Defendant fined 6*d*. for false claim.

The same inquisition finds that, in the last customary tallage, John de Schepley was charged 20d. over and above his proper proportion on his land, because William de Tothill held ⅓ thereof in dower with his wife, mother of the said John, who is therefore to recover the 20d. against William. And William is amerced 6d.

Cecilia and Amabilla, daughters of Elyas de Sourby, sue John the Milner del Bothes for one-fourth of ½ bovate in the Bothes, as their inheritance, after the death of Richard, s. of Symon del Bothes, their uncle, who died without issue lawfully begotten. The above jury find that Cicilia del Bothes, mother of the said Richard, acquired ½ bovate in the Bothes from one Julian de Bothes . . . . . to hold to herself and her said son Richard, and Richard died without issue . . . .

[*The end of the membrane is in rags, but from the few words that remain here and there it seems to be said that* Cicilia continued to hold the bovate, and married William del Bothes, and that . . . . . . Matilda . . . .]

───────

[*mem.* 12 *dors.*]

TOURN there the same day, viz. at Brighouses.

12 JURORS.—Master Thomas de Dalton, Alexander del Fryth, John the Fleming of Dalton, John de Lokwod, senior, John the Clerk of Hertesheved, John de la Rode, John de Byrstall, Thomas Dines of Dalton, Roger de Aula, Thomas del Wode of Fekesby, Lovecokes de Nettelton, John, s. of Adam de Lokwode, who say :—

BAILIFF.—Thomas, s. of Thomas the Milner, living in Holne-frith, drew blood from Matilda, wife of Roger the Milner, 12d.

Jouwetta, wife of John de Stourleye [?], from Beatrice, hand-maid of the Dame del Bothem, 12d.

Thomas de Tothill raised the hue on John, s. of Henry de Fekesby ; and John is fined 12d. for breaking Thomas's fold, and taking his cattle, and 12d. for raising the hue without cause on the said Thomas, for taking a pledge of him, when tres-passing.

John de Avenlay, 12d. for blocking up a pathway within the bounds of Barkesland, between Willestrichell and Evotestrichell.

Sum total of this Tourn : 5s., all from the Bailiff.

COURT at Byrton, on Thursday before the Feast of
St. Dunstan [May 19], 6 Edw. II.

HOLNE.—William de Ryeley and Gilbert the Litster of Byrton
[6d.] agree.

Roger, s. of Matthew de Schepeley, and William Brid [6d.] agree.
William finds sureties that he will not trespass in the wood or
meadows of William de Schefeld, viz. Thomas Brid and Adam
Keneward.

Henry de Hoton and Richard de Byrton surrender 33½ acres
with buildings in Fouleston, and afterwards pay 2s. to take the
same again for their lives, with remainder to Elias, s. of the
said Richard, or to Robert, his younger brother, if Elias should
die without issue ; and, in default again, to the right heirs of
Richard de Byrton. Sureties : Henry de Hoton and Richard
de Byrton.

. . . . . .—. . . . . . la Rode sues John, s. of Adam de
Heppeworth, Thomas, s. of Richard, Nicholas, s. of John s. of
Gilbert, and Richard, his brother, for destroying the ditches
and fences of a certain royd that he took from the lord . . . . .

. . . . . .—[John] . . . . . sues Richard del Bothe for a rood
of land which he asserts belongs to certain lands which Thomas,
s. of Margery, father of the said John, took from the lord
. . . . . . says that 16 years ago the present Steward granted
the land to John de Byrstall until someone else should take
the same lands. Richard says he had the lands from John
de Byrstall, who took the same in full court. The rolls are to
be examined.

Alan del Dam, 6d. for blocking up a lane in Wlvedale with
his timber and dung-heap, so that cattle cannot water.

An inquisition finds that Thomas de Elwardhilles suffered
a certain room he held of his wife's dower to be injured by
want of maintaining the roofing ; he is to keep the house up
and satisfy Adam de Butterley for the damages ; fine, 6d.

Robert Wades gives 6d. for license to take an acre in Fouleston from Emma del Storthes, for 8 years.

Adam Robuk, 2s. to take a house and 5 acres in Twong
from Hugh del Hole. Sureties for his maintaining the same in
proper order : Hugh del Hole and John, s. of Geoffrey de
Littelwod.

Riginald, s. of William the Turnur, 12d. as a heriot on 6
acres and buildings in Holne, after his father's death.

John, s. of Michael de Holne, 6d. to take an acre in Holne from Thomas de Bouderod to him and his heirs.

Thomas, s. of Gilbert de Alstanley, 6d. to take ⅜ acre in Alstanley from his father.

John Baron, 12d. to take 2 acres in Alstanley from Thomas, s. of Gilbert, who gives 2s. to take 4 acres from the said John.

Matilda, d. of Adam de Carlecotes, 2s. as a heriot on 8 acres in Wlvedale, after her father's death ; and, as she is under age, she is committed to the guardianship of Alice, her mother.

William del Flosche, 12d. to take 4 acres in Littelwod from Adam del Grenewod, for 8 years.

Matthew, s. of Thomas, 6d. for false claim against Adam, s. of Jordan, and John de Loukes.

Adam, s. of [A]d[am] [?] the Milner . . . . . . acre of land of the said Matthew, s. of Thomas, as he gave mainprise on behalf of a certain stranger ; 6d.

. . . . to take an acre in Alstanley from Adam del Grene, in exchange.

[*Three entries at any rate are torn away at the bottom of the page.*]

[*mem.* 13.]

COURT at Wakefeld, held on Friday before the Feast of St. Dunstan [May 19], 6 Edw. II.

ESSOINS.—Hugh the Nodder, attorney of dame Margaret de Nevill, by German Cay. Surety : Robert de Hegherode.

John de Lepton, by Thomas de Wytelay. Surety : John de Mora.

Thomas de Thornton, by German Cay. Surety : William de Castelford.

John de Schypedene, by Richard Alman. Surety : William del Okes.

William de Rastrik, by William de Floketon. Surety : William Ingrays.

Eadmund the Normaunt, by John Patrikes.

BAILIFF.—A jury at the tourn at Burton testify that Symon de Thurstanland had concealed [the matter of] the path for which he had been indicted at the previous tourn ; which path is now straightened. Amerced 6d.

Roger Beel, 12d. for many defaults.

John the Carpenter of Paynelhoton essoins against Roger Viron, by German Swerd   Surety : Ivo the Smith.

D

Thomas de Tothill sues John, s. of Henry de Fekesby, for damage done by his cattle to plaintiff's grass in a place called the Oldrode ; damages, 5s., and grass consumed, 6s. 8d. John wages his law, but fails to make it ; fine, 6d.

SOURBY.—An infirm mare, found waif, sold to Henry de Saltonstall for 2s.

BAILIFF.—Roger Viron sues Richard the Carpenter for assaulting him as they were leaving Ivo the Smith's house in Snaypthorp, striking him with a stick on his head and shoulders; damages, £10. Richard wages his law. Surety : Ivo the Smith.

John Patrikes and Thomas, s. of Peter Lewyn [6d.], agree ; likewise John and Eadmund the Normaunt.

. . . . .—Adam Cappe, 6d. for not coming to answer Robert the Sclatter.

ALVIRTHORP.—John Dade, 4d. for false claim against Henry the Stunt, Adam Gerbot, and William, servant of Margery.

THORNES.—William, s. of Roger de Sneypthorp, plaintiff, and Robert, s. of Ivo and John Baret [12d.], agree.

BAILIFF.—Adam de Wlfwro, 12d. for not prosecuting his suit against the township of Schellay.

ALVIRTHORP.—John Dade to be summoned to answer William Templer in a plea of land. William appoints Henry Ganton his attorney.

BAILIFF.—Matilda Harpur [12d.] and William, s. of Robert de Hegherode, agree.

HIPRUM.—Roger de Clyfton gives 5s. to take 10½ acres in Haselhirste from John de Birstall, Symon del Dene, and Richard, s. of Walter.

New rent.—Adam Pocokes gives 6d. to take a piece of the waste in Brighous, 20 feet by . . . . . . ; rent, 1½d.

HOLNE.—Henry the Waynwright, 12d. for the custody of the lands of John, s. of John . . . . . . nd for 12 years . . . . .

BAILIFF.—William de Botterworth, taken for trespass committed in Sourbyschire, gives 40s. [to be acquitted thereof]. Sureties : Henry de Walda and John, s. of Robert the Mercer.

[ALVIRTHORP.]—Thomas, s. of Laurence, 6d. to take a rood of meadow in Alvirthorp from Quenilda, d. of Hugh, for 20 years.

. . . . . .—John Poket, 2s. 6d. for defamation against Henry de Walda, William de Locwod, and Philip the Syour, of which he is convicted by inquisition.

Richard, s. of Bate de Osset, 12*d.* for license to give in marriage Agnes, his daughter.

[*mem.* 13 *dors.*]

OSSET.—A waif calf, found in the graveship of Osset, sold by the Steward to William de Lokcewod for 3*s.*

Sum total of this Court : 74*s.* 1*d.*, and new rent, 1½*d.*

	i.e. Bailiff,	56*s.* 9*d.*	Sourby,	2*s.* 6*d.*
	Hiperum,	5*s.* 6*d.*	(and new rent, 1½*d.*)	
	Holne,	12*d.*	Alvirthorp,	10*d.*
	Osset,	4*s.*	Thornes,	12*d.*
	Stanley,	2*s.* 6*d.*		

TOURN at Wakefeld the same day.

12 JURORS.—Robert de Wyrunthorp, William Ingrays, John Patrikes, Thomas de Wytlay, Thomas de Seyvil, Richard de Birstall, William de Deusbery, German Filkoces, Robert the Walker, Henry de Chevet, Thomas Alayn, and William Grenhod, who say —

BAILIFF.—Paulinus de Emeley brewed contrary to the assize, viz. at 1½*d.*; amerced 2*d.*

Richard Cosin drew blood from Haukin the Mareschall ; 12*d.*

Robert, s. of William the Sonnyor de Floketon, from Adam Pawe of Emmelay ; 12*d.*

John de la Chapele of Emmelay from John Fraunceys ; 12*d.*

Richard the Styrter from William, s. of Richard de la Haye.

William, s. of John Munkes, from Henry de Ketelsthorp ; 12*d.*

James, s. of John Munkes, from the same ; 12*d.*

Thomas, s. of Peter de Walton, and John de Reygate, 12*d.* each for the same.

Richard the Shepherd, John de Thornhill in Heton, and Henry de Eland, servant of Thomas de Heton, were taken by William Lighthesels to assault William Haliday, and they received two sheep for beating him, and they violently drew blood from the said William.

William de Clayton and William Haliday in self-defence drew blood from Richard the Shepherd and Henry de Eland.

Thomas Pes from Robert Pes, 12*d.*; and Robert from Thomas, 12*d.*

The wife of Richard the Litster of Deusbery, for brewing, etc., 6*d.*

Hugh Modisaule and Robert del Okes, 12*d*. each for mutual assault.

John Caynok drew blood from Hugh Danyel, 12*d*.

Robert the Harpur of Walton, 6*d*. for baking bread to sell without weight.

William de Heyrode drew blood from Malina the Harpere ; 12*d*.

Roger, s. of Thomas Viron, from Hugh his brother.

Richard and John Carpenter from Roger Viron ; 2*s*.

William del Spen from Odam de Stanley, 12*d*.; and *vice versa*, 12*d*.

Richard Longschankes' wife commonly brews at 1*d*.; amerced 6*d*.

. . . . . . has a grudge against Robert Pees of Osset, and followed and assaulted him . . . . . .

. . . . . . John de Morl [?] killed [?] Thomas Laverok de Morlay in the house of Hugh the Chapman of Wakefeld . . . . . he is sent to York Gaol.

. . . . . . Drake and Mariota, widow of Henry Archor, drew blood from Joan Baba ; 12*d*.

William Fenne from Johanna Pymme ; 12*d*.

John de Heton assaulted John the Bocher, pursuing him into his own chamber ; amerced 12*d*.

William Fenne levied the hue without cause on John the Bocher ; he is to be attached when he can be found.

Robert de Ludham, 6*d*. for not coming.

Gilbert le Tincker came and walked about the town at night ; he is not obedient to law, and has no sufficient property with which to answer ; he is to be attached.[1]

Hugh the Chapman, his wife, and all his family receive evildoers into their house ; they are to be attached.

Isabel, d. of Hugh the Chapman, drew blood from Gilbert the Tincker.

Elizabeth, d. of Alan, is constantly raising disputes with her neighbours, and insulting them. She is to be attached.

Henry de Adingham created a nuisance on the King's highway in Wrennegate, with his dung-heap ; amerced 12*d*.

---

[1] The subsequent order for his attachment is given   because he is not obedient to regulations, and is not of sufficient means (*sufficiens*) to live in the town.''

William del Clogh raised a bank round a piece of meadow in the town-common, which was presented at a previous tourn, since then he has raised the bank afresh ; amerced 12d.

Richard Peger drew blood from Robert Codeling ; 12d.

[*Three lines, at any rate, are destroyed at the bottom of the sheet.*]

[*mem.* 14.]

COURT held at Wakefeld on Friday in Whitsun-week, 6 Edw. II.

ESSOINS.—Thomas de Thorneton, by Hugh de Thorneton. Surety : Richard de Salsamara.

Nicholas de Caylly, by Henry de Metheley. Surety : Adam Hood.

Robert the Draper, by William de Castelforth. Surety : Richard de Birstall.

John de Lepton, by Thomas de Wytteley. Surety : Robert de Heyerode.

John de Schipedene, by Adam de Tothill. Surety : Henry de Ganton.

Elias de Birton, by Thomas Grenhod. Surety : Eadmund the Normaund—afterwards he came.

Thomas de Bellhous, by Roger Bele. Surety : John de Mora.

BAILIFF.—William del Cloghe, 6d. for many defaults. And the imparlance between Nicholas de Bateley and the said William is removed into the Burgess Court, because they are burgesses.

Roger Viron sues John Carpenter of Painelhoton for assault ; damages, £10. John wages his law. Surety : Ivo the Smith.

HOLNE.—John Kenward, one of the jurors on the inquisition between Adam Strekeyse and Richard del Bothe, 12d. for not coming.

John de la Grene, 12d. for the same.

BAILIFF.—Henry Ganton sues Roger Bele, John Isabel and Philip Isabel for 14s. 2d., being part payment for a horse bought by Roger of plaintiff last year, for 26s. Defendants cannot deny ; amerced 18d.

SOURBY.—Richard Alman, 6d. for not prosecuting Adam Capper.

ALVERTHORP.—Adam, s. of Thomas de Flansaue, sues Quenilda, d. of Hugh de Alverthorp, for 3s. 6d. for sundry amercements for which he was made responsible in his accounts. An inquisition was to be taken, but defendant does not attend ; she is therefore considered convicted of the debt ; amerced 3d.

SOURBY.—Matilda, formerly wife of Thomas de Counale, 6*d.* for not proceeding in the prosecution of Robert de Saltonstall in a plea of dower ; is amerced 6*d.*

HOLNE.—Emma, d. of Alice de Holne, plaintiff, William Benet and Cecilia, his wife, defendants, agree. The fine, due from Cecilia, pardoned because it was in the turn.

. . . . . .—John, s. of Jordan de Warlolay, sues Henry the Clerk of Warlolay for trespass. Surety : Adam [?], s. of Ivo de Warlolay.

[STAN]LAY.—Thomas, s. of Stephen, sues Richard, s. of Robert de Bateley, for assault ; damages, 100*s.*; defendant cannot deny it ; amerced 12*d.*, and 6*d.* for withdrawing his suit against the said Thomas.

WAKEFELD.—The booth [*selda*] in Wakefeld held by Master Robert Tyrsi taken into the lord's hand, because he is dead.

. . . . . .—Richard Child and Adam Benne [3*d.*] agree.

[ALVERTHORP.]—William Grenhod gives 6*d.* to take a " brod-dole " of meadow in Alverthorp, for 20 years, from Richard Wythoundes.

[SANDALE.]—Henry Fox, 2*s.* to take 4 acres, with the meadow thereto belonging, in Westenges in Crigleston, from John, s. of William de Plegwyk.

[THORNES.]—Thomas de Wytley, 6*d.* to take 2¾ acres in Thornes from Margery, formerly wife of John Malyn, for 9 years.

[SOURBY.]—Elias, s. of Ivo de Warlolay, 18*d.* to take 3 acres in Sourby, on Wildeborhill, from Robert, s. of John Hodde.

[SANDAL.]—John, s. of Robert the Smith of Dritkar, 6*d.* to take ¼ of a rood in Dritker from William, his brother.

Roger, s. of Henry de Dritker, and Alice, his wife, 12*d.* to take 3 roods in Crigleston from Thomas, s. of Roger.

Adam, s. of Jordan, 18*d.* to take 6¾ acres with buildings in Wlfdale from Elyas, s. of Adam Cadman, for 20 years.

Mary, wife of Peter de Wildborleye, 6*d.* to take an acre

. . . .

[*mem.* 14 *dors.*]

ALVIRTHORP.—Henry del Bothem and John Broun, 3*d.* each for one white thorn.

Henry Quitthard, 2*d.* for dry wood.

Thomas Assolf, 6*d.* for breaking the palings ; Ellen Attekyrk, 2*d.*; Robert the Taillur, 2*d.*; Symon Ward, 12*d.*; William, s.

of Thomas, 4*d.*; Adam Gerbot, 6*d.*, for escapes ; Richard, s. of Broun, 6*d.* for dry wood.

John Waltbaly, 6*d.* for vert. Surety : John Broun.

WAKEFELD.—Robert, s. of Gelle, Henry the Nauthird, 2*d.*; William the Theker and William de Sandale's son, 2*d.* each ; John Tasse, the handmaids of Elyas Tyrsy and Nicholas del Toun, 2*d.* each ; John de Amyas's maid, 4*d.*; Robert Capoun's maid, 2*d.*; Philip Chacer, 3*d.*; John Dade's handmaid, 2*d.*, and the handmaid of Richard, brother of Henry, 2*d.*, for dry wood and escapes.

Alexander, servant of German Filcokes, for a green staff cut in the Hagge, 12*d.* Surety : German Filcokes.

THORNES.—William Dolfyn, 1*d.* for a green staff ; Roger Frayllment, Thomas Viron's son, Roger Viron's wife, 2*d.* each for dry wood.

Thomas Viron's son, John Baret, the daughter of Margery del Haghe, and Ivo the Smith's son, 2*d.* each for taking birds.

SAURBY.—William de Stodelay, 6*d.*; John de Hertlay, 3*d.*; William del Foldes, 3*d.*; John Culpun, 6*d.*; John del Redeker, 6*d.*; William del Bothem, 6*d.*; Thomas del Rode, 6*d.*; Robert de Saurby, 1*d.*; Roger, s. of German de Grenwod, 6*d.*; Roger, s. of Amabilla, 1*d.*; John de Miggelay, 1*d.*; Thomas, his son, 1*d.*; Magota de Scyrcote, 4*d.*; Hugh de Baliden, 2*d.*; William, s. of Bateman, 2*d.*; Henry del Holgate, 3*d.*; Robert de Saurby, 2*d.*; John, brother of Roger Seward, 1*d.*; Alice de Illingworth, 2*d.*; Richard de Witteleghe, 2*d.*; Ote the Smith, 1*d.*; Thomas Otes, 2*d.*; Adam del Grefes, 1*d.*; Ivo del Hole, 1*d.*; Peter del Grefes, 1*d.*; Matthew del Wod, 6*d.*, for escapes of cattle.

OSSETE.—Henry the Cobbler [*sutor*] of Gaukthorp, 2*d.* for dry wood.

BAILIFF.—Alice Barill sues Richard Tilly and Alice his wife, for detaining a chest. Surety : Elyas de Birton.

ALVERTHORP.—Roger Preest sues Richard de Colley for debt. Surety : John Attebarre, senior.

BAILIFF.—William Erl sues Margery, formerly wife of Henry Erl, for seizing a mare. Surety : William the Goldsmith.

John, s. of Sybil, and William Cussing sue Walter del Hill for trespass. Surety : William de Castelford.—In the Burgesses' Court.

John Cay sues Adam Gerbot, William Nelot, John Tasse, Thomas, s. of Laurence, Roger Beele and John Pollard for debt. Surety : William the Goldsmith.

John Cay also sues Dom. Radulph de Emelay for debt.

STANLAY.—John Bull sues Robert Gunne for land. Surety:
Thomas Bull.

Sum total of this Court : 36s. 2d., and new rent, 3s. 7d.

i.e. Alvirthorp,	5s. 1d.	Bailiff,	2s.
Osset,	2d.	Sandale,	2s. 6d.
Thornes,	21d.	Stanlay,	18d.
Holne,	10s. 2d.	(and new rent, 3s. 7d.)	
Sourby,	8s. . . .	Wakefeld,	4s. 3d.

From herbage during the winter in Stanley Coppice, 11s. 10d.

[*mem.* 15.]

COURT held at Wakefeld on Friday, the Feast of SS. Peter
and Paul [June 29], 6 Edw. II.

ESSOINS.—Robert de Wyrunthorp, by William de Castelford.
Surety : Thomas the Seyvile.

Robert de la Grene, by Thomas de Witlay. Surety : John de la
More.

Eadmund the Normaunt, by William, s. of Margery. Surety
William del Okes.

Richard de Birstall, by William the Goldsmith. Surety:
William de Castelford.

William de Rastrik, by Thomas de Tothill. Surety: William
the Goldsmith.

RASTRIK.—The waif mare in the keeping of the grave of
Rastrik is dead ; her skin was sold for 6d. by the grave.

HOLNE.—Adam Strekaise and Richard del Bothe agree, on
condition of Richard's surrendering to Adam all his right in 1½
acres in Twong, Adam paying Richard 6s. 8d., and abandoning
all his actions and charges against him ; Adam gives 6d. for
admittance.

BAILIFF.—William Erl sues Margery, formerly wife of Henry
Erl, for driving his mare from a place called the Holmes in the
town of Crigleston, to the town of Wakefeld, where she kept it
in Hugh Cay's fold till it was delivered by William the Goldsmith, the sworn bailiff ; damages, 40d. Defendant wages her
law. Surety : German Filkoces.

STANLAY.—John Bull and Robert Gunne agree by John's
surrendering to the said Robert, to Margery his wife, and to
Emma their daughter, all his claim in a garden in Ouchthorp,
which Robert bought of Thomas Bull, John's brother. Robert
pays 6d. for the recognition.

HOLNE.—Adam the Wainwright del Rode, plaintiff [6*d.*], John, s. of Adam de Heppeworth, Thomas, s. of Richard, Nicholas, s. of John s. of Gilbert, and Richard,· his brother, defendants, agree.

SOURBY.—John, s. of Jordan de Warlolay, sues Henry the Clerk of Warlolay for giving him the trunk of a tree to burn for Christmas time a year ago, for which trunk he was afterwards amerced 13*s.* 4*d.*, Henry having failed to warrant him. Both parties request an inquisition.

Robert de Bentlayrode sues Agnes, d. of Emma de Asserlay, and Richard de Asserlay and Emma, his wife, for burning an oak in Sourby wood on plaintiff's land, for which he was amerced 13*s.* 4*d.* Agnes cannot deny the fact, and the forester swears the other defendants received Agnes contrary to the forester's prohibition. They are therefore to answer for her trespass, and are amerced 12*d.*

. . . . . .—John Cay sues Adam Gerbot for 2*s.* for arrears ; this is acknowledged ; amercement, 6*d.*

John Cay sues William Nelot for 25*s.* arrears ; fine, etc., as above.

[STANLAY.]—John Bunny gives 12*d.* to take 2 acres in the graveship of Stanlay from Thomas de Wytlay.

[SOURBY.]—Ellen Goos of Migelay gives 6*d.* to take 3 roods in Sourby, with buildings thereon, from Robert, s. of John s. of Richard, junior, for her life.

William Templer, by Henry Ganton, his attorney . . . . [*All but a few words of this entry is torn away at the bottom of the membrane.*]

[*mem.* 15 *dors.*]

SOURBY.—Ivo del Hole, 2*d.*; John, s. of Robert, 1*d.*; Alan de Miggelay, 2*d.*; Richard del Dene, 2*d.*; Alice de Illingworth, 3*d.*; John de Sunderland, 3*d.*; William de Sunderland, 2*d.*; Hugh de Ovenden, 1*d.*; Thomas de Illyngworth, 2*d.*; Thomas de Ovenden, 1*d.*; Big Hugh of Ovenden, 1*d.*; John de Ovenden, 1*d.*; John Fox of Illingworth, 2*d.*; William de Haylay, 2*d.*; John Peukes, 2*d.*; John Moddry, 2*d.*, for escapes at Saltonstall.

Henry de Holgate, 6*d.*; William de Stodlay, 6*d.*; Adam, s. of Ivo, 4*d.*; Henry the clerk of Warlolay, 3*d.*; Adam del Wroo, 2*d.*; Thomas de Saltonstall, 3*d.*; Richard del Wyteleye, 3*d.*, and William del Bothem, 6*d.*, for escapes in the Frith.

HOLNE.—The township of Holne, 6s. 8d. for vert in Holne fields.

John de Haropp, 6s. 8d. for timber cut without permission.

ALVIRTHORP.—John Rate, 6d.; John Graffard, 6d., and Alice Graffard, 4d., for escapes in fence-time.

WAKEFELD.—Robert de Fethirston, 12d. for a cart-load of wood.

Robert Marescall, 6d.; John the Sotheron, 2d.; William Peger, 6d.; Adam Torkatro, 6d.; John Dade, 6d.; Nicholas Nodger, 2d.; Thomas Forester of Kergate, 2d.; the daughter of Robert Broun of Kergate, 2d.; Adam de Castelforth's daughter, 6d.; Roger Wasse, 2d.; Johanna Leget, 2d.; Ellen Cort, 2d.; William Pope, 3d., surety, Henry de Adyngham ; the daughter of Alexander de Aula, 2d.; Alice, wife of Richard Peger of Erdes-lawe, 2d.; Robert the Litster, 4d.; Robert Capon, 2d., and Robert Liftfast, 2d., for dry wood and vert.

Roger del Mere, 12d. for breaking the lock of the park gate.

Jordan the Litster, 12d., and Thomas the Waruner, 6d., for a cartload of wood each.

SANDALE.—John, s. of Adam s. of Penne, gives 6s. 8d. to take a messuage, 18 acres of land, and meadow, in Crigleston from Henry de Panteria, his brother.

HOLNE.—John, s. of Thomas Pees, and Richard del Bothe agree by Richard's surrendering to John all his claim in the rood of land in dispute. John fines 6d. for the recognition. Surety : John de Holne. Richard amerced 6d. for wrongful detention.

ALVERTHORP.—Adam, s. of Robert de Castilsted, gives 2s. as a heriot on villein [nativa] land, which his father held in the graveship of Alverthorp.

WAKEFELD ; new rent.—John Sibson gives 6d. for license to enlarge his booth in Wakefeld Market, in the direction of Biche-hil, on a piece of waste land the length of the booth, i.e. 33 feet, and 3 feet broad ; rent, 1½d.

The Steward grants permission to Robert the Walker to make a drying-ground [?] on a waste piece of land outside Kergate, as long as he farms the fulling-mill from the lord.

BAILIFF.—Thomas, s. of Roger de Crigelston, sues Margery, formerly wife of Henry Erle, for seizing cattle. Surety : John Erle. Margery is attached by Hugh Kai.

SOUREBY.—William the Mercer and Alice, his wife, sue Matilda, d. of Pirneis, on an agreement. Surety: Thomas, s. of John de Miggeley.

OSSET.—William Cole sues Henry de Curia for trespass. Surety: Robert Pees.

Sum total of this Court: 53s. 9d.; and new rent, 16d.

i.e. Rastrik,   6d.   Hyperum,   2s. 6d.

Alvirthorp,   6s. 4d.   Osset,   12d.

Sandale,   6s. 8d.   Stanley,   18d.

Holne,   18s. 8d. (and yearly rent, 2½d.)

Wakefeld,   9s. 11d. (and yearly rent, 13½d.)

Sourby,   6s. 8d.

COURT held at Wakefeld on Friday, the Feast of St. Margaret the Virgin [July 13], 7 [Edw. II].

ESSOINS.—Thomas de Thornton, by Gilbert de Thornton. Surety: William de Hokes.

Thomas the [*le*] Seyuil, by William Cussing. Surety: William de Castelford.

Henry the Nodder, attorney of Margaret de Nevil, by William de Castilford. Surety: Robert Heyrode.

Robert de la Grene, by Thomas Grenhode. Surety: Thomas de Witteley.

John de Schipedene, by Thomas the Clerk. Surety: Richard de Salsa-mara.

Nicholas Cailli, by Henry, his son. Surety: William de Castilford.

John de Lepton, by Thomas de Witteley. Surety: William Wildebor.

[*Four lines, at any rate, are almost entirely destroyed at the end of the membrane, but are apparently only records of postponements of business.*]

[*mem.* 16.]

BAILIFF.—Margery, formerly wife of Henry Erle, makes the law she waged against William Erle ; he is amerced 6d. for false claim.

Thomas, s. of Roger de Crigelston, sues the said Margery in a similar suit [see above, p. 58]., Margery says the seizure of cattle was made not in Thomas's house in Crigelston, but in a place called the Holmes, which forms part of a bovate of land held of the said Margery by John, s. of Gilbert, for homage, fealty, and free service of 14s. yearly, which is a year in arrears ; she seized the cattle by way of distraint. The parties have a love-day at their own request.

HOLNE.—Agnes, formerly [? wife] of Thomas Pymme, for entry into 2 acres leased for a term, the term being expired ; amerced 6d., and 6d. for license to marry.

SANDALE.—Matilda, Matilda and Alice, daughters of Alexander the Shepherd del Wodthorp, give 2s. to take a bovate and 5½ acres in Sandale as a heriot after the death of their father.

Thomas, s. of Thomas de Dorkinge, gives 12d. as a heriot on ½ bovate with buildings in Crigelston, after his father's death.

William the Wilde, 6d. as heriot, to take a rood in le Neubigginges, after the death of Adam, s. of Peter, his father.

RASTRIK.—William, s. of Adam de Wodehouses, gives 12d. to take 6½ acres in Rastrick from Adam, s. of Ivo, his father.

SOURBY.—Matilda, d. of Elias del Frith, 12d. to take 2¼ acres in Sourby from William the Mercer and Alice, his wife.

William the Horseknave of Licthesils gives 3s. 4d. to take a bovate and a half except 3 roods in Soland, from Thomas, s. of Sabina, who pays 3s. 4d. to take 17 acres with buildings from William Horsknave in Licthesils.

OSSET.—Adam de Goukethorp, 12d. for the marchet of Johanna, his daughter.

HOLNE.—Adam, s. of Robert Stirk, 12d. to take 2½ acres in Wlvedale from . . . . . .

. . . . .—John Kay and Dom. Ralph, parson of Emmeley church [2s.], agree.

SOURBY.—William the Mercer and Alice, his wife, and Matilda, d. of Pirneys, agree ; 3d.

OSSET.—William Cole [6d.] and Henry de Curia agree.

HOLNE ; new rents.—John Barun has license to take 2 acres of the waste in Alstanley ; rent, 8d.

Thomas, s. of Emma, to take a rood of waste in Fouleston common wood ; rent, 1d.

Adam de la Mere, an acre in the same ; rent, 4d.

SOURBY.—Thomas, s. of Cecilia de Halifax, 1d. [?] ; Adam del Schaye, 3d.; Adam de Routonstall, 4d.; Richard del Dene, 1d.; Richard, s. of Robert de Cheswellay, 3d.; William de Stodeley, 1d.; John Culpon, 1d.; Henry the Clerk of Werlullay, 2d.; Roger the Taillur, 2d.; Roger de Grenwode, 1d.; William, s. of Roger del Foldes, 2d.; Jokyn's wife, 2d.; Henry de Holgate, 3d.; Adam, s.

of Ivo, 2*d*.; Thomas de la Rode, 2*d*.; Richard de Sourby, 2*d*., for escapes.

[*Four names, at least, are torn away at the bottom. Three are apparently* Richard de Saltonstall, [?] 2*d*.; Alice de Illingworth, 2*d*., and Henry del Ryding, . . . *d*.]

HIPERUM.—John del Clif, 3*d*.; Henry de la Rode, 6*d*.; Thomas the Webster, 2*d*.; Henry Marwe, 2*d*.; Walter de Adrychegate, 3*d*.; John de Holway, 3*d*.; Hugh, s. in law of Walter, 2*d*.; Robert de Ourum, 1*d*.; Michael de Hadegreves, 1*d*.; John the Pynder, 2*d*.; Peter del Barm, 2*d*.; John Wodelome, 6*d*.; Thomas del Northend, 6*d*.; Thomas del Belhous, 6*d*.; John Fildingmay, . . . ; William Talvace, . . . , for vert and escapes.

[*Four names, at any rate, have been torn away at the bottom of the membrane.*]

[*mem*. 16 *dors*.]

Sum total of this Court : 35*s*., and 13*d*. annual rent.

i.e. Sourby,   14*s*. 10*d*.   Bailiff,   2*s*. 6*d*.
     Rastrik,   12*d*.   Hiperum,   6*s*. 11*d*.
     Osset,   18*d*.   Sandale,   3*s*. 6*d*.
     Holne,   3*s*. 9*d*. (and new rent, 13*d*.)
     Thornes,   12*d*.

ALVIRTHORP.—Agnes, formerly wife of William Whitackoc, sues Ralph, s. of Nicholas, for dower. Surety : John Attebarre.

Richard Wythundes sues Matilda, formerly wife of John the Boteler, on an agreement.

John Attebarre sues John Torald for debt. Surety : Thomas de Whitteley.

THORNES [void].—Philip de Castelforth sues Elyas Bulnays for trespass. Surety : Philip Wlf.

THE EARL'S MEADOWLAND.—John de Amyas gives 21*s*. for the [*relucro* ?] of the herbage in the Earl's meadow land, after the hay has been mowed and carried. Surety : Philip Wlf.

COURT held at Wakefeld on Friday, the Feast of St. Laurence,
7 Edw. II.

ESSOINS.—Thomas de Thornton, by William de Wodesom. Surety : Thomas de Wyttelay.

John de Schipedene, by Thomas de Wytteley. Surety : William del Okes.

. . . . . .—[John the Carpenter of H]oton Paynell withdraws from the law he waged against Roger Wyron ; and is therefore to pay damages to be taxed. Surety : Robert de Wyrunthorp.

Thomas, s. of Roger de Crigelston [6d.], and Margery, formerly wife of Henry Erl, agree.

BAILIFF.—-Robert, s. of Geoffrey de Stanley, 3d. for default.

[*Four lines, at least, destroyed at the end of the membrane, but they appear to be only records of postponements, similar to previous entries not transcribed here.*]

[*mem.* 17.]

STANLAY.—John Bul released and quitclaimed to John, s. of Robert the Mercer, all his possible rights in the lands, etc., bought by John, s. of Robert, from Thomas Bul, brother of John, in Ouchephorp fields in the graveship of Stanley ; John fines 6d. for the recognition.

HOLNE.—Mariota, formerly wife of Peter del Wildeborleghe, gives 12d. to take a toft with buildings and 2 acres of land in Alstanlay from John de Harope ; to hold to herself and Robert, her son.

William, s. of Hugh de Thurstanland, 12d. to take a toft and 9 acres in Wlfdale, left unoccupied by the heirs of Adam Cosyn.

William Totty, 18d. to take the said land from William, s. of Hugh, for 20 years, undertaking to keep the buildings in proper repair.

HIPERUM.—John the Milner del Bothes, 6d. to take an acre in the Bothes from Cecilia, d. of Elias de Werlulley.

HOLNE ; new rent.—William, s. of Wylkes, junior, 10d. to take 1¾ acres of waste new land in Heppeworth common, at a rent of 4d. an acre.

ALVERTHORP.—John Attebarre, villein [*nativus*], sues John Torald, villein [*nativus*], who is amerced 3d., and is to be distrained, for not coming.

WAKEFELD.—Elyas Tirsy and William, his brother, agree as follows :—that Elyas shall release and quitclaim to William and Matilda de Hoby and their heirs a stall in Wakefeld market, which was in dispute between the said Elyas and William after the decease of Master Robert Tirsy, their brother. William and Matilda fine 2s. for admittance.

ALVERTHORP.—Robert Gerbot gives 40d. as a heriot on 11 acres in Alverthorp fields, after the death of Adam Gerbot, his uncle, whose heir he is, the said Adam dying without issue.

HOLNE.—William, s. of Wilkes, junior, has license to take 1¼ acres in Heppeworth from Adam the Waynwricht, who took the land from the common.

WAKEFELD.—Robert Swerd, 6*d.*; Hugh Chapman's wife, 2*d.*; Beatrice de Aula, 1*d.*; Gilbert the Tinkler, 2*d.*; Peter Lorimor, 2*d.*; Robert the Yong, 6*d.*; Peter the Pynder, 6*d.*; Thomas Alayn, 4*d.*; Thomas Brodfot, 6*d.*; Walter the Yong, 4*d.*; Henry de Adyngham, 12*d.*; William Pichak, 6*d.*; Symon Fox, 6*d.*; Adam, s. of Roger the Turner, 6*d.*; Robert Jose, Adam de Castelforth, Broun Robyn's son, Roger Wasche, John Dun, Idonea Pollard, Henry de Ayketon, John Tenet, and William Bul, 2*d.* each ; Adam Torkatro, 3*d.*, for dry wood and vert, and palings broken.

OSSET.—Richard the Pynder, 4*d.*; Robert, s. of Soñ, 4*d.*; Adam, s. of William, grave of Osset, 2*d.*, and John, s. of William, 2*d.*, for escapes.

HORBIRY.—John Dypsy, 6*d.*; Hugh Modysaul, 6*d.*, and the wife of Adam Dobbeknave, 2*d.*, for vert and dry wood.

THORNES.—John de Northwode, 2*d.*; Roger Traylment, 6*d.*; Robert, servingman of John de Mora, 4*d.*, for dry wood, etc.

ALVIRTHORP.—William the Carpenter of Alvirthorp, 2*d.*; John Rate, 6*d.*; William del Holmes, 2*d.*; Richard de Colley, 2*d.*, and Peter the Pynder, 3*d.*, for escapes.

STANLAY.—Adam Spinkes, 3*d.*; the handmaid of Thomas, s. of Stephen, 2*d.*; Philip the Syour, 3*d.*; Matilda de Haleyes, 2*d.*; Robert Spivy, 4*d.*; Thomas de Hayleys, 2*d.*; William de la Grene, 2*d.*; Adam de Okerodes and his associates, 12*d.*; surety, Hugh Skayf,— for dry wood and escapes, and breaking palings of coppice.

Sum total of this Court : 30*s*. 7*d*., and yearly rent, 7*d*.

i.e. Bailiff,	21*d*.	Thornes,	12*d*.
Holne,	4*s*. 4*d*. (and new rent, 7*d*.)		
Osset,	12*d*.	Hiperum,	6*d*.
Alvirthorp,	8*s*. 4*d*.	Stanlay,	3*s*.
Wakefeld,	9*s*. 6*d*.	Horbiry,	14*d*.

THORNES.—John Kyde sues Philip Damysell for trespass. Surety: Thomas de Whytteley.

Christiana, formerly wife of Richard, s. of Junne, sues Eda, formerly wife of John de Aula, for trespass.

Henry, s. of Eva, sues Robert P[eger] and Amabilla, his wife, for trespass. Surety : Adam, s. of Walter.

. . . . . . [void].—John the Rased sues Richard W . . . . . . for trespass. Surety : John de Heton.

. . . . . .—William, s. of Gotte, sues Richard, s. of R . . . . . .
. . . . thwode for land. Surety : Thomas Pees.

. . . . . .—Julian de Thornes sues William del [?] Ro[des] on
an agreement. Surety : William the Goldsmith.

John Dade sues Agnes Wlf for seizing a horse. Surety : William
de Castelforth.

————

COURT held at Wakefeld on Friday after the Feast of the Decollation of St. John the Baptist [Aug. 29], 7 Edw. II.

[ESSOINS].—Hugh the Nodder, attorney of Margaret de Nevill,
by William de Birton. Surety : John de Mora.

John de Lepton, by Thomas de Whitteley. Surety : William
del Okes.

Thomas del Belhous, by William de Castelforth. Surety :
William Wyldebore.

Thomas the Seyuill, by Henry de Wakefeld. Surety : William
de Castelforth.

William de Rastrike, by Thomas de Tothill. Surety : William
de Castelforth.

Richard de Birstall, by William, servant of Margery. Surety :
John de Mora.

Nicholas de Caylli, by Henry de Metheley. Surety : William
Wyldebore.

John, s. of Henry de Fekesby, . . . d. for sundry defaults.

Thomas de Tothill sues the said John for damage done to his
oats in Fekesby . . . .

[*Four lines gone, at least, at the end of the membrane.*]
[*mem. 17 dors.*]

ALVERTHORP.—Agnes, wife of William Whitackoc, amerced 4d.
for not prosecuting Ralph, s. of Nicholas.

John Torald, 3d. for not coming to answer John Attebarre.

THORNES.—The bailiff to distrain on Philip Damysell, for satisfaction to John Kyde, etc., for corn of his seized by Philip, though
Thomas de Whytteley, the sworn bailiff, had prohibited the seizure
in the lord's name.

Christiana, formerly wife of Richard, s. of Junne, and Eda,
formerly wife of John de Aula [2d.], agree.

Henry, s. of Eva, sues Robert Peger and Amabilla, his wife, for
assaulting him, and preventing him from impounding their cattle
found in the meadow of Adam, s. of Walter, his master. An inquisition is to be taken.

OSSET.—William, s. of Gotte, sues Richard, s. of Robert de Southewode, for ½ acre, which he says belongs to half a bovate, which he formerly held from Sir [Dño] John de Horbiry, and now holds from the Earl. Defendant says [he is] a free man, and that his father held the ½ acre from time immemorial as a free tenement. The bailiff and the grave of Osset are to summon an inquisition for the next court.

SOURBY.—Henry de Werlulley, grave of Sourby, 12d. for not attending the court.

HIPERUM.—Symon del Dene, grave of Hyperum, 12d. for the same.

RASTRIK.—Alexander de Wodehous, grave of Rastrik, 12d. for the same.

OSSET.—Robert Gunne sues John Moloc of Osset for debt. Surety : Thomas de Wytteley.

STANLEY.—Robert Gunne sues Richard del Kere for debt.

SOURBY.—John de Holgate, 18d.; Alice Jonkyn, 12d.; Roger, s. of German de Grenwode, 12d.; William, s. of Roger del Foldes, 6d.; William de Stodeley, 6d.; Peter, s. of Anot, 6d.; . . . . . . , 3d.; . . . . . . , s. of Wymark, . . . ; Hugh de la Lawe, . . . ; John del Rediker, . . . ; [?] Thomas de Waddeworth [?], clerk, . . . ; John del . . . . . of Northland, . . . ; William Horsknave, . . . ; . . . . . . , s. of Ivo, 4d.; Richard, s. of Stephen, 18d.; Henry de Holgate, 6d.; Michael Sourmilk, 4d.; Elyas the Couper, 2d.; Roger, s. of Amabilla, 2d.; Ivo, s. of William, 3d.; John Milner, 4d.; John de Holgate, 2d., for escapes in the Frith and Haderschelf.

Alexander, s. of Symon de Ovendene, 6d.; John Fox of Illingworth, 2d.; Roger, s. of Adam de Illingworth, 6d.; John de Sundreland, 4d.; William de Sunderland, 2d.; Symon de Schipedene, . . . ; John de Northenes, . . . ; Roger del Kyrk of Houwrth, . . . ; John, s. of Robert de Cheswellay, 2d.; John Sourmilk, 2d.; Hugh, s. of Evot, 2d.; John, servant of Thomas de Wylly, 4d.; William the Carpenter of Ourum, 2d.; Robert Pek, 2d.; William, s. in law of Otes, 1d.; Adam, s. of Ivo de Werlulley, 2d.; John Dughty, 1d.; Henry del Hill, . . . ; Hugh, s. of John . . . . . . , 2d.; Thomas Sausemer, 2d.; Henry Coli . . . . . . , 2d., for escapes.

Sum total of this Court : 23s. 4d.; i.e. Rastrik, 12d.
Sourby, 17s. 1d. Hyperum, 12d.
Thornes, 2d. Bailiff, 3s. 6d.
Alverthorp, 7d.

E

[*mem.* 18.]

COURT held at Wakefeld on Friday, the Feast of St. Matthew the Apostle [Sept. 21], 7 Edw. II.

ESSOINS.—Elyas de Byrton, by John Pycard. Surety : Richard de Salsa-mara.

Thomas de Thorneton, by William de Thorneton. Surety : Robert de Heyerod.

John de Lepton, by Thomas de Wytlay. Surety : William del Okes.

Hugh the Nodder, attorney of Margaret de Nevill, by Thomas Grenhode. Surety : William de Castelford.

John de Schipedene, by John de Migelay. Surety : Adam Hood.

Nicholas de Caylly, by John Patrikes. Surety : Henry de Cheuet.

OSSETE.—Richard Passemer, 6*d.* for not having William de Lyghthesels in court, according to his surety.

BAILIFF.—Gilbert Tynkler is acquitted by an inquisition of receiving malefactors coming to the town by night.

Hugh the Chapman and his family are also acquitted of the same.

THE TOWN COURT.—Thomas, s. of Laurence, essoins against John Kay, by German Swerd. Surety : Henry del Bothem. The matter is removed into the town court, because they are burgesses.

Also the suit of John Cay against John Tasse.

BAILIFF.—Adam Cappe, 6*d.* for sundry defaults.

ALVERTHORP.—John Torald, 6*d.* for detaining 4*s.* from John Attebarre ; he is to pay the debt before next court. Surety : Robert Gerbot, grave of Alverthorp.

Richard de Collay's amercement forgiven for detaining 12*d.* from Roger Preest.

BAILIFF.—Philip Damysell, 6*d.* for contempt of the lord in carry-ing away corn on which a prohibition had been put by him. Surety : Robert de Wyrumpthorp.

THORNES.—John Kyd sues Philip Damysel for ousting him from the crop of a rood in Thornes, being one of 3 roods which John took for 4 crops from John the Drapour, after 2 crops which Philip had therein. An inquisition is to be taken.

. . . . . .—Adam Sprigonel, 40*d.* for default.

Richard, s. of Robert de Southwod, [?] 2*s.* for contempt in court.

THORNES.—Henry, s. of Eva, and Roger Peger and Amabilla, his wife [6*d.*], agree.

TOWN COURT.—Agnes Wlf to be attached to answer John Dade, in the town court, *re* detention of a horse.

The grave of Hiperum to attach William del Hinganrodes and Alexander, his brother, to be before the steward at Rastrik tourn, for making a rescue and threatening Andrew the Forester, when he found them committing evildoing in his graveship.

. . . . . [?]—John Maunsel and Richard Snart agree ; fine, . . . *d.*

[*Three lines, at least, are torn away from the bottom of the membrane.*]

[*mem.* 18 *dors.*]   Attachments.

HOLNE.—Thomas Oldman of Twong, 6*d.*; the son of Peter de Scoles, 4*d.*; Gilbert Schaylhorn, 3*d.*; Gilbert del Dene, 3*d.*; Hugh, s. of Adam de Thurstanland, 2*d.*; William, s. of the said Hugh, 2*d.*, for escapes.

HIPERUM.—John Fox of Bayrstow, 6*d.*; William Scharp of Bayrstow, 12*d.*; Peter del Clohges, 1*d.*; Henry de Northclyffes, 1*d.*; Agnes, widow of Astay, 2*d.*; Thomas Band of Brighous, 1*d.*; Cecilia, widow, of Brighous, 3*d.*; William the Milner, 1*d.*; John de Skulcotes, 2*d.*, for dry wood and escapes.

SOURBY.—Elyas de Waddesworth, 3*d.*; Thomas Chapeleyn, 3*d.*; William, s. of Wylkes, 2*d.*; Ivo del Hole, 2*d.*; Richard, s. of Adam, 2*d.*; Henry, s. of Robert de Grenhirst, 1*d.*; Juliana de Aula, 1*d.*; William del Rydinge, 1*d.*; John de Heton, 2*d.*; John del Lum, 3*d.*; Henry, the grave, 2*d.*; Alexander, s. of Symon, 3*d.*; William de Sunderland, 2*d.*, for escapes.

WARDROBE.—Thomas de Tothill, £10 for a certain fine made with the Earl on behalf of himself, his brothers, and their followers, and for a certain quitclaim by the Earl of all villein service [*omn' servitute nayvitatis*], with which he and his brothers were charged. The £10 was paid into the wardrobe to Dom. William Gascelyn, keeper of the wardrobe of the said Earl, and the receipt is in the hands of Dom. Matthew de Halyfax, receiver.

Sum total of this Court : £11   18*d., i.e.* Wardrobe,   £10

Sourby,	2*s.* 9*d.*	Wakefeld,	40*d.*
Osset,	12*d.*	Alverthorp,	6*d.*
Thornes,	6*d.*	Sandale,	18*d.*
Bailiff,	6*s.* 4*d.*	Stanley,	18*d.*
Holne,	20*d.*	Hyperum,	2*s.* 5*d.*

ALVERTHORP.—William Cussing sues Henry del Bothem and Richard Wythoundes for trespass. Surety : John, s. of Sybilla.

STANLEY.—Robert Broun of Wyrnthorp and Edusa, his wife, sue Margery, d. of Adam Cote, for trespass. Surety : Roger Beel.

BAILIFF.—John, s. of Robert the Clerk of Sandale, sues Robert, s. of Henry, and William, his brother, William Layroun, and John Attewelle for trespass. Surety : Robert the Clerk of Sandale.

OSSETE.—John, s. of Richard the Pynder of Osset, sues William Hernyng for trespass. Surety : Richard Wythoundes.

BAILIFF.—William Tyrsi sues William de Castelford for trespass. Surety : John Erle. In the town court.

[*mem.* I.]

PLEAS and PERQUISITES of the Soke of Wakefeld from Michaelmas, 8 Edw. II, to the Michaelmas of the following year ; in the time of Henry de Walda, then Steward.

COURT held at Wakefeld on Friday after Michaelmas in
the year abovesaid.

ESSOINS.—William de Tothill, by Thomas de Tothill. Surety : Peter Swerd.

Robert de Wirnthorp, by John Cay. Surety : William Marjoriman.

Robert the Drapur, by Thomas de Wytlay. Surety : Richard de Salsa-mara.

Robert Patrikes, by John Patrikes. Surety : William Eyre.

Richard de Crosseland, by John de Crosseland. Surety : Matthew del Wod.

Adam Sprigonel, by William Marjoriman. Surety : Peter Swerd.

Thomas de Dronsfeld, by Robert the Clerk of Sandale. Surety : William Wildbor.

Richard de Birstall, by John de Schepeley. Surety : Thomas del Belhous.

SANDALE.—Renewal of order to take into the lord's hand the villein [*nativa*] land held by John Dande, and all goods and cattle found on the said land, because John had despoiled it of 18 oak-saplings, 4 ashes, and other timber.

BAILIFF.—Henry de Wakefeld, surety for the essoin of Margaret de Schepelay at the last court, amerced 3*d.* for not having her present. The said Margaret, 6*d.* for not coming to make her law against John de Schepeley.

John the Clerk of Schepeley, 6*d.* for withdrawing his suit against Margaret de Schepeley ; he acknowledges himself liable to the whole of the above amercements. Surety : William Marjoriman.

ALVERTHORP.—German Swerd and John Broun [6*d.*] agree in the matter of wood carried off.

BAILIFF.—Thomas de Tothill opposes himself against William, s. of Adam del Leye, in a plea of trespass, who has been distrained by 12 acres of oats, and 5 marks in the hands of William del Boure, but does not come ; further distraint to be made. Thomas appoints John Patrikes or Henry de Wakefeld his attorney.

William Marjoriman presents that William del Leye and William del Boure have carried off the corn attached by him as bailiff.

SANDALE.—William del Grene, 3*d.* for not prosecuting his suit against John Dande.

THORNES.—John de Heton and Alice Graffard [6*d.*] agree.

ALVERTHORP.—Dom. William the Receiver and John Swan [3*d.*] agree. Surety : Henry del Bothom.

SANDALE.—Adam, s. of Laurence, sues Robert del Neubigginges and Robert, s. of Pelle, for 2 thraves of corn of St. Peter's [*blad' beati Petri*], which they took this year from the manor of Walton, having no right in the said corn this year. Defendants say the bailiff of the said manor paid them nothing for the said grass last year, when they had it by demise of the plaintiff, and that the grass in question was paid them in satisfaction therefor. They were to have come to warrant this assertion at this court ; by default they are judged convicted, and are amerced 12*d.*

BAILIFF.—Hugh de Gildesome and Amabilla, his wife, 6*d.* for withdrawing their suit against Alice del Wro in a plea of trespass. William de Gildesom, surety for the prosecution, and Hugh and Amabilla are amerced.

ALVERTHORP.—Robert Gerbot, 6*d.* for carrying his hay on which a prohibition had been laid by the grave of Alverthorp.

Amabilla de Flansau sues Robert Gerbot for ousting her [*destornavit ei dotem suam*] out of a certain piece of meadow assigned her in dower by John, her son. An inquisition to be taken.

An inquisition finds that Walter del Hill's cattle fed on and trampled a rood of oats belonging to Richard de Collay ; damages, 6 sheaves. For this, and breaking Richard's enclosure and carrying off his cattle, Walter is amerced 2*s.*

BAILIFF.—Robert the Mareschal of Wakefeld sues John the Carpenter of Walton for carrying off a young bull worth 10*s.* from the new park of Wakefeld, which Robert had agisting there, and detaining it ; damages, 20*s.* An inquisition to be taken. Sureties : William Wytbelt and Robert de Heyerode.

THORNES.—Ralph de Lupesheved surrenders a bovate in Snaypthorp, and afterwards Philip, s. of Roger de Snaypthorp, fines 5s. to take 3 acres thereof immediately, and the remainder of the said bovate after the said Ralph's death.

WAKEFELD.—William Cussinges gives 8s. to take 8 acres in the graveship of Wakefeld from John Cussinges, his father.

ALVERTHORP.—William de la Grene, 12d. to take a house and ½ acre in Alverthorp from John Tupe.

SOURBY.—Hugh del Lowe, 2s. 6d.; Adam del Schaye, 12d.; William de Stodelay, 12d.; William del Bothem, 12d.; Richard del Estwod, 6d.; Robert, s. of John Hodde, 6d.; Robert, his brother, 3d.; William, servant of Thomas de Stodelay, 2d.; Adam, s. of Ivo, 3d.; Elias the Couper, 3d.; John del Rediker, 3d.; John, s. of Robert, 3d.; Robert de Saltonstall, 6d.; Adam de Routonstall, 6d.; Philip de Soland, 3d.; Roger del Foldys, 3d.; John, son-in-law of Richard del Dene, 3d.; Richard the Shepherd, 6d.; Thomas the Hird of Miggelay, 3d.; Matilda del Barm, 1d.; Elyas de Haderschelf, 1d.; Adam the Shepherd, 2d., for escapes in the Frith.

HIPERUM.—Thomas de Hemmingway, 6d.; John de Birstall, 3d.; Symon, s. of Jordan, 2d.; John del Rode, 2d.; William, s. of Peter, 6d.; Henry the Milner, 2d.; William the Milner, 2d.; Alexander the Tailor, 2d.; the widow [?] del Brighouse, . . .d.; Roger del Brighouse, . . .d.; John de Schepeley, 3d.; Henry del Rode, 3d., for escapes.

Richard, s. of John, 3d.; John de Northwod, 3d.; Agnes, d. of William s. of Jordan, 2d., for vert.

WAKEFELD.—Agnes Melyn, 3d.; Alice Preest, 2d.; Magota Preest, 2d.; Adam Torkatro, 4d.; John Dun, 2d.; Roger Wasse, 2d., Idonea Pollard, 2d.; and Brounrobyn's wife, 1d., for dry wood.

SOURBY.—Robert del Wyndybankes, 6d.; Matthew de Southourum, 1d.; John Drake, 1d.; William de Haylay, 4d., Thomas del Belhous, 2d.; Nicholas the Milner, 3d.; Thomas Hird of Miggeley, 3d.; John del Bothem, 4d.; Henry del Loue, 4d.; Hugh de Lygthasels, 6d.; Hancoke de Soland, 1d.; John de Waddesword, 3d. and 4d.; Alan de Miggelay, 6d.; William, s. of Ivo, 3d.; Richard the Smyth, 1d.; Henry, s. of Beatrix, 2d.; John de Notschagh, 6d., surety, Richard the Smith—for dry wood.

HYPERUM.—John, s. of Ralph de Bairstow, 6d.; William del Rode, 2d.; William Hare, 2d.; Symon del Dene, 2d., for escapes and dry wood.

ALVERTHORP.—Richard, s. of Broun, 4d.; Henry del Bothem, 4d.; Walter del Bothem, 2d.; Richard, s. of Broun, 2d., for escapes.

STAYNLAY.—Richard Longschankes, 3*d.* for an escape.

OSSETE.—Richard de Gaukthorp, 2*d.*; Robert Sunman, 2*d.*, and Amabilla [?] Tonclok, 2*d.*, for the same.

ALVIRTHORP.—Isolda Wlf, 2*d.* for vert.

HORBERY.—Hugh del Wro, 3*d.* for breaking the paling.

WAKEFELD.—Richard the Milner, 2*d.*; John Leche, 2*d.*; Henry Fauconberg, 2*d.*, and Adam Halfmark, 3*d.*, for dry wood.

[*mem.* 1 *dors.*]

WAKEFELD.—John Cay and William Wiles amerced for not coming to elect the grave, being tenants of villein [*nativa*] land.

STANLAY ; the lord's will.—Henry de Bennyngs has the lord's license to take a bovate of land in Stanlay, into which Margery Moyce entered after her father's death, and which she subsequently demised to divers freemen of Wakefeld.

WAKEFELD ; grave.—The whole of the graveship of Wakefeld elected John Cay as grave of Wakefeld ; he refused office, and his land was seised into the lord's hand.

SEIZURE.—An acre of land and meadow under the Falbankes, into which John Cay entered without license, to be seized into the lord's hand. The land was demised to Cay by one Robert Hipel, bastard.

HOLNE ; new rents.—Matthew de Langlay gives 18*d.* to take 3 acres of new land in Langlay common, at 4*d.* an acre.

Thomas, s. of Elkoce de Hepword, gives 6*d.* to take an acre of new land in Hepworth common, at 4*d.* an acre.

HIPERUM.—William del Bothes sues Richard, s. of Ivo, on an agreement. Surety : Thomas de Whitley.

William, s. of Henry, the grave of Eland, sues Henry de Godelay for trespass. Surety : Roger del Brighouse.

STANLEY.—John Rate sues Hugh Tagge for trespass. Surety : Richard Bullokes.

BAILIFF.—Dom. William the Receiver sues Robert Lorimar for trespass.

William, s. of Henry de Eland, sues Robert de Rysseworth for trespass. Surety : Roger del Brighouse.

Sum total of this Court : 48*s.* 4*d.*; and yearly rents, 16*d.*

i.e. Osset,	14*d.*	Horbery,	3*d.*
Wakefeld,	10*s.* 3*d.*	Alvirthorp,	5*s.* 5*d.*
Sandale,	15*d.*	Hyperum,	4*s.* 1*d.*
Stanley,	3*d.*	Thornes,	5*s.* 6*d.*
Sourby,	16*s.* 2*d.*	Bailiff,	2*s.*
Holne,	2*s.*		

COURT at Halifax on Monday after the Feast of St. Luke
the Evangelist [Oct. 18], 8 Edw. II [1314].

SOURBY.—Henry del Holgate, grave of Sourby, Richard de Saltonstall, grave of Sourby after said Henry, William the Horsknave,
grave after said Richard, Henry de Saltonstall, grave after said
William, and Thomas de Rothelsete, grave after said Henry, successively graves of Sourby, 6s. 8d. each, for not taking into their
keeping the lord's wild pigs in Sourbischire, and giving no account
thereof to their successors.

Thomas de Rothelsete, 12d. for giving up without authority
a sow·[treetum] by which he had distrained John de Counale to
answer Henry de Saltonstall.

Robert, s. of John s. of Richard, 6d. for breaking an agreement
with John del Toun of Northland, with regard to an exchange of
cattle, and also for refusing [quia dedixit] an inquisition ; and 6d.
for refusing to be sworn on the inquisition on Adam Attetownend
[ad capud ville] de Miggeley, stockkeeper [instaurator].

Emma, wife of Richard de Asserlay, and Juliana Wade
amerced 6d. each for slandering one another.

John Pikeston, 6d. for contempt, is amerced 6d.

Adam de Routonstall, 40d. for not coming at the lord's command.

John the Milner of Sourby sues John Pykeston for putting one
of his oxen to the yoke at night without his consent ; this is acknowledged by the defendant, and damages are taxed at 3d. Sureties :
Henry de Luddyngdene and Robert de Saltonstall. Fine, 12d.

The inquisition on Adam Attetownend [ad capud ville] de Miggeley, formerly the lord's stockkeeper in Sourbyschire, finds that he
kept 11 sheep on the lord's hay during the winter in the vaccary
at Saltonstall ; sentence is at the lord's will.

The township of Sourby, 13s. 4d. for not repairing Sourby
bridge, as presented at the last tourn. The bridge is to be put into
repair before next tourn under a penalty of 100s.

Adam del Wro gives 8s. to take 6 acres in a royd called Satilworth in Warloley from Henry the Clerk of Warloley.

Adam, s. of William de Northland, 18d. to take 3 acres in Lyghthesels from Alice, formerly wife of . . . . . de Lyghthesels, and
which Alice holds in dower. Adam is to hold for the term of the
life of Alice.

Henry del Loue, 12d. to take a rood of meadow in Sourby from
Robert de Saltonstall.

An inquisition of twelve jurors finds that John de Migeley was charged by Henry de Soland before Jordan de Wirkeslay, formerly Receiver of the Green Wax in the county of York, with having sold 11 beasts from the township of Soland, with which he satisfied the King for the share he had had of the goods of Philip the Walsse, and with afterwards causing the township of Soland to be amerced for the said beasts, of which the aforesaid John was elsewhere acquitted by a Jury of 24 ; the said charge against him led to his being sued and annoyed.   The damages are taxed at 2s., which Henry is to pay, and he is amerced 6d.   Surety : Henry, s. of Say de Soland.

The said John de Miggelay, charged with receiving from the Earl 10s. in money, and two oaks worth 10s., for the purpose of repairing a certain chapel and kitchen (built aforetime by the grandfather of the present Earl in the said John's courtyard), and with not having completed the repairs to the said chapel and kitchen as ordered, finds the following sureties for paying the 20s., unless he can obtain easier terms from the lord, viz.:—John del Toun de Northland, John the Harpur de Northland [?], Richard del Whiteleye, Thomas de Heytfeld, and William, s. of Ivo de Warlolay.

William de Wlrunwall, 3d.; Eva de Wolrunwall, 3d.; William, s. of Hugh, 2d.; John, son-in-law of Richard del Dene, 9d.; Michael de Routonstall, 2d.; Jonkyn's wife, 3d.; John de Holgate, 6d.; Richard Fichet, 18d.; Richard the Smith of John Culpon's forge [de forg' Joh' Culpon], 3d.; and Michael de Lyghthasels, 2s., for escapes in Saltonstall and elsewhere.

John Sourmylk gives 3s. to take 4 acres in Sourby from Elyas, s. of Philip, and Avice, his wife.

Sum total : 107s. 11d.—all from Sourby.

[mem. 2.]

TOURN there the same day.

12 JURORS.—Richard de Waddesworth, Matthew del Wod, William de Counale, Adam de Midelton, John de Northland, William de Skyrcote, Alan de Heptonstall, Bate the Lytster, John Fox, Robert del Haye, Richard del Whyteleye, and Richard de Saltonstall, who say :—

SOURBY ; Bailiff.—John Pikeston, Henry del Loue, and John the Cobbler drew blood from one another ; 12d. each.

William de Wynter raised the hue on John, s. of Mokoce, for coming to his house to ravish his daughter ; John amerced 40d.

William de Sothill, senior, amerced 40*d.* for deflecting a water-course in Waddesworth to the injury of the neighbours, and for raising a bank. The latter is to be levelled.

SOURBY.—Matthew, serving-man of Henry de Saltonstall, drew blood from Adam, serving-man of Ivo; amerced 2*d.*

Robert de Midelton, a common malefactor in the Earl's free chaces, came, together with other malefactors, to the vaccary of the Wythenes, and lodged there the night, and the keeper of the said vaccary fled and hid himself in the hay, and in the morning they carried off the boy of the keeper of the vaccary aforesaid as far as Turneleye mosse.

BAILIFF.—Henry the Fuller [or Walker] of Halifax drew blood from Cecilia de Wygan; 12*d.*

William del Foldes drew blood from the wife of Richard de Heptonstall; 2*s.*

Roger Spillewood did not come to the tourn; he is amerced, but is forgiven at the instance of the vicar of Halifax.

Magota de Rypun, Robert Spillewode's wife, and the wife of Henry de Sourby, 12*d.* each for brewing, etc.

Roger de Bedeforth stole a tunic, worth 6*d.*, from Adam de Coventre, and Adam went to the constable, and the constable and several others followed Roger, and he cast away from him the tunic and escaped. He is to be attached when found.

Adam, s. of Roger de Walssedene, killed a doe at Haderschelf, and took the carcase to his father's house with his father's knowledge, and dealt with it at his will. They are both to be attached. Adam constantly trespasses in the free chace, with his father's knowledge. Roger, the father, fines 2 marks to be acquitted. Sureties: Roger Rotel and Richard, s. of Alota.

SECOND INQUISITION.—Richard de Counale, John de Northland, Thomas de Waddesworth, John de Noteschaye, William, s. of Henry, John de Cockecroftes, Thomas, s. of Sabba, Adam del Schaye, William de Sothill, junior, Hugh de Whiteleye, John the Harpur of Stanysfeld, and William de Estwode, who say :—

Amabilla, wife of Henry the Fuller, together with her said husband, drew blood from Cecilia de Wygan; 6*d.*

This was concealed by Bate de Halyfax, Richard, s. of Bate, John the Webster, German de Grenewod, and John the Badger, jurors of the township of Halifax in the first inquisition; they are therefore amerced 5*s.*

Sarah, wife of Bate the Litster [*tinctor*] of Halifax, brewed at 1*d*.; and this was concealed by Bate and the other jurors ; she is amerced 6*d*.; and they, 5*s*.

Juliana, the widow of Thomas de Aula, brewed at ½*d*.; her amercement is forgiven, because the ale was good.

Margery, wife of Jordan Spyvi, 3*d*. for brewing at ½*d*.

Alice, d. of Robert de Sourby, 12*d*. for the same at ¾*d*. This was concealed in the first inquisition by Robert de Sourby, John the Milner, Richard del Field, John, s. of Henry, and Robert, s. of John, jurors in the said inquisition ; they are amerced 5*s*.

Richard the Tynkler, 6*d*. for not coming to the tourn. This was concealed in the first inquisition by Thomas, the Grave, John Gretword, Roger de Illyngworth, William de Haldworth, and Peter del Bathe ; amerced 5*s*.

Richard, s. of Roger de Estwode of Stansfeld, 40*d*. for not coming at the lord's command, and for not attending the tourn. The township of Stansfeld, 6*s*. 8*d*. for concealing it.

Richard, s. of Christiana de Northland, and the township of Northland, 40*d*. and 6*s*. 8*d*. for a similar offence.

Henry de Byri of Halifax is guilty of the same ; his amercement is forgiven because he is poor, and the township of Halifax for concealing his default is amerced 40*d*., but forgiven because it is poor.

Henry Stelyng of Waddeworth, and the township of Waddesworth, 40*d*. and 6*s*. 8*d*. as above.

William del Foldes of Heptonstall, and the township of Heptonstall, 12*d*. and 40*d*. as above.

Adam de Walssedene of Sourby, and the township of Sourby, for the same ; the township pays 40*d*.; his fine is forgiven because he has fled.

Sum total : 107*s*. 7*d*., *i.e.* Bailiff,   104*s*. 7*d*.
Sourbi,   3*s*.

MILLS.—Soland Mill is let this year to Adam del Olderode for 5 marks. Sureties : Roger de Sourby, Henry del Seye, Richard atte Townend of Sourby, and Henry del Loue.

Warlolay Mill is let for the year to William de Warlolay for 2 marks. Sureties : Roger, s. of Amabilla, Ivo de Saltonstall, and Henry de Saltonstall.

COURT held at Rastrik on Tuesday after the Feast of St. Luke the Evangelist [Oct. 18], in the year abovesaid.

HYPERUM.—Roger de Brighouse, grave of Hyperum, is amerced a mark for not having seised into the lord's hand, nor entered on the Steward's roll, the land held by Richard, s. of Walter of Northourum, who died before Whitsuntide.

John, s. of Thomas s. of Cecilia of Halifax, gives 5s. as a heriot on 7 acres in the graveship of Hyperum after his father's death.

Walter, s. of Richard s. of Walter de Northourum, gives 13s. 4d. as a heriot on 22 acres with buildings in Northourn after the death of his father, whose heir he is.

RASTRIK; Grave.—Matthew de Tothill is elected grave of Rastrik.

A waif beast in the custody of Andrew Forester is sold for 2s.

Beatrix, d. of Henry s. of Elyas de Rastrik, gives 6s. 8d. to take 9 acres in Rastrik from her father.

[HYPERUM.]—William de Sunderland, elected grave of Hiperum, fines 6s. 8d. to have respite of office this year.

Thomas, s. of Thomas de Hiperum, 6s. 8d. for contempt, and 6s. 8d. in order not to be grave this year.

GRAVE.—John de Sunderland is elected grave of Hyperum.

Henry de Coppeley, Robert del Laue, and Thomas de Lyghtclyfes, 12d. each for encroachments along the edge of Hyperum wood.

The township of Hyperum, for concealing these encroachments at the last tourn, is amerced . . .

William del Rode, Thomas, s. of Thomas, Henry de Northclifes, John, s. of Ralph de Bayrstowe, John de Schepeley, Alexander del Brighous, and Alexander the Waynwricht, 6d. each for encroachments.

Thomas de Slaghwayt, 40d. for license to take 6 acres in the Bothes from William del Bothes, to hold during the life of Isabel del Bothes, who had them in dower, and sold her life-interest to William.

William del Bothes, 12d.; Adam, s. of Henry de Hyperum, 12d.; Alexander del [sic] Waynwricht, 3d.; John de Northclyfes, 2d.; John, s. of Ralph de Bayrstowe, 6d.; John de Birstall, 6d.; Thomas, s. of Eliote, 4d.; Alice, formerly wife of Richard s. of Walter de Northourum, 3d.; Alice del Northclifes, 2d.; Thomas, s. of Thomas, 12d.; John, s. of Pynder, 3d.; Roger de Northclifes, 2d., for escapes in the Hagge.

RASTRIK.—Richard, s. of John del Apelyard, 2s.; William, s. of Adam del Leye, and Henry de Tothill, 2s. each, for escapes of cows and sheep.

HYPERUM.—John the Pynder of Hyperum, 2s. for the same.

Richard del Rokes, Roger de Preestley, and John del Clyfes give 12d. to be respited from the charge made against them by . . . . . . del Bothes and other of their neighbours until the next tourn.

. . . . . . de Adrichgate for contempt is amerced . . .

BAILIFF.—Roger del Grene, 2s. for refusing to come to the tourn. [*mem. 2 dors.*]

HYPERUM.—Beatrix de Tothill gives 40d. to take 16 acres with buildings in Brighouse from John de Schepeley, for 8 years. And the aforesaid Beatrix shall keep in repair the buildings on the said land, as is befitting.

Sum total : £4 3s. 8d., *i.e.* Bailiff,   2s.
        Hyperum, 69s.   Rastrik,   12s. 8d.

TOURN at Rastrik the same day.

12 JURORS.—John de Querneby, Thomas de Tothill, John the Flemmyng of Clyfton, John the Flemmyng of Walton, Alexander del Firth, John the Clerk of Hertesheved, William de Sunderland, John del Rode, Thomas del Wode of Fekesby, Matthew de Bosco of Tothill, John, s. of William de Steynland, who say :—

BAILIFF.—The Abbot of Fountains [*de Fontibus*] is bound to keep Bradeley bridge in order ; and it is now in disrepair. He is amerced 40s., and is distrained by 13 horses.

The wife of John, s. of Dyan of Querneby, and Agnes, d. of said Dyan, 6d. each for brewing.

HIPERUM.—Thomas Bande's wife presented for brewing, etc., but pardoned, because she was amerced unjustly on another occasion.

The wives of William the Milner of Hyperum, of Roger the grave of Hyperum, of John Pynder, of John del Rode, and of John Speght, and Alice, wife of William Swyer, 6d. each for brewing, etc.

BAILIFF.—Thomas, s. of John de Dalton, drew blood from Thomas, s. of Master Thomas ; 12d.

Alot' Balle, from Adam del More ; 12d.

RASTRIK.—The wife of Alexander de Wodhouse, 3d., and Matilda, wife of Nicholas de Rastrik, 6d., for brewing.

BAILIFF.—Richard de Avenley drew blood from Thomas de Tothill ; 12d.

John Godayre ; John, s. of Alan ; John, s. of William de Barkes-land ; Hugh, s. of Wymark ; Adam, s. of Sarah ; Thomas, s. of Christiana ; Alan de Bothemley ; Adam de Bothemley ; William de Stokkhill ; John del Wode ; Christian[a] del Wode of Querneby ; Robert de Fekesby ; Robert, s. of Magge ; Roger de Lynneley ; Robert, s. of Hugh ; Hugh, s. of Isabel ; Adam the Smith [*faber*] ; Thomas de Mora ; Peter, s. of Adam ; Jordan, s. of Robert ; Nicholas del Heliwelle ; William de Qwytakres ; Richard, s. of Watter ; William de Baa ; William, s of Dokefot ; Adam del Leye ; Henry, s. of Thomas ; Thomas Asschalf ; Robert de Lyghtriche ; Richard, s. of Modde ; John Webster [*textor*] ; Adam Salter ; Richard de Querneby ; Alan the Milner ; Alexander de Hertisheved ; William de Rothelsete ; John de Nettilton ; William del Schagh ; John del Schagh ; Henry, s. of Gilbert ; William del Leghe ; Adam Coly ; Roger, s. of Jordan ; Peter de Dalton ; Thomas de Quytakres ; Robert de Collreslay ; Thomas de Aldonley ; John de Southwode ; William, s. of Adam ; Thomas the Smith ; Matthew the Tailor ; William, serving-man of the Abbot ; Thomas de Lynley ; John, s. of Richard ; William Seliheved ; Henry de Tothill, and John de Dyghton, 3*d.* each for not coming to the tourn.

HYPERUM.—The house of William, s. of Adam de Hyperum, was burglariously broken into in August, and sundry goods and chattels stolen from it. The township of Hyperum would not arrest, nor follow the thieves with the hue ; they are amerced 6s. 8*d.*

BAILIFF.—The above burglary was presented at this tourn by the township of Hyperum, and the twelve jurors were unwilling to enter the said burglary as it was presented to them by the aforesaid township. Therefore they are amerced half a mark.

The township of Fekesby, 6s. 8*d.* for concealing that Thomas de Tothill drew blood from Richard de Avenley.

Sum total : £4 15s. 4*d.*, *i.e.* Bailiff, £4 4s. 11*d.*

Hyperum,   9s. 8*d.*   Rastrik,   9*d.*

HOLNE.—John, s. of Nicholas Kenward, sues Gilbert del Dene for trespass. Surety : Adam, s. of Jordan.

Gilbert the Litster [*tinctor*] sues Dyonisia Crabbe for trespass. Surety : William de Ryeley.

Roger, s. of Mokoc de Schelley, sues Margaret de Schepeley for trespass. Surety : John, s. of Thomas the Smith.

William Wastel sues Richard de Lynne for debt. Surety : Richard del Bothe.

Henry Wade sues Richard, s. of Michael, for debt ; and also Thomas, s. of Richard del Rode.

Emma del Storthes and Thomas de la Rode severally sue Richard, s. of Michael.   Surety : Richard, s. of Richard.

Richard, s. of Michael, sues Adam, s. of Jordan, for debt.

Henry de Cartworth sues Matthew, s. of Thomas, for trespass.

———

[*mem.* 3.]

COURT held at Birton on Thursday after the Feast of St. Luke the Evangelist [Oct. 18], 8 Edw. II.

HOLNE.—Richard de Lynne, 6*d.* for putting Richard del Bothe as his surety against Thomas, s. of Thomas de Honley, for 2*s.* 10*d.*, and for not acquitting him thereof.

Roger, s. of Matthew [6*d.*], and Margaret de Schepeley agree. Surety : John the Clerk of Schepeley.

Gilbert del Dene, 6*d.*, and to pay damages to John, s. of Nicholas Kenward, for damage to his corn, amounting to the loss of 12 sheaves, by Gilbert's cattle.   Surety : John the Couper.

William Wastel proves [? himself and two others] by three witnesses [*tertia manu sua*] that Richard de Lynne owes him 10*d.* on a cow bought from William ten years ago ; amerced 3*d.*

Richard del Bothe, 12*d.* for imparting a counsel confided to him [*quia intimavit consilium sibi revelatum*].

William Huthe gives 2*s.* 6*d.* to take an acre in Rommesdene, left unoccupied by Peter Peede.

John de Rommesdene, 2*s.* 6*d.* for a similar acre.

An inquisition finds that Thomas, s. of Richard de la Rode, owes Henry Wade 5*s.* 10*d.*; amerced 6*d.*

An inquisition finds that Richard, s. of Michael, was surety for John de Castel for the return to Holnefrith of a brass dish [*patella*]. an iron dish, and a towel belonging to Alice, d. and heir of William del Storthes, and taken by Emma del Storthes, mother of the said Alice, to the said John's house when he married her.   Richard is answerable ; and is amerced 6*d.*

Adam, s. of Jordan, 6*d.* for unjustly detaining a skep [*skeppa*] and a half of oats for which he was surety for Henry de Crigleston from Richard s. of Michael ; and 3*d.* for withholding 6*d.* from the same.

Agnes, formerly wife of Thomas Pymme, sues Matthew, s. of Thomas de Cartworth, for her dower in 5 acres in Cartworth after her husband's death ; Matthew cannot deny her claim ; amerced 6*d.*

Matthew, s. of Thomas, 6d. for unjustly evicting [*deforciandi*] Henry de Cartworth.

Robert, s. of Thomas de Foughleston, gives 6s. 8d. to take 5½ acres with buildings in Foghleston from Adam Fernoule.

Robert de Langley, 2s. to take 3 acres in Hepworth from William de Hallumschire.

Thomas de la Rode [6d.] and Richard, s. of Michael, agree.

Richard de Birton gives 12d. to take 6¼ acres in Foghleston from William de Butterley, Adam the Waynwright, Richard, s. of Herbert, and Robert, s. of Thomas, who pay the same to take an equal quantity in exchange from him.

Adam Botchecollok, 18d. to take a curtilage and ½ acre in Overthwong from Adam Strekeyse.

Nicholas, s. of Nicholas Kenward, 12d. to take 1½ roods in Wlvedale from Adam del Scoles.

Robert de Wades, 12d. to take ½ acre in Wlvedale from Adam de la Grene.

Roger del Oldfeld, 2s. to take 2 acres in Heppeworth from Elyas, s. of Henry.

John del Holokes, 18d. to take 1½ acres in Heppeworth from Henry del Mere.

William, s. of Thomas del Brig, 5s. to take 4 acres in Cartworth from Thomas Carpenter.

Richard, s. of Richard de Cartworth, 5s. to take 5 acres in Cartworth from William, s. of Richard de Cartworth.

William de Cartworth, 2s. to take 2¼ acres in Carteworth from Richard de Carteworth.

John, s. of the Smith [*faber*] de Thwong, 18d. to take 1¾ acres in the Scoles from Robert del Scoles.

Sum total of this Court : 42s. 2d.—all from Holne.

————

TOURN there the same day.

12 JURORS.—Adam de Heley, Richard de Thorteley, Henry de Schelley, Robert de Wlfwro, William de Ryeley, John Wyther, John de Braytwayt, Henry de Birton, Richard de Birton, John, s. of Adam, Adam, s. of Adam de Wlvedale, Adam de la Grene, and Hugh del Hole, who say :—

HOLNE.—William, s. of Wilkes, junior, blocked up a certain path by Heppeworth spring, 12d.

BAILIFF.—Christiana de Schelley and Amabilla the Badger, 12*d.* each ; Robert Somer's wife, 6*d.*, for brewing, etc.

HOLNE.—William the Fuller's wife, 12*d.* for the same.

BAILIFF.—Richard, s. of Robert de Birton, drew blood from Richard Wlvet with a knife ; 2*s.*

HOLNE.—Matthew, s. of Thomas, exchanged one ½ acre of new land for another, without license ; fine, 6*d.*

BAILIFF.—John, s. of Nicholas de Schellay, and John, s. of John s. of Alice, for fighting together ; 2*s.* Both are attached.

The wives of Adam the Badger and of William the Sagher, 3*d.* each for brewing at ½*d.*

John Typupp of Schelley, 3*d.* for not coming.

HOLNE.—The wife of Robert del Scoles, 3*d.*; Margaret, wife of Richard del Holme, 3*d.*; Margery, d. of John the Brewer [*bracerii*], 12*d.*; Thomas the Smith's wife, 12*d.*, and Cecilia de Whitstones, 3*d.*, for brewing.

Adam, s. of Jouuet, 3*d.* for not coming.

BAILIFF.—William, s. of Hugh de Thurstanland, drew blood from Simon the Clerk of Thurstanland, amerced 2*s.*

HOLNE.—Robert Argent of Skelmerthorp, 3*d.* for not coming.

Ellen, wife of Adam de Holne, four years ago stole 9*s.* in silver and half a stone of wool from the chest [*huchia*] of John Honheved, and this has been concealed up to the present by the township of Holne. She is to be taken ; and the township amerced 6*s.* 8*d.*

The wife of William de Alstanley, 2*d.* for brewing, etc.

John de Holne stole and killed a waif pig in the last pannage. He is to be taken.

Henry de Cartworth blocked up a lane in Cartworth to the injury of Matthew, s. of Thomas. It is to be seen by the Steward.

Adam, s. of Jordan, and Gilbert del Dene, 12*d.* each for drawing each other's blood.

Margaret del Storthes and Margery, d. of the Smith, 12*d.* each for brewing, etc.

Adam Cheward and William Wlfes, the latter of Alstanley, 3*d.* for not coming.

. . . . . . wife, 3*d.* for brewing, etc.; and John de Kesseburgh, Robert, s. of Nicholas, Robert the Milner, and Adam the Shepherd, 2*s.* for concealing the same.

Sum total of this Tourn : 29*s.* 4*d.*, *i.e.* Bailiff, 9*s.* 3*d.*

                                        Holne, [20*s.* 1*d.*]

F

[*mem.* 3 *dors.*]

COURT held at Wakefeld on Friday after the Feast of St. Luke
the Evangelist [Oct. 18], 8 Edw. II.

ESSOINS.—John de Lepton, by Walter de Toftclyf. Surety:
Richard de Salsa-mara.

Thomas de Thorneton, by Thomas de Whitlay. Surety: Walter
de Toftclyf.

John de Schypedene, by William del Bothes. Surety: Matthew
del Wode.

Adam de Stanclyf, by Henry de Wakefeld. Surety: Thomas
le Seyvil.

Thomas de Dronsfeld, by William de Dronsfeld. Surety: John
de Leek.

Nicholas de Caylly, by Henry de Metheley. Surety: Richard
de Birstall.

William de Rastrik, by Thomas de Tothill.

Robert Patrikes, by John Patrikes. Surety: William the Eyr.

William, s. of Thomas de Tothill, by Henry de Wakefeld.

Thomas de Heton, by Richard de Thornhill. Surety: John
de la More.

John de Soland, by Thomas de la Sale. Surety: Thomas del
Belhouse.

BAILIFF.—John the Flemmyng gives 4s., and Thomas de Langfeld, 40d., for respite of suit till Michaelmas.

HOLNE.—Gilbert the Litster [*tinctor*] of Birton essoins against
Dyonisia Crabbe, by William Marjoriman. Surety: William del
Okes.

John de Holne, taken for stealing a waif pig, whereof he was
indicted at the tourn of Birton; gives 20s. [*pro suavitate prisone
habend*] until the delivery of York Gaol. Sureties: John de
Heppeworth, Richard del Bothem, Richard Michel, Adam [de] la
Grene, Adam Kenward, and Matthew, s. of Thomas.

Ellena, wife of Adam de Holne, 13s. 4d. for the same.

BAILIFF.—Peter Swerd gives 12d. to have respite of suit till
Michaelmas.

Thomas del Holgate, the grave, 40d. for allowing John Dande
to waste villein [*nativa*] land of oak, ash, and other timber, bought
from the said John.

Robert, s. of Isolde, 40d. for buying part of the said timber.

It is ordered that the villein land held by John Dande be seized and all the goods and chattels found thereon, because the said John committed waste on the said land in regard to 18 oaks, 4 ash trees, 4 sloes [?] [*bullect*] and ——? [*tremell'*], and was convicted thereof by the inquisition.

Robert, s. of Isolde, 40*d.* for buying part of the same timber.

William, s. of Adam del Leye, 6*d.* for sundry defaults.

Thomas de Tothill sues the said William under an agreement by which William was to remove a certain house belonging to the said Thomas in Fekesby for 18*d.*; and he received as a god's-penny, 12*d.*, and did part of the work, but went off, leaving the house unfinished. William makes no defence ; damages, 20*s.*; fine, 6*d.*

STANLEY.—Hugh Tagge, 6*d.* for not coming.

BAILIFF.—An inquisition of 12 finds that Richard, s. of John de Osset, Robert Pees, Richard Passemer, and John, s. of Richard, and Robert Scote procured Reginald Snart to assault John Maunsel. Reginald and those who procured him to go to prison. They afterwards find sureties for making amends, viz. Richard, s. of John, Richard, s. of Robert de Southwod, William Wyldebor, John de Northewod, William Graffard, Robert de la Grene ; Richard Snart and Jordan Elyot being sureties for Reginald himself.

An inquisition of twelve jurors of Wakefeld and Walton finds that Robert Marescall made a false charge against John the Carpenter of Walton, in saying that he had unjustly taken a young bullock from the New Park, for the said young bullock was calved from a cow of the said John there grazing. Amerced 6*s.* 8*d.*

John, s. of John de Soland, gives 2*s.* to have respite of suit till Michaelmas.

ALVERTHORP.—Amabilla de Flansawe, 3*d.* for false claim against Robert Gerbot.

Robert Gerbot gives 2*s.* for license to take ⅓ of 4 acres in Flansawe, held in dower by Amabilla de Flansawe, from the said Amabilla.

SOURBY.—Richard, s. of Alice de Sourby, gives 2*s.* to take 10 acres in Saurbyschire from Elyas the Couper, for 20 years.

SANDALE.—Peter, s. of Robert the Wayte del Neubygging, 2*s.* to take 6 acres in the Neubigging from Adam the Wayt.

OSSET.—Swayn de Osset gives 12*d.* for license to give in marriage Eva, his daughter.

BAILIFF.—Dom. John de Thornhill, 4*s.*; John de Querneby, and Matthew del Wode, 2*s.* each, for respite of suit till Michaelmas.

The township of Schellay, 6s. 8d. for concealing for the last six years a rent of 2s., which the Earl used to receive from land lately belonging to Richard del Rodes, the Earl's villein [*nativus*].

WAKEFELD ; new rent.—Robert Estrild gives 6d. for license to lengthen his solar [*solarium*] towards the street by 4 feet ; rent, 1½d. a year.

Laurence the Clerk, 6d.; the wife of Nicholas del Toun, 4d.; Robert Walker, 2d.; Robert the Tailor, 3d.; Nicholas Nodger, 3d.; Agnes Chepe, 2d.; the wife of Robert the Goldsmith, Alice de Castelforth, the handmaid of Robert the Goldsmith, junior, John Harehill, Adam Torkatro, Alice, d. of Alexander, John Leget's handmaid, Christiana Coly, John Clement's handmaid, Richard Man, Richard Fegald, Nicholas Hogge, John Torald, and Robert Hodde, 2d. each, for dry wood and escapes of swine.

STANLEY.—Walter del Spen's wife, John de St. Swythin, Robert del Spen's wife, Walter Gunne, Beatrix Gunne, and Walter Odam, 2d. each for the same.

WAKEFELD.—William Dun, Ralph Bate, German Hodelyn, Matilda de Sourby, Geoffrey, s. of Robert, Agnes Melyn, John Torald, John Rosselyn, Gilbert Gayrokes, Henry Fauconberd, Robert the Couper, the wife of Richard the Servant, and William Lacer's wife, 3d. each ; Margery Archur, 2d.; William Badger, 3d.; Agnes, d. of Roger, 2d.; Henry the Nauthird, 2d.; William the Theker, 3d.; John Richard, 3d.; Thomas Molle, 2d., and Hugh Chapman, 2d., for the same.

STANLEY.—Philip, s. of Agnes ; Alice, wife of Martin Dede ; Richard Bullokes, Thomas Thore, and Broun de Wirnthorp, 2d. each for the same.

ALVIRTHORP.—John Rate, 3d., and John Swan, 2d., for the same.

STANLEY.—Eva, d. of Agnes de Wyrnthorp, 1d. for the same.

WAKEFELD.—Thomas Alayn, 2d. for the escape of 2 cows in Moseley Hay.

William the Theker, 3d.; Gilbert Gayrokes, 3d., and John Richard, 2d., for dry wood.

STANLEY.—Emma the Long, 2d.; Richard Spynk's wife, 3d.; Eva, d. of Richard Spynkes, 3d.; John the Turnur's son, 6d.; Philip, s. of Agnes, 3d.; John Cort, 2d., and Martin Dede's wife, 1d., for escapes and vert.

ALVERTHORP.—Avice, wife of John the Smith of Neuton, [?] 2d. and William, s. of Walter, . . d., for dry wood.

STANLEY.—The wife of Thomas de Hey, . . . of Lofthous, 3*d.* for escape of a horse.

Matilda the Webester and Agnes, d. of Hugh de Lofthous, 3*d* each for dry wood.

Sum total of this Court : £6 15*s.* 9*d.*; and rent, 1½*d.*

i.e. Bailiff,	79*s.* 4*d.*	Sandale,	2*s.*
Alvirthorp,	3*s.* 1*d.*	Holne,	33*s.* 4*d.*
Stanley,	4*s.* 10*d.*	Osset,	12*d.*
Wakefeld,	10*s.* 2*d.*	(and new rent, 1½*d.*)	
Sourby,	2*s.*		

[*mem.* 4.]

TOURN there the same day.

12 JURORS.—Walter de Grimeston, Thomas de Seyvile, Thomas de Qwitlay, Robert de Wyrnthorp, Richard Tylli, John Patrikes, Thomas Alayn, Robert the Walker, Walter Scottes, William de Dewisbery, Richard de Salsa-mara, German Filcokes, who say that—

BAILIFF.—Agnes, wife of Robert the Clerk, brews at 1*d.*; 12*d.*

Adam de Lynne drew blood from John Fox ; 12*d.*

Peter Thrumbald from William, s. of Gilbert.

The King's highway in Wrennegate is impaired by the dung-hills of Henry de Adyngham and William Wlmer ; 12*d.* each.

The highway in Kergate by Symon Fox's dung-hill ; fine, 12*d.* Also by the dung-hills of William Pichakes and John de Kendale ; 6*d.* each.

Ibbota Ilhore stole an overtunic, worth 8*d.*, and a sheet, worth 2*d.*, from John the Piper's house at Plegewykes. She is to be taken.

John the Smith of Clifton drew blood from William Fox ; 12*d.* Peter Humbloc from William the Milner ; 12*d.*

Reginald Snart from John Maunsel. No amercement here because the matter is before the Court.

William Wiles from Laurence, s. of Odam ; 12*d.*

Robert Marescall raised the hue on Alice Graffard ; she [*sic*] is amerced 12*d.*

Agnes Peger drew blood from Juliana, wife of Gelle ; 12*d.*

Robert Marescall, 12*d.* for blocking up a public path leading past [*ultra*] Godwynrode.

John Torald, 12*d.* for marrying his daughter to John Gerbot without license.

Thomas Bunny drew blood from William Dodde ; 12*d.*

Walter de Monte from Alice Mokoc ; 12*d.*

Juliana, wife of Adam Cosin ; Agnes, wife of William Molle ; Richard de Colley's wife ; Richard de Bretton's wife, and the wife of John, s. of Erkyn, 12d. each for brewing, etc.

Alice, wife of John the Clerk, 12d. for raising the hue on Matilda de Hopton, and on the King's bailiff, who was delivering to the said Matilda her dower in Walton.

Thomas, s. of Henry, John the Leeche, and the other jurors of the town of Wakefeld, for concealing an encroachment made by Walter Adam, under his solar, 6s. 8d.

Robert Estrild and Philip Pykescull, 6d. each for not coming.

The jurors of the town of Wakefeld, 40d. for concealing their absence.

Sum total of this Tourn : 33s.—all on the Bailiff's account.

STANLEY.—Henry Gunne sues John, s. of Robert del Spen, for trespass. Surety : John Poket.

SANDALE.—Thomas de Holgate sues Henry Truncer for trespass. Surety : William de Osset.

ALVERTHORP.—William, s. of Walter, sues Richard Bunny for seizing a cow. Surety : William de Birkynschaye.

Richard Bunny sues Eva, formerly wife of William de Ouche-thorp, for breaking the lord's fold.

HOLNE.—Robert, s. of Hancoke de Wlvedale, sues Robert Jolyfe for land. Surety : Adam Kenward.

As far as this in the time of William the Goldsmith.

Sum total : £15 15s. 1d.

COURT held at Wakefeld on Friday after the Feast of
St. Martin [Nov. 11], 8 Edw. II.

ESSOINS.—John de Lepton, by Thomas de Wytley. Surety : William the Goldsmith.

Richard de Birstall, by William Marjoriman. Surety : William del Okes.

Adam Sprigonel, by Gilbert the Litster [*tinctor*]. Surety : Robert Drapur.

Thomas de Thorneton, by William de Thorneton. Surety : Robert de la Grene.

Thomas le Seyvile, by John Patrikes. Surety : Thomas de Bellehous.

Hugh the Nodder, attorney of Lady Margaret de Nevill, by Henry de Wakefeld. Surety : the aforesaid John Patrikes.

HOLNE.—Matilda del Apelyerde, for not producing Dyonisia Crabbe, for whom she was surety. Dyonisia afterwards came, as appears below.

SOURBY.—Mabel de Holynworth proved a cow seized by the forester of Sourbyschire was hers ; valued at 5s. Surety : John the Harpur of Northland. She paid a fine of 2s. 6d. for custody, herbage and view, and the grave of Sowerby is charged therewith.

BAILIFF.—John de Schypedene and Adam de Steynclif give 12d. each for respite of court-suit till Michaelmas.

HOLNE.—Gilbert the Litster [tinctor] and Dyonisia Crabbe [3d.] agree.

BAILIFF.—John, s. of John de Chikynley, appears against Robert Pees ; and because the said Robert appeared at last court, but did not come [sic], and made default after appearing, he is to be distrained to answer for default, etc.

Thomas de Dronsfeld, 2s., and Thomas de Heton, 40d., for respite of suit till Michaelmas.

Henry de Paldene comes and says he bought a cow from William de Balne, bailiff of Dom. John de Merkynfeld ; and it escaped from the custody of Jordan, s. of Symon, his own bailiff, and was seized at Schepeley by John de Schepeley's bailiff ; and when the said Jordan found it there, John and his bailiffs refused to give it up, but removed the cow into the Earl of Lancaster's fee. An inquisition taken finds John not guilty. [No record of amercement.]

William, s. of Henry de Eland [12d.], and Robert de Risseworth agree.

William de Tothill appoints Thomas de Tothill his attorney to do suit of court till Michaelmas.

William, s. of Hugh the grave of Eland, and Henry de Godeley [6d.] agree.

Henry de Schelley gives 6s. 8d. for license to remain on the land he acquired from Adam del Rodes, the Earl's villein [nativus], till the Earl come into these parts.

A reckoning is made between the graves of Wakefeld and Elizabeth del Rodes as to the rent of Adam del Rodes' land, which has been concealed, and it is found to be 5 years in arrears last Michaelmas.

William, s. of Adam del Leye, and his father, 40d. for removing a crop on which the lord's bailiffs had laid a prohibition on his behalf.

THORNES.—Robert, s. of Ivo, gives 3s. to take 5½ acres in Snaypthorp from Margery Hawe, for 12 years.

HOLNE.—Robert, s. of Hancok of Wlvedale, and Robert Jolyf [6d.] agree.

STANLEY.—Thomas Hancok gives 4s. to take a toft and 6 acres of land in Wyrnthorp from Richard Cade for 20 years, after a term of 3 years that Richard Spynk has therein.

HOLNE.—Robert, s. of Henry de la Grene, quitclaims to Thomas, his brother, all right he has or could have in a bovate in Wlvedale, formerly held by Robert Jolyf. Thomas fines 4s. for the recognition.

Richard del Bothe, grave of Holne, pays 40d. to be removed from his bailiwick.

STANLEY.—John, s. of Richard del Bothem, gives 12d. to take 2 acres with a toft in Stanley from Henry de Ayketon. [mem. 4 dors.]

HOLNE ; grave.—Thomas de Elwardhuls is elected grave of Holne.

ALVIRTHORP.—Alice, d. of Richard Gerbot, gives 6d. for license to marry.

STANLEY.—Robert, s. of Ralph, elected grave of Stanley, gives 2s. that his appointment may be postponed this year.

WAKEFELD.—Roger Preest and Rosa, his wife, sue William Cussing on a plea of land. Surety : Robert Carpenter.

SANDALE.—An inquisition of twelve finds that Henry the Truncer and his wife cursed [maledixerunt] Thomas de Holgate, the grave, because he struck Henry, and drew blood from him. And the said Henry struck the said Thomas in return, and drew blood from him. Both of them amerced 12d.

OSSET.—Richard Snart and Reginald, his son, wounded William Graffard so that he lies in peril of death ; they are fined 6s. 8d., to be under the mainprise of Jordan Elyot, Richard de Southwod, Walter de Southwod, Robert de Milkelfeld of Stanley, John Broun, and John de Northwod, until the next court.

ALVIRTHORP.—An inquisition finds that William de Neuton consented to the throwing up of a bank in Neuton fields, for which the township of Neuton was amerced in the tourn ; he is therefore to pay the grave for his share of the amercement, and is amerced 6d. for false claim.

Richard Bunny gives 12d. for license to retire from the office of grave.

STANLEY.—John Broun, 3d. for false claim against Hugh Tagge.

GRAVE.—Robert, s. of Robert s. of Walter, is elected grave of Stanley.

WAKEFELD.—John Dade gives 6*d.* to take a rood of land in the graveship of Wakefeld from John Teuet.

ALVIRTHORP ; grave.—Henry del Bothem is elected grave of Alvirthorp.

WAKEFELD.—John Nelot, 40*d.* for contempt.

OSSET.—Thomas the Pynder, the son of Richard Atte-tounende, and the son of William, s. of Gotte, 2*d.* each for dry wood.

THORNES.—The wife of Richard Carpenter, Margery Hawe, and John Graffard, 2*d.* each for the same.

Ivo the Smith, 12*d.* for breaking down palings.

ALVIRTHORP.—Richard, s. of Broun, 2*d.* for dry wood ; John Rate, 3*d.*, and Robert Gerbot, 3*d.*, for escapes of swine.

WAKEFELD.—Robert Marescall, Cecilia Buckes, the son of John the Sotheren, and German the Gardiner, 2*d.* each for dry wood.

SANDALE.—Henry, servant of the Constable, 2*d.*; William the Eyr, 2*d.*; Robert del Neubigging, 8*d.*; Thomas, s. of Pelle, 4*d.*; William, s. of Ralph, 2*d.*; William de Donecastre, 6*d.*, for vert, escapes, etc.

Alice Gerbot, 4*d.*; Gilbert de Sandale, 3*d.*; Margery del Hill, 2*d.*, and Richard, s. of the grave, 2*d.*, for the same.

HOLNE.—Peter de Wildborleye, 2*d.*; John, s. of Magge de Littelwod, 4*d.*; John the Hewer, 4*d.*; Ada Mirpel, 2*d.*; Adam the Schepehird, 4*d.*; William Pyntel, 4*d.*, for vert and escapes.

WAKEFELD.—John Cussing, for vert, 6*d.*

STANLEY.—Emma Dully, 2*d.* for dry wood.

WAKEFELD ; grave.—John Nelot is elected grave of Wakefeld.

BAILIFF ; Increased rents.—John Cay, who held 5 acres of land and ½ acre of meadow of the Bordland, fines 2*s.* 6*d.* for license to retain the said land at 12*d.* an acre ; and he will make the mill-pond of Wakefeld and the service [*auxilium*] of the chace in the old park as he has been accustomed to do, but will be relieved of the office of grave, and from tallage and all other claims of service ; increased rent, 4*s.* 1½*d.*

William Wiles, who held 5½ acres of land, and ½ perch of the Bordland, pays a fine of 2*s.* 6*d.* for a similar license ; increased rent, 4*s.* 2*d.*

Robert the Walker, who held 2 acres of the Bordland, pays 12*d.* for a similar license ; increased rent, 18*d.*

Adam de Castelforth, 6*d.* for 2 acres of same ; increased rent, 18*d.*

John Dade, 12*d.* for the same on 2¼ acres of the Bordland ; increased rent, 19*d.*

William Filche, 6*d.* for the same on ½ acre ; increased rent, 4½*d.*

William, s. of Robert s. of Hugh, 6*d.* for the same on one acre ; increased rent, 9*d.*

John Wyclof, 12*d.* for the same on 3 acres ; increased rent, 2*s.* 3*d.*

William, serving-man of Margery, 6*d.* for the same on 1½ acres ; increased rent, 13½*d.*

Robert Estrild, 40*d.* for the same on 7½ acres ; increased rent, 5*s.* 7½*d.*

The Earl enfeoffed Master Robert Carpenter of Wakefeld, by charter, in 3 acres in the graveships of Alverthorp and Thornes, at a rent of 3*s.* for all services, Robert paying an extra 6*d.* beyond the accustomed rent as compensation for the accustomed services incidental to Bordland, which cease under the said charter.

Total of this Court : 75*s.* 7*d.*; and increase of rent, 23*s.* 6*d.*

i.e. Sourby,	2*s.* 6*d.*	Bailiff,	31*s.* 8*d.*
Thornes,	4*s.* 6*d.*	(Increased rents, 23*s.* 6*d.*)	
Holne,	9*s.* 11*d.*	Stanley,	7*s.* 5*d.*
Sandale,	4*s.* 11*d.*	Alvirthorp,	2*s.* 8*d.*
Osset,	7*s.*	Wakefeld,	5*s.*

ALVIRTHORP.—John Broun sues Walter del Bothem for seizing cattle. Surety : John Graffard.

HOLNE.—Thomas Whatmod sues Emma del Storthes for land. Surety : Richard de Langley.

THORNE.—William Peger sues Alice, formerly wife of Roger Traylment, for debt. Surety : John, s. of Philip. Void, because Alice has nothing.

Matthew de Osset sues John, s. of Margery, for debt. Surety : Richard, s. of John de Osset.

Johanna de Thornes sues William del Rodes for debt. Surety : Thomas de Whitley.

SOURBY.—Thomas the Clerk of Waddesworth sues Robert de Saltonstall, Richard, s. of Alot, Henry de Luddingdene, Adam [son of Ivo, William] the grave of Warloley, for seizing cattle. Surety : John Sourmylk.

[*mem.* 5.]

COURT held at Wakefeld on Friday, the Feast of
St. Nicholas [Dec. 6], 8 Edw. II.

SANDALE.—William the Wylde, charged with being a neif, and
arrested on that account at Wakefeld, fined 5s. to have respite
until this court ; for which the grave of Sandale is answerable.

WAKEFELD.—A waif beast sold to John de Gayrgrave for 3s.

HOLNE.—Thomas del Ryding of Hopedale proved that a heifer,
reputed to be a waif and stopped in Holnefrith, was his property.
He fines 12d. for the custody.   Surety : John de Rylay.

ESSOINS.—Richard de Crosseland, by William Marjoriman.
Surety : William del Okes.

Adam Sprigonel, by John Patrik.   Surety : Robert de la Grene.

William de Rastrik, by Thomas de Whitlay.   Surety : William
del Okes.

BAILIFF.—John, s. of John de Chyckynley, sues Robert Pes for
4s. 6d. residue of 5s. owing for 3 quarters of oats ; damages, 6s. 8d.
Robert makes no defence ; fine, 6d., and 6d. for divers defaults.

Dom. William Receiver, chaplain, and Robert Lorimer [6d.] agree.

William de Roueley proves his ownership of 19 beasts stopped by
the Earl's bailiffs at Hiperum ; they are valued at £6 ; he fines 40d.
for the custody and escape.   Sureties : William del Clogh and Peter
Spynkes.

John, s. of John Skinner, and Robert Munk have a love-day.

Robert Munk, 6d. for sundry defaults.

Nicholas de Caylly, 40d. for respite of suit till Michaelmas.

John de Lepton, 6d. for default.

John Stelyng gives 3s. to take 3 acres with buildings in Sourby
from Richard, s. of Alot, for 20 years.   Surety : Robert, s. of John,
junior.

Thomas del Feld gives 12d. to take [3 acres] in Sourby from Robert, s. of John, who pays 12d. to take another 3 acres with buildings
in exchange from Thomas.

HOLNE.—The land held by John, s. of Nicholas Kenward, to be
seized into the lord's hands, because he is dead.   And as Nicholas,
his elder son, was born before marriage, and Thomas, his younger
son, after,—counsel is to be taken thereon with the Earl's advisers
[*consuland' est inde cu' consilio d'ni Com'*].

Richard de Aslay gives 4s. to take 6½ acres in Elwardhuls from
Emma Attelydyhate, for 19 years.

SANDALE.—Eva, d. of Elyas, gives 12*d.* to take a place of land to [? for] a house and curtilage in Crigleston from Thomas, s. of Pelle.

BAILIFF ; prison.—William de Bradeley and William de Kellet, bailiffs of William de Mallom and of the Abbot of Fourneys, are attached by John de Gairgrave and William de Notton, sureties for their prosecuting William de Roweley for stealing 19 cattle, belonging to their masters and to William, chaplain of Gairgrave. Defendant says he bought the said cattle in good faith from one Nicholas, s. of Roger de Overton in Westmerland ; and as the said William de Rowley had not the said Nicholas forthcoming to warrant the said cattle, he and the beasts are arrested till next court.

STANLEY.—Henry Gunne, 6*d.* for not prosecuting John, s. of Robert del Spen, on a plea of slander.

Three waif lambs sold to John de Gayrgrave for 18*d.*

THORNES.—William, s. of Roger, grave of Thornes, 12*d.* for not entering on the Steward's roll the land formerly held by Roger Traylment, who died before Michaelmas.

[? ALVIRTHORP.]—John Broun, 6*d.* for damage done by his sow in Walter del Bothem's garden, by breaking his gate and trampling down the oats ; damages, ½ quarter of oats. Surety : Walter del Hill.

Walter del Bothem, 3*d.* for keeping the said sow impounded, contrary to his pledge and promise.

THORNES.—William Grenehod took an acre and a quarter from Elyas Bulnays for 6 years, without license ; 12*d.*

John Tasse similarly took 3 roods ; fine, 12*d.*

William del Rodes, 6*d.* for not paying 4*s.* 4*d.* due to John de Thornes. Surety : William, s. of Thomas.

OSSET.—The whole of the graveship of Osset, 40*d.* for not coming when summoned.

John, s. of Margery, 3*d.* for not paying 8½*d.* due to Matthew de Osset.

THORNES.—Robert Mareschall, 3*d.*; Robert de Fery, 6*d.*; Richard, s. of Mille, 12*d.*; German Hareward, 6*d.*; John Tasse, 6*d.*; Richard the Wayte, 6*d.*, for not coming when summoned, to answer for taking land from Elyas Bulneys and Robert Peger and William del Rodes.

William Gardiner, senior, summoned for the same, is ill ; his land therefore to be seized.

William del Rodes acknowledges he demised land without license ; amerced 9*d.*

Magota, wife of William Peger, and German Hodelyn summoned for the same, amerced 6*d*. each for not coming.

[*mem. 5 dors.*]

Richard, s. of Mille, summoned to answer for taking for a term an acre from Thomas Lilman ; fines 18*d*. for entry. Thomas amerced 3*d*.

Amabilla, wife of William Lacer, 3*d*.; John the Cobbler [*Sutor*], 6*d*., and Alice, wife of Thomas Nundy, 3*d*., for not coming to answer as above. Thomas Lilman fined 6*d*. for leasing out of court.

John the Cobbler [*Sutor*], 6*d*.; the wife of Elyas de Swilington, 6*d*.; Robert de Fery, 6*d*., and Jordan the Mawer, 6*d*., for the like, for land taken from John, s. of Richard, who is fined 14*d*.

William Grenhod, 12*d*., and Robert de Fery, 6*d*., for the like, for land taken from William, s. of Thomas, who is amerced 8*d*.

Richard, s. of Robert, 3*d*. for land taken from Richard del Rodes ; 3*d*.

The wife of Elyas de Swilington, 3*d*. for land taken from Robert de Lupesheved ; 3*d*.

John the Cobbler [*Sutor*], 3*d*. for land taken from William Malyn ; 2*d*.

Thomas, servant of German, gives 6*d*. to take ½ acre in Thornes from William Malyn, for 6 years.

The wife of Walter Bille, 3*d*.; Richard Wayte, 6*d*.; Henry Gontoun, 12*d*.; John Tasse, 12*d*., for not appearing to answer for land taken from William Malyn, who is amerced 10*d*.

John, s. of Roger Traylment, has nothing in goods, and fines 6*d*. as a heriot on a bovate and 5½ acres in Snaypthorp, after his father's death.

STANLEY.—Richard Spinkes amerced 6*d*. for taking 6 acres to farm without license from William Cade, who also is amerced 6*d*.

ALVIRTHORP.—Thomas, s. of Laurence, gives 18*d*. to take 3 roods from John Swan in Alvirthorp, for 12 years.

WAKEFELD.—John Cussing, 6*d*. for vert.

STANLEY.—Emma Dully, 2*d*. for dry wood.

SANDALE.—Henry Achard, 4*d*.; John, s. of Nalkes, 6*d*.; Symon the Paytur, 6*d*.; Thomas, s. of Bate, 2*d*., for vert, dry wood, etc.

HORBERY.—John the Clerk of Horbery, 6*d*.; Hugh Cort, 3*d*., and his son, 3*d*., for vert.

John Dypsi, 6*d*. for receiving wood cut by his brother.

WAKEFELD.—Robert de Chedill, 8*d*.; the serving-man of Robert the Yung, 3*d*., for vert, etc.

OSSET.—Henry the Styrter, 2d. for vert.

STANLEY.—A woman of Lofthous, who went beyond the paling, 2d. Surety : Henry Forester.

ALVIRTHORP.—Thomas, s. of Philip, 3d.; Adam Wlf, 2d.; William Carpenter, 3d., and John Bullokes, 3d., for dry wood.

WAKEFELD.—Hugh Chapman, 2d. for the same.

ALVERTHORP.—Isabel, d. of Hugh, 1d. for the same.

OSSET.—Thomas Bull, 3d. for the same.

WAKEFELD.—William Lacer's wife, 2d.; Christiana, wife of Richard the servant, 1d.; Alice Wythoundes, 2d.; John Rosselyn's handmaid, 1d.; Henry Drake, Robert Swerd, Cecilia de Castelforth, Peter Spinkes, Richard Man, Robert Hodde, John Leche, Juliana Roper, William Mannolfstygh, William Mawer, and William Nelot, 2d. each for vert and dry wood.

Jordan the Mawer, 6d. for breaking palings.

William Mannolfstygh's wife, William Thrift, William Twenti-payr, John Cussing, Margaret Preest, and the handmaid of Christiana Coly, 2d. each ; Alice, d. of Alexander, 3d., and John the Bogheir's wife, 4d., for dry wood, etc.

Emma Pymme, 2d. for vert.

STANLEY.—Richard the Long, 6d.; William, his son, 2d.; John, his serving-man, 2d., for vert.

WAKEFELD.—Robert Swerd, for trespass with his cart, 2d.

Johanna Ladyknave, Magota, d. of John Tournur, Rosa, wife of Thomas the Masson, Roger de Silkeston, John the Tayllour, and Alice de Alvirthorp, 2d. each for dry wood.

STANLEY.—Robert Bele, Richard Longschankes, John Isabel, Philip Isabel, 2d. each ; William, s. of Adam, and Thomas, s. of Stephen, 3d. each, for dry wood.

WAKEFELD.—Hugh Chapman ; Agnes, d. of Roger ; the d. of Richard, s. of Junne, 2d. each ; Henry the Nauthird and Alice Wythoundes, 3d. each ; the wife of Richard the servant, William the Lacer's wife, and Agnes, sister of Matilda Bull, 2d. each ; Adam, s. of Ralph ; Matilda de Sourby and Ralph Bate, 3d. each ; German Hodlyn and William Dun, 2d. each ; John Rased, 3d., and Robert the Yonge, 2d., for dry wood.

STANLEY.—Robert de Mickylfeld and William . . . . . . , 2d. each for vert and dry wood.

[mem. 6.]

The Earl's villeins [nativi] of Stanley complain, as they have frequently done before, that Richard del Ker has lived an incestuous life amongst them, and has allowed the harlot, forbidden by the Steward, to return again, the penalty assigned being 40s. He was, therefore, attached and came, saying it was true the harlot lived in the house with him, to bring up his children [*pueris*], but he had no relations with her. An inquisition is taken of the whole graveship, who find otherwise. He pays 6s. 8d. of the above penalty at once, and the remainder is held over to see how he conducts himself.

THORNES.—William Graffard gives 13s. 4d. to take 34 acres in Sneypthorp left waste by Adam Besk and his heirs.

Margery Pygge, 2d. for leasing ½ acre to John de Gayrgrave without license of the court.

STANLEY.—Robert Leeper, 6d., and Richard Isabel, 2d., for the same.

John de Gaygrave gives 6d. to have the land above demised.

Henry Bull gives 12d. to hold 1½ acres for a term of years from William Tagge.

Richard Poket, 6d. for demising an acre for 6 years to Henry Bull, who is amerced 18d.

Laurence the Clerk, 2s. for license to keep his term of years in 2½ acres taken from William Tagge.

John Leche, 7d. for 2 crops [*vestura*] of ½ acre from William Tagge.

Thomas, s. of Molle, 18d. for 3 crops from 3 roods from the same.

Richard Poket, 6d. for leasing an acre for 3 years to Thomas the Roller ; amerced 6d.

Isolda Roo, 2d. for leasing a rood for 6 years to Henry Gontoun, amerced 9d.; also 2d. for an acre for 6 years to John Mous, who is amerced 18d.

Richard Poket, 6d. for 3 roods for 6 years to John the Rased, who pays 2s.

Robert de Mickelfeld, 6d. for an acre to Henry Bull ; Henry pays 12d.

Henry Bull gives 6d. for license to hold ½ acre which he took from Ellen Pygge, for 3 years.

Isolda Roo, 2d. for leasing a rood to Laurence the Clerk for 3 years ; he pays 6d.; also 2d. for 1½ roods for 3 years to John Leche, who pays 12d.; and 2d. for ½ acre to Henry Drake, who pays 12d.

Robert, s. of Walter, 6d. for leasing ½ acre to Robert the Leeper without license.

Robert the Leeper, 6d. for leasing the said ½ acre for 6 years to Robert Hoode, who pays 12d.

HIPERUM.—Alexander the Tailor [*Cissor*] del Briggehous sues William, s. of Agnes of Halifax, for debt. Surety: Andrew Forester.

ERROR [*sic*].—John de Schipleye, John, s. of Roger, and Alexander del Briggehous sue John de Sonderland and William del Bothes for seizing cattle.

BAILIFF.—John Cay sues Henry Tyting on an agreement. Surety: John Lerl.

Robert the Yongh sues Roger Bele and Mariota, his wife, Philip Isabele, and John Isabele for debt. Surety: Thomas de Wytley.

Total of this Court: 118s. 11d., *i.e.* Sourby, 5s.

Sandale,	7s. 6d.	Wakefeld,	13s. 4d.
Horbery,	18d.	Stanley,	34s.
Holne,	5s.	Alvirthorp,	3s. 3d.
Ossete,	3s. 9d.	Bailiff,	9s. 2d.
Thornes,	36s. 5d.		

COURT held at Wakefeld on Friday, the Vigil of St. Thomas the Apostle [Dec. 21], 8 Edw. II.

ESSOINS.—Thomas de Tothull, attorney of William de Tothull, by Hugh de Thothull. Surety: Thomas de Wytleye.

John de Lepton, by John Patrikes. Surety: Thomas de Wytleye.

Hugh the Nodder, attorney of Margaret de Neville, by William Marjoriman. Surety: John atte More.

Thomas de Thornton by Robert de Horbery. Surety: Thomas del Bellehus.

BAILIFF.—Robert the Herde Dalkenden,[1] indicted at Halifax tourn for breaking into the house of . . . . . . Pede of Walscheden, fines 13s. 4d. to have favour and leniency [*pro favore et suavitate habend*]. Surety: Dom. John de Thornhull.

Robert Monk is to pay John, s. of John the Skinner, the debt of 4s. for which he is sued. Amerced 6d. Surety: Robert de Newebiggyng.

HOLNE.—Thomas Whatmod sues Emma del Storthes for land; and as Emma is married, and her husband not included as defendant, she is acquitted. Thomas amerced 6d. Surety: Richard del Langheley.

HIPERUM.—Alexander the Taillour del Briggehous, 6d. for not prosecuting suit against William, s. of Agnes de Halifax.

----

[1] Of Alcomden ?

SOURBY.—Thomas the Clerk of Waddesworth, plaintiff, 12*d*., and Robert de Saltonstall, Richard, s. of Alice, Henry de Luddyngdene, Adam, s. of [Ivo, and William] the grave of Warlouley, agree.

HIPERUM.—John de Schepeley, 6*d*. for making a rescue from the grave, in contempt of the lord.

SANDALE ; new rent.—Adam, s. of Roger, the Earl's villein [*nativus*], who had acquired 7 acres of free land by two charters in his possession, fines 40*d*. to take the said land from the lord, and will pay 1*d*. new rent.

[*mem. 6 dors.*]

William de Roulay taken and arrested at the suit of William de Bradley and William de Kelet, who do not appear, pleads not guilty to the charge of stealing 19 cattle. An inquisition is taken by the oaths of William de Dewesbury, John Patrik, Richard de Salsamara, Robert de Heirode, John de Mora, Richard de Crosseland, Adam Sprygonel, John Dade of Wakefeld, William del Okes, Richard de Bristall, German Swerd of Wakefeld, and Richard, s. of John de Osset, who find him not guilty, and he is acquitted.

BAILIFF.—Elias de Birton gives 2*s*. for respite of suit till Michaelmas.

Robert the Yongh sues Roger Bele and others (above-named) for 7*s*. 8*d*., which they acknowledge. Amerced 12*d*.

RASTRIK.—Peter, s. of Henry de la Croiz of Rastrik, gives 40*d*. as a heriot on 5 acres with buildings in Rastrik, after his father Henry's death.

Thomas, s. of John Reyner, gives 2*s*. as a heriot on 4 acres in Fykesby, after his father's death.

Three acres of free land which the said John Reyner, villein [*nativus*], purchased are taken into the lord's hand ; and afterwards the said Thomas fines 12*d*. as a heriot thereon.

SANDALE.—John Cokewald and Idonea, his wife, give 13*s*. 4*d*. to take 1½ bovates of land in Plegwyk from John, s. of William de Abbathia, after 9 years that Henry de Holgate has therein.

SOURBY.—William de Lytheseles gives 7*s*. to take 12 acres in Soland from Alice, formerly wife of Thomas de Lyhtheseles, for 10 years.

BAILIFF.—William de Roulay, arrested here with 19 beasts, as recorded above, gives £6 13*s*. 4*d*. for an aid [*auxilium*]. Sureties : Ralph de Scheffeld, parson of the church of Thornton in Cravene, John de Gayrgrave of Wakefeld, William del Clogh, and Robert the Yongher.

G

SOURBY.—Alice, formerly wife of Thomas de Lyhtheseles, sues Michael, s. of Nicholas de Wordhull, on an agreement. Surety: William de Lyhtheseles. Michael is distrained by 4 stirks in Alice's custody.

Adam, s. of Ivo de Warmelee, bought an ox seized into the lord's hand, which was stolen by a thief, beheaded at Sourby, for half a mark. And the rest of the value of the ox was handed over to a certain boy, who procured sentence on the said theft [*qui fecit predicto latrocinio judicium* [or ? *indicium*] *suum*].

SANDALE ; increased rent.—Thomas, s. of Thomas s. of Pelle, the Earl's villein [*nativus*], having acquired by two charters, in his possession, ½ bovate of free land in Crigeleston, and a toft, a croft and 3 acres of free land in West Bretton, fines 10s. for license to hold the same ; and will pay an increase of 6d. rent.

SEIZED INTO THE LORD'S HANDS.—The land of John, s. of Nicholas Kenward, is to be seized into the lord's hands, because he is dead, and because that one Nicholas, his eldest son, was born before marriage was contracted, and Thomas, his younger son, was born after marriage, and counsel is to be taken thereon with the lord the Earl.

OSSET.—The inquisition between Matthew de Osset and John, s. of Marjory, postponed till next court, because John is still [away] in the lord's service.

SANDALE.—Robert Ster of Sandale, 2s. for breaking down and carrying off the fences of the Earl's garden.

HIPERUM.—Agnes de Astay, 4d.; Ibbota Tilly, 4d.; Adam de Bothes, 3d.; Bate del Bothes, 2d.; Thomas Thalthewayt, 3d.; William de Hayllay, 3d.; John the Milner, 2d.; Elyas de Knottinglay, 4d.; Thomas de Northclif, 4d., surety, John de Wythill ; Henry de Coldlay, 3d.; Roger de Prestlay, 3d.; Roger de Waveray del Loue, 4d.; Jordan Bithebrokes, 3d.; the widow del Deuebankes, 2d.; Thomas, s. of Jordan, 2d.; William Scharp, 3d.; Richard Meste, 3d.; William de Bairstaw, 2d.; John Blade, 2d.; William, s. of Adam, 2d.; John de Holway, 2d.; William de Aderichgate, 2d.; William de Yngandrod, 2d.; Thomas del Clif, 2d.; Henry de Finchedene, 4d.; for escapes, dry wood, and vert.

WAKEFELD.—William Goldsmith, 6d. for dry wood.

STANLAY.—Walter Gunne, 3d. for the same.

WAKEFELD.—William Lacer's wife, 6d.; Ibbota Fuller, 3d.; John Pollard, 2d.; Robert Lipestast's [sic] sister, the handmaid of

Beatrix Cay, Robert Peger, Robert the Taillour's sister, and Robert Goldsmith's handmaid, 2d. each, for dry wood.

STANLEY.—William Spen, 2d. for the same.

WAKEFELD.—The son of Walter Cook, Johanna Pymme, and the son of Elias, s. of Peter, 2d. each for dry wood.

SANDALE.—William Cort, 4d.; William de la Grene, 2d.; William del Okes, 6d.; John, s. of John Patrike, 4d.; Alice de la Grene, 2d.; Thomas Monikes, 2d.; Thomas, s. of Bate, 2d.; Thomas, s. of Magota, 2d., and William Leyr, 3d., for dry wood.

SANDALE.—An inquisition finds that William de la Grene encroached on the lordship, by erecting a fence farther on the common than he ought to have done. He is amerced 12d. for this and for felling a young oak on villein [nativa] land.

The township of Crigeleston, 2s. for concealing the encroachment at the last turn.

INCREASE OF RENT.—Adam de la Grene, who had purchased a bovate and 3 acres of free land, fined 6s. 8d. for license to hold the same from the lord, and will pay 3d. yearly in addition to the ancient rent.

[? WAKEFELD.]—John Pollard, jun., and William Nelot, 6d. each for not coming.

[? ALVIRTHORP.]—John de Wraggeby gives 6d. for license to hold 1½ roods in Alvirthorp, which he took outside the court from Marjory Wynter for 3 crops. Margery amerced 3d. for making the lease out of court.

. . . . . .—Margery, wife of John Peger, 6d. to take an acre from William del Rodes for 4 crops.

. . . . . .—Richard del Bothem, pale setter in Stanley wood, 12d. for not making an adequate paling.

John, s. of Thomas de Lytlewode, gives 4s. to have 4 beasts feeding on the hollins [ad husetum] in the Holnefrith, during the winter.

Richard del Bothem, 6s. for 9 beasts feeding in the same in winter time.

Total sum of this Court : £10 5s. 6d., and increased rent, 10d

i.e. Thornes,   6d.   Bailiff, £7   10s. 2d.
Holne,   10s. 6d.   Hyperum,   6s. 10d.
Sourby,   14s. 8d.   Rastrik,   6s. 4d.
Sandale,   10s. 7d. (and increase of rent, 10d.)
Wakefeld,   3s. 9d.   Stanley,   17d.
Alvirthorp,   9d.

[*mem. 7.*]

SANDALE.—Robert, s. of Richard Beausir, sues Juliana, formerly wife of the said Richard.   Surety : Hugh del Holyns.

BAILIFF.—Roger Beel and Mariota, his wife, sue John de Heton for trespass.   Surety : Robert Beel.

COURT at Wakefeld on Friday after the Feast of the Epiphany [Jan. 6], 8 Edw. II.

ESSOINS.—Richard de Crosseland, by William Marjoriman. Surety : William del Okes.

John de Lepton, by Thomas de Whitley.   Surety : Robert de Heyrode.

Thomas de Thorneton, by William Cussing.   Surety : German Cay.

Adam de Schypedene, by Thomas Clerk.   Surety : John Patrikes.

BAILIFF.—Thomas the Seyuile is in the King's service ; he is therefore pardoned for default.

SOURBY.—Alice, wife of Thomas de Lyghtheseles, 6*d.* for not prosecuting her suit against Michael, s. of Nicholas de Wordhill.

RASTRIK.—William de Rastrik gives 40*d.* to take 5 acres with buildings in Rastrik from Peter, s. of Henry de la Croyce.

SOURBY.—Adam, s. of Nelle s. of Ivo, gives 34*s.* as a heriot on 2 bovates in Sourby with buildings, after his father's death.

Richard, s. of Alan the Fool, gives 12*d.* as a heriot on a house and a toft in Sourby, after his father's death.

HOLNE.—Alice, formerly wife of John, s. of Nicholas, gives 2*s.* for an inquisition on land for which she sues John, s. of Nicholas. Surety : Richard, s. of Michael.

SANDALE.—Robert, s. of Adam, grave of Sandale, 6*s.* 8*d.* for concealing 1½ bovates held by William de Abathia, for which service has not been rendered in court.

John, s. of William de Abathia, gives 6*s.* 8*d.* as a heriot on 1½ bovates with buildings in Plegwyk, after his father's death.   Surety : John Cokewald.

HOLNE.—Nicholas, s. of John Kenward, gives 40*d.* as a heriot on 4½ acres with buildings in Wlvedale, after his father's death.

Thomas, s. of John Kenward, 6*s.* 8*d.* as a heriot on 14 acres with buildings, after his father's death.

William del Bothe, 12*d.* for license to take an acre in Alstonley from Gilbert de Alstanley and William, his son.

OSSET.—Robert the Couper, 18*d.* to take a rood of meadow in Osset from Thomas Pees, for 12 years.

BAILIFF.—Henry de Schellay gives 100*s.* as a fine on a bovate of land formerly held by Richard del Rodes and Adam del Rodes, the Earl's villeins [*nativi*], whereof the said Henry has the Earl's charter.

HOLNE.—The land of Henry del Mere, which he surrenders, is taken into the lord's hand until, etc. [*sic*]. And, afterwards, John Wlnet fines 2*s.* to take the said land, viz. 1¾ acres, with buildings from Henry del Mere.

OSSETE.—Thomas Pees and John, s. of Margery, give 6*d.* to agree with Matthew de Osset *re* a plea of debt.

ALVIRTHORP.—William de Birkinschagh gives 12*d.* to take an acre of land and meadow in Alvirthorp from Alice, d. of Gerbot.

STANLEY.—John, s. of Richard del Bothem, gives 2*s.* to take 2 acres and a toft in Stanley from Ellen and Isabel, daughters of Symon de Everyngham.

HOLNE.—Adam del Grene gives 4*s.* 6*d.* to have six beasts feeding on the hollins in the Holnefrith for the winter.

Richard del Dene and William de Cartworth, 3*d.* each for 4 beasts apiece, at the same.

Adam Strekeys, 6*s.* for eight beasts, at the same.

STANLAY.—Henry Tyting, 3*d.* for not coming to answer John Cay in a plea of agreement, is amerced 3*d.*

WAKEFELD.—Roger Preest of Wakefeld and Rosa his wife sue William Cussing for 5½ acres in the graveship of Wakefeld, as the inheritance of Rose from Gerard Cussing, her uncle, whose next heir she is. William, by his attorney John Cussing, his father, replies that Gerard gave him the land in question in a town called Wentebrigge, in the Earl of Lyncoln's land, in the presence of William the Taillour, then bailiff, who took the said land to the use of the aforesaid John Cussing, who did the Earl's will in the presence of the Steward ; which precludes plaintiffs' claim. They deny this. Upon this the said John, executor of Gerard Cussing, says the deceased owed a number of debts, and that the present Earl gave him permission to retain the land till these were paid. The plaintiffs say the Earl was deceived therein, because Gerard was a free man, and the villein [*nativa*] land of the Earl cannot be charged with the debts of a free man. An inquisition is taken by the oath of Robert de Flansawe, Richard [?] del Bothem, Robert de Lupesheved, Symon de Monte, Simon Tytyng, Elyas, s. of Peter, Philip Wlf, John Kyde, Robert del Grene, Philip de la More, Henry, s.

of Ellen, Thomas, s. of Pelle, Hugh Skayfe, Robert Pescy, Robert Ricard, Robert de Mik[elfeld ?], Philip le Ciour, Robert Gunne, William, s. of Thomas, Adam de Flansowe, William del Rodes, William de Overhall, William Peger and Robert the Leper, who say the surrender of the land in the Earl of Lincoln's fee ought not to prejudice plaintiffs' claim ; that native land ought not to be charged with the debts of a free man, unless he is in arrears or otherwise in debt to the Earl ; also that Gerard left sufficient goods at his death to discharge his debts. Plaintiffs are therefore to recover seisin, and give 6s. 8d. for admittance. Surety : John Cay. William's amercement is forgiven by Dom. Thomas de Scheffeud.

INCREASE OF RENT.—William Cussing, who holds 2½ acres of Bordland, has Dom. Thomas de Scheffeud's license to retain the same at an increased rent of 12d. per acre, paying suit to Wakefeld mill, give aid in hunting in the Old Park, but to be quit of serving the office of grave, and from tallage and other servile claims.

ALVIRTHORP.—John Bunny gives 18d. to take an acre of land and meadow in Neuton from John Attebarre, for 14 years.

STANLAY.—Richard, s. of John Poket, gives 6d. to take a perch of land in Stanlay from his father, John Poket.

ALVIRTHORP.—Thomas Thorald, 2s. to take ⅓ of a bovate and of 2½ acres of Rodland from Matilda, his mother, to hold after her death.

Henry the Nautherde, 18d. to take an acre in Neuton from Robert Gerbot, for 12 years.

THORNES.—Alice, formerly wife of Thomas Nondy, gives 6d. to take ½ acre in Thornes from Thomas Lylman, for 3 crops.

John Cobbler [Sutor], 12d. to take ½ acre in Thornes from said Thomas, for 6 years.

SANDALE ; new rents.—William de la Grene, 6d. to take a place of new land under Thurstanhawe, 102 feet by . . . . . . ; rent, 2d.

John Kyde, who held 1½ acres of the Bordland, commutes as above, for 12d. an acre.

[mem. 7 dors.]

WAKEFELD ; new rent.—Robert the Walkere, who bought ½ acre of meadow from William Nelot, the Earl's villein [nativus], has license from Dom. Thomas de Scheffeud to retain the same ; he is to pay 18d. increase of rent, on the former rent of 6d. William is pardoned for selling without license, because he is poor.

THORNES.—Ivo Smith [faber], 6d. for escape of pigs.

HORDBYRI.—John, s. of Hugh, 6d. for the same.

OSSET.—Richard, s. of John, and Richard Snart, 4*d*. each for the same.

THORNES.—John, s. of Magge, 2*d*. for carrying away 2 posts of the old paling.

WAKEFELD.—Walter Preesteson, 12*d*. for blood.

STANLEY.—Sibil Hamond's son, 2*d*.; Richard Poket, 2*d*.; Henry the Dyker, 2*d*.; Agnes, d. of Hugh de Lofthous, 3*d*.; Matilda Hayley's, 2*d*.; Philip the Syour, 3*d*.; John, s. of Philip, 6*d*., for dry wood.

Thomas Assolf and Robert, s. of Nicholas Nodger, 6*d*. each for refusing to shut the gates of the wood.

WAKEFELD.—John Russelyn's wife and Margaret, d. of Richard Junne, 2*d*. each for dry wood.

STANLAY.—William, s. of Adam Coc, 12*d*. for ivy [*edera*].

Roger Carter, 4*d*.; John Isabel, 2*d*.; Philip Isabel, 2*d*.; Emma Long, 2*d*., and Richard Spynk, 3*d*., for dry wood.

WAKEFELD.—Emma the Zoughe, 2*d*.; Henry the Nautherde's son, 2*d*.; Robert Tropenel, 2*d*.; Robert the Zoughe, 3*d*.; William de Hevensale, 6*d*.; Adam Torcatro, 6*d*.; Alota, d. of John s. of Sibbe ; Richard Peger's wife, 2*d*.; Robert de Rypun, 3*d*.; John de Haseley's son, 2*d*.; Nicholas Nodger, 2*d*.; John Nelot, 6*d*.; Margery Preest, 2*d*.; Elyas, s. of Peter, 6*d*., and William the Dykere, 2*d*., for dry wood, etc.

STANLEY.—John Pykehuskes, 6*d*. for vert.

WAKEFELD.—Henry de Ayketon sues Isabel de Everyngham and Ellen, her sister, for debt. Surety : Thomas Alayn.

SANDALE.—Robert, s. of William, sues William Quert [?] for trespass. Surety : Thomas, s. of Pelle.

Total sum of this Court : £10 7*s*. 4*d*., and increase of rent, 4*s*. 8*d*.

i.e. Bailiff,	100*s*.		Sourby,	25*s*. 6*d*.
Rastrik,	40*d*.		Holne,	31*s*. 6*d*.
Sandale,	13*s*. 10*d*. (an increase of rent, 2*d*.)			
Osset,	2*s*. 8*d*.		Alvirthorp,	6*s*.
Stanley,	8*s*.		Hordbiry,	6*d*.
Wakefeld,	13*s*. 10*d*. (and new rent, 4*s*. 6*d*.)			
Thornes,	2*s*. 2*d*.			

BAILIFF.—Adam Torcatro and Avice, his wife, sue Robert Coker for trespass. Surety : Thomas de Wytleye.

Robert Coker sues Henry de Adingham and William de Kyrkeby for trespass.

Memorandum that John Fox began to work in a forge in Hyperum wood on Monday after the Feast of the Conversion of St. Paul for 8s. for the week, and discontinued at the end of the said week.

FORGE.—The said John Fox took a forge in Hyperum wood at 9s. a week, to begin working on Monday after the Octave [of the Purification] of the B.V.M.

William Yonghare took a forge in the said wood at the same rent, to begin working on Monday after the Octave of the Purification.

[*mem.* 8.]

COURT held at Wakefeld on Friday after the Feast of the Conversion of St. Paul [Jan. 25], 8 Edw. II.

ESSOINS.—Thomas de Tothull, attorney of William de Tothull, by Hugh de Tothull. Surety: Richard the Saucemier.

Richard de Crosseland, by William Marjoriman. Surety: John de Toftclive.

William de Rastrik, by Thomas de Wytley.

Richard de Byrstall, by Adam de Emeley. Surety: William atte Grene.

BAILIFF.—Thomas, s. of Erkyn de Bretton, sues Robert, s. of John de West Bretton, for 16s. 8d. debt under the following circumstances: In 6 Edw. II Thomas agreed to buy all Robert's land, and paid him 26s. 8d. as an instalment of the purchase price of £12; afterwards Robert wished to withdraw from the bargain, and promised to return the 26s. 8d., of which he has repaid only 10s.; damages, 13s. 4d. Robert is ordered to pay 16s. 8d. and 12d. damages, and is amerced 12d.

SANDALE.—John Dande's land is again ordered to be seized. He is fined 12d. [being poor], for the offence of cutting down timber from villein [*nativa*] land. Sureties: Robert, s. of Isolde, and Thomas de Holgate.

BAILIFF.—Thomas de Sottoun, taken in the Earl's free chase in Sourbyschire, having entered it with other malefactors to commit a trespass, is fined 26s. 8d., paying a moiety thereof at each of the next courts. Sureties: John, s. of Adam de Locwod, and Richard de Crosselaund.

Roger Bele and Mariota, his wife, 6d. for not prosecuting suit against John de Heton.

Henry de Ayketon, 6d. for the same against Isabel de Everyngham and Ellena, her sister.

SANDALE.—Robert, s. of Richard Beausire, gives 16s. to take ⅓ of half a bovate in Sandale, which was seized into the lord's hand, because Juliana, formerly wife of Richard Beausire, who held the said land in dower, is free, and is living out of the lord's fee.

Roger, s. of Roger Milner of Crigeleston, gives 2s. to take 2½ acres in Crigeleston from Peter del Newebygging, after 6 years that Henry de Vallibus has therein, by demise of one Roger, s. of Amabilla, who formerly held the land.

WAKEFELD.—Master Robert of Wakefeld, carpenter, gives 12d. to take an acre in Wakefeld from Roger Preest and Rosa, his wife.

HOLNE.—Richard de Lynne gives 6s. 8d. to take 15 acres in Thwong from John de Holn, guardian of John, s. of Thomas de Thwong, who is under age and cannot act, for 9 years. Surety: Thomas de Elwadholes.

John Wolnet gives 2s. 6d. to take 1½ acres in Hepworth from John de Hollokes.

Adam del Quyk gives 5s. to take 4 acres in Holne from John de Rommesdene.

ALVIRTHORP.—Philip de Stanlay gives 12d. to take 2½ acres in Alvirthorp from Thomas Torald.

SOURBY.—William de Sothill, 1d.; Adam, s. of Ivo, 3d.; William del Waterhous, 6d. and 12d.; John del Fryth, 6d.; Robert de Wildeborleye, 4d.; Eva de Avonley, 6d.; William de Stodlay, 2d., and Robert the Scauberkes, 6d., surety, Roger, s. of Amabilla—for escapes in Scammendene.

Robert de Saltonstall, 3d. for an escape in Sourbyschire.

William de Staynland, 5d. for an escape in Skamenden. Surety: Alexander del Fryth.

John de Redykere, 3d.; William, s. of Adam s. of Nalkes, 3d., and Robert de Sourby, 3d., for escapes in le Firth.

HOLNE.—Agnes, formerly wife of John, s. of Hugh, 4s.; Henry de Cartworth, 3s., and Matthew, s. of Adam, 4s., for hollins [hussel] for cattle in Cartworth.

HYPERUM.—Henry [Smith] [faber], 6d.; John Sourmylk, 3d.; Adam, s. of William Drake, 3d.; the son of Henry del Rode, 3d.; the wife of Richard, s. of Walter, 3d.; John del Wythill, 3d.; John Milner, 2d., and Thomas, s. of Elyot, 3d., for vert and escapes.

HOLNE.—John de Holne, 6d.; Juliana, his daughter, 3d.; John Baroun, 3d.; Robert Chopard, 6d.; Thomas Fairber of Cartworth, 3d.; Thomas Fynion, 2d., and Adam the Waynwrycht of Hepworth, 3d., for vert, etc.

BAILIFF.—Adam de Byrchough, taken in the Earl's free chase in Sourbyschire, is fined 33s. 4d. Surety : John Dade.

SANDALE.—Thomas del Holgate sues Henry Sprigonel for trespass. Surety : William de Locwode.

Henry Sprigonel amerced 12d. for a gallon pot unmarked and false measure.

OSSETE.—Richard Snart, 12d. for a pottle unstamped and false.

BAILIFF.—Meggota de Rypun of Halifax, 12d.; Adam Sprigonel ; Robert, s. of Isolde ; Robert, s. of William s. of Alan ; Robert de la Grene ; John Plouman ; Margery Carpenter [*Carpentatrix*] ; Robert, s. of Pell ; William Molman ; Sygroda de Horburi ; and John, s. of Hugh, 3d. each, for unstamped gallon pots. [The first pays 12d. because it was also a false measure.]

STANLEY.—Robert, s. of Walter, 3d. for the same.

BAILIFF.—Nellota, d. of the clerk of Dewesbury ; Richard Litster [*tinctor*] ; Agnes, wife of the clerk of Dewesbury ; Robert Pees ; Thomas Pees ; Adam de Wodesom ; Matthew atte Welle of Walton ; Matilda, wife of Andrew ; Adam Carpenter's wife, and Henry de Sourby of Halifax, 6d. each for unstamped gallons and pottles.

STANLEY.—Richard Longschanke of Wyrunthorp, 3d. for the same.

John Page, 12d.; Robert, s. of Walter, 3d.; Robert the Leper, 2d.; Richard del Ker, 2d., and Robert Spyny's wife, 2d., for escapes.

. . . . . .—Robert de Chedelay, 2d.; John Cussing, 2d.; William de Kyrkeby, 2d., surety, Henry the Stirter; Margery Harchur, [?] 2d.; William Olyve, [?] 6d.; William de Middelton, 3d.; Richard, s. of John Poket, 6d.; Richard, s. of Robert, 6d.; Adam Spynk, 3d.; Walter de Bothem, 3d.; John Rate, 4d.; Richard de Gaukthorp, 6d.; Roger del Brighous, 3d., and three others [*illegible*], 3d. each, for vert, dry wood, etc.

THORNES.—Ivo Smith [*faber*], 3d. for an unstamped gallon measure.

STANLEY.—Henry Gonne, 3d.; the wife of Gilbert the Thekere, 3d.; Richard Isabel, 3d.; Nicholas de Bateley, 3d.; and Adam Spynk's wife, 3d., for gallons and pottles unstamped.

BAILIFF.—Julian Marmion of Normanton ; John Pycard ; William Jordan ; Adam the Bagger of Birton ; Robert Clerk of Birton ; Amabilla the Baggere ; Christiana de Schellay ; William Seger ; William the Hyne of Emeley ; the widow of Emeley, and Adam Cosyn, 6d. each for the same.

SANDALE.—Robert, s. of William s. of Alan, 4*d.*; William Petit, 2*d.*; Henry, s. of Cecilia, 4*d.*; Thomas, s. of Roger, 4*d.*; Thomas de Donecastre, 2*d.*, and Thomas de Holgate, 4*d.*, for escapes.

WAKEFELD.—Alice de Aula, 2*d.*; the son of John de Heselay, 2*d.*; Robert Top, 6*d.*; Richard Fegald, 6*d.*; the handmaids of John Tailor [*cissor*] and John Clement ; Robert Faucons ; Twentipair ; Walter Pollard's wife ; and Ibbota, d. of Hugh Chapman, 2*d.* each ; John Clement, 3*d.*; Margery Preest, 3*d.*; Johanna, her sister, 2*d.*; the wife of Simon Thrombald, 2*d.*; Robert Hod's handmaid, 2*d.*; Gilbert Tyncler, 2*d.*; Marjory Skall, 2*d.*, and John de Grenegate, 6*d.*, for vert and dry wood.

. . . . . .—. . . . . . Avice, his wife, and Robert Coker have a love-day.

. . . . .and Henry de Adyngham and William de Kyrkeby have a love-day.

. . . . .gives 12*d.* to take 3 acres in Thornes from Henry Poyde, for 6 years.

Sum total of this Court : £7 10*s.* 10*d.*, *i.e.* Bailiff, 76*s.*

Sandale,	[?] 21*s.* . .	Wakfeld,	. . ..
Holne,	27*s.* 4*d.*	Sourby,	[?] 5*s.* 3*d.*
Alvirthorp,	2*s.* . .	Stanley,	. . ..
Osset,	18*d.*	Rastrik,	12*d.*
Thornes,	15*d.*	Hyperum,	.. 2*d*

[*This membrane is the longest in the roll, and has consequently been the outside sheet, and some of the words are too much rubbed to decipher.*]

[*mem. 8 dors.*]

BAILIFF.—Richard Fylly sues Richard de Birkestalle for taking a mare. Surety : Thomas de Wytlay.

ALVIRTHORP.—John atte Barre sues Richard Bonny for taking cattle. Surety : Thomas Alayn.

WAKEFELD.—John Cay sues William Nelot for debt.

SOURBY.—John del Gledeholte sues Hugh, s. of Reginald de Warloulay, and Richard, his son, for assault. Surety : William de Locwode.

SANDALE.—Robert, s. of Adam, sues John, s. of William Hare, for trespass. Surety : Thomas de Holgate.

John, s. of Thomas, sues severally Thomas, s. of Roger, Alexander Shepherd [*bercarius*], John, s. of Hugh, John, s. of Alexander, and Alexander de Dritkere for trespass.

Robert the Yonghe sues John, s. of Margery, for debt.

BAILIFF ; void.—Richard, s. of Thomas de Aunlay, sues Thomas de Tothulle for trespass.

STANLAY.—Robert, s. of Ralph Ters, sues Walter Hog for land. Surety : John, s. of Gelle.

Philip, s. of Thomas de Stanley, sues Richard, s. of John Poket, for debt.

THORNES.—Juliana, formerly wife of William the Westerne, sues Johanna Dade, Henry de Lupesheved, and Richard de Lupesheved for dower. Surety : William Marjoriman.

COURT held at Wakefeld on Friday after the Feast of St. Matthias the Apostle [Feb. 25], 8 Edw. II.

ESSOINS.—John de Lepton, by Thomas de Wytlay. Surety : Thomas del Bellehous.

Thomas de Thorntone, by John de Rilay. Surety : William del Okes.

Hugh the Noddere, attorney of Margaret de Neville, by William Marjoriman. Surety : Richard the Saucemer.

William de Rastrik, by Thomas de Tothille. Surety : Thomas de Wytlay.

Thomas de Seynille, by John Patrikes.

BAILIFF.—Richard Tylly, plaintiff, essoins against Richard de Birkstall, by John Woderoue.

HOLNE.—Alice, formerly wife of John, s. of Nicholas, 6d. for not prosecuting her suit against John, s. of Nicholas, and her surety for prosecuting Richard son of Michael is also amerced.

John Kenward of Hepworth summoned by Master Ralph de Coningburgh to come here, on account of Alice, d. of Simon de Hepworth, whom he holds in adultery, and for whose sake he drove his wife from his house ; fined 6s. 8d. for not coming.

BAILIFF.—Robert Coker, plaintiff, and Henry de Adyngham and William de Kyrkeby [8d.] agree.

Adam Torcatro and Avice, his wife [4d.], agree with Robert Coker.

Richard, s. of Thomas de Aunlay, 12d. for not prosecuting his suit against Thomas de Tothulles.

John del Russcheleye attached for receiving goods and chattels of Thomas de Langfeld, from Ellen, wife of the said Thomas, fined 20s. to have peace thereon. Surety : Thomas Alayn.

Henry, s of Hychecokes de Rachedale, indicted at a tourn at Halifax for thieving oxen, cows, etc., fines 26s. 8d. for an auxilium. Sureties : Thomas de Aula and John de la Rode.

PRISON.—The said Henry is taken for stealing an ox and a cow, at the suit of Emma del Storthes, who says he stole them in Feb., 7 Edw. II, from Wolvedale fields. Henry begs the decision of a jury, viz.:—Thomas del Bellehous, Robert le Drapour of Stanlay, Robert de la Grene of Osset, William del Okes, Richard de Salsa mara, Robert de Heirode, Henry de Adyngham, Richard de Crosseland, John Hod, Adam Sprigonel, and Richard, s. of John de Osset, who find Henry innocent ; Emma is therefore sent to prison.

SOURBY.—John del Gledeholt sues Hugh, s. of Reginald, and Richard, his son, for assaulting him ; the father held him by the throat while the son beat him on the head with a stick ; damages, 100s. An inquisition finds defendants guilty; fined, 13s. 4d.; damages taxed at 10s. Sureties : Ivo de Saltonstall, ... , s. of Ivo, and Thomas de Roldesheved.

Richard, s. of Hugh, is amerced 6d. for cutting up an oak blown down by the wind, worth 18d., without license ; and for taking the profit thereof to himself. He has also to pay the value of the oak.

HIPERUM.—John de Astay holds 3 acres of villein [native] land in Hiperum, and finds sureties for building houses thereon between Easter and Michaelmas [9 Edw. II], and for paying the rent of the said land at the usual terms, and for dwelling on the land, viz.:— John de S[onder ?]lland and William de Hyperum.

John, s. of Ralph de Bairstaw, holds 5 acres of the same land, and William, s. of Henry de Astay, 2 acres ; they find sureties as above.

Henry de Northclif holds 2 acres of the same, and does not come.

RASTRIK.—William del Waterhous, 12d. and 6d.; Robert de Wildborleye, 4d.; William de Stainlande, 5d.; John del Firth, 7d., and Emma de Batelay, 6d., for escapes and husset.

HOLNE.—Richard del Bothe, 3s. for cattle grazed without agistment fee.

Matilda, d. of [?] Thomas, 2s., Richard del Dene, 12d.; Adam del Grene, 6d.; William de Cartworth, 12d.; Henry de Cartworth, 12d.; Warin de Twong, 12d., John, s. of Margery, 12d.; Matthew del Mersh, 6d.; Henry de Birton, 6d.; Richard de Cartworth, 3d.; William [?] Flosch, 3d. . . . . . . [three or four other names entirely rubbed away] . . . . . for escapes.

SOURBY.—Richard de Saltonstall, 3d., John del Dene, 4d.; Richard, s. of Adam, 3d.; Robert de Cheswallay's wife, 2d., Richard,

s. of Robert de Cheswallay, 2*d*.; Adam, s. of Ivo, 3*d*.; Alice, d. of Annota, 2*d*.; William, s. of Alcok, 3*d*.; Elias Milner, 2*d*.; William, s. of Elyas, 3*d*.; Richard, s. of Cecilia, 2*d*.; Wymarka, d. of Seye, 1*d*.; Anabilla del Bothe, 1*d*.; the wife of Thomas de Lyhtheseles, 2*d*.; William de Wolrunwall, 2*d*.; Eva de Godelay, 2*d*.; Henry de Holgate, 2s., and Richard de Wadesworth, 3*d*., for escapes.

HYPERUM.—William, s. of Peter, 4*d*.; Alexander Tailor [*cissor*], 2*d*.; William Milner, 2*d*.; Richard Taylor [*cissor*], 2*d*.; John de [*six names illegible*] . . . . . . for escapes, etc.

ALVIRTHORP.—Thomas Bonny, 3*d*.; John Broun, 3*d*.; Richard Broun, 2*d*.; William Carpenter, 3*d*.; Alice, d. of Richard Broun, 3*d*.; John Swan, 2*d*., and John Bonny, 2*d*., for dry wood.

STANLEY.—Richard, s. of Robert, 2*d*.; John Isabel, 2*d*.; Robert Broun, 2*d*.; Philip, s. of Agnes, 3*d*.; John . . . . . . , 2*d*.; and the wife of [?] Martin, 1*d*., for dry wood.

WAKEFELD.—Agnes, wife of Hugh, 2*d*.; . . . . . . [*nine names torn away*] . . . . . for dry wood.

[*About twelve lines at the end of the membrane are quite illegible ; the writing is only just visible at all.*]

[*mem.* 9.]

SOURBY.—Thomas de Wadesworth, clerk, elected grave of Sourby on account of the land he holds in the Mythumrode and in the Blacker, has not sufficient property to serve that office ; he therefore made a fine of 40s so that he may not be grave nor stockkeeper all his life, on account of the said land. Sureties : Roger, s. of Amabilla de Sourby, and Ivo de Saltonstall.

HIPERUM.—William de Sonderland is amerced 6s. 8*d*. for having entered into 12 acres of land in the graveship of Hiperum, the dower of Matilda, his sister, about 8 years ago, without license.

William, s. of Ivo de Saltonstall, 12*d*. for leasing land without license to Adam del Bothes, who is amerced 12*d*. for not coming, when summoned, to answer thereupon.

SANDALE ; warrener.—Henry Sprigonel is made forester of the town in Thurstanhaghe, Southwode, Blacker, and warenner of land and water throughout the whole graveship [*sic*] of Crigeleston, and is sworn.

ALVIRTHORP.—Richard Bonny, 6*d*. for contempt in court.

STANLAY.—Philip, s. of Thomas de Stanlay, plaintiff, and Richard, s. of John Poket, defendant [4*d*.], agree, *re* a plea of debt

ALVIRTHORP.—An inquisition finds that Richard Bonny wrongfully impounded sheep belonging to John atte-Barre, in his common of Neuton ; to the damage of one puncheon [*punchetti*].   He is to make satisfaction, and is amerced 6*d.*

SANDALE.—Thomas, s. of Roger ; John, s. of Hugh, and John, s. of Alexander, 3*d.* each for not coming, when summoned, to answer John, s. of Thomas.   Alexander Shepherd and Alexander del Dritker to be resummoned for the same.

STANLEY.—Walter Hog, 3*d.* for not coming to answer Robert, s. of Ralph Ters.

Robert de Mikelfeld gives 2*s.* to take 2 acres of land in Stanley from John Pollard.

OSSETE.—John de Heton gives 13*s.* 4*d.* to take a bovate of land with buildings in Erleshetone from Richard, s. of Adam Broun ; and finds sureties for the fine and for keeping up the same, viz. Richard Broun of Erlesheton and William de Hetone.

THORNES.—John Pymerich of Thornes, villein [*nativus*], arrested, fines 13*s.* 4*d.* for license to dwell out of the Earl's fee, at Mekeslorgh, for 6 years, and finds sureties for returning with his goods and cattle to the neif land at the end of that time, and for keeping up his land properly, viz. John Dade and German Swerd.

HIPERUM.—William de Sonderland surrenders to Robert, s. of Alexander de Sonderland, 2 parts of a bovate in Hiperum, for 6 years ; and Robert fines 6*s.* 8*d.* for admittance, and will sufficiently keep the buildings in repair.

WAKEFELD.—Master Robert Carpenter has license to take an acre of land on Borwemantoftes from Roger Preest and Rosa, his wife, for 3 years ; 6*d.*

HOLNE.—Alan del Dam gives 4*s.* to take 4 acres of land in Cartworth from Emma del Storthes, for 10 years.

Thomas del Holwey gives 13*s.* 4*d.* to take 16¾ acres in Litlewode from John de la Grene ; and 12*d.* to take 3 roods in Wolwedale from Richard Child.

Peter Bole and Agnes, his wife, give 3*s.* to take 7 acres in Litlewode from Adam de Wolvedale, guardian of William, s. of John de Craven, a minor, for 6 years.

THORNES.—Richard del Rodes gives 12*d.* to take a rood in Thornes from John Pymerich.

BAILIFF.—John de Bolling and Alice, his wife, sue Ingellard, vicar of Halifax, for withholding a gold ring.   Surety : Thomas de Tothull.

THORNES.—Nicholas, s. of Robert de Batelay, sues John Pymme, heir of Robert Pymme, his brother, for debt.   Surety : Peter de Achom.

OSSET.—Richard, s. of John de Osset, elected grave of Osset, fines 10s. for postponement of office this year.

HORBURY.—Hugh Cort and Robert atte Oke successively elected graves of Horbiry, fine 3s. and 5s. respectively for a like postponement.

SOURBY.—John del Redykere and Thomas de Solande successively elected bailiffs of Sourby, fine 13s. 4d. each for similar postponements.

Henry de Saltonstalle, 12d. for not coming ; he is to be distrained to come to next court because he has not completed Sourby chamber [*quia non perfecit cameram de Sourby*] as he was instructed.

Adam, s. of Ivo, is elected grave of Sourby, and received and sworn.

Sum total of this Court : £13 16d., *i.e.* Holne, 40s. 8d.

Bailiff,	48s. 8d.	Stanlay,	7s. 6d.
Sourby, £4	8s. 4d.	Rastrik,	3s. 4d.
Wakefeld,	6s. 4d.	Hiperum,	17s. 3d.
Alvirthorp,	2s. 10d.	Sandale,	9d.
Ossete,	23s. 4d.	Thornes,	14s. 4d.
Horbury,	8s.		

ALVERTHORP.—William de Locwode sues John Rate for carrying away wood. Surety : Thomas Alayn.

John de Gairgrave sues Richard del Houndes for unlawfully impounding. Surety : Henry del Bothem.

THORNES.—Robert Pegar sues William Dolfyn on an agreement. Surety : Thomas Lilman.

———

COURT held at Wakefeld on Friday after the Feast of St. Gregory the Pope [March 12], 8 Edw. II.

ESSOIN.—John Hod, by Thomas de Locwode. Surety : Thomas de Wytlay.

SANDALE [?].—Robert, s. of William, and William Cort [6d.] agree.

Robert, s. of Adam, sues John, s. of William Hare, for causing him to be amerced 6s. 8d. for not coming to pay heriot on the land . . . . . . after the death of his . . . . . . , when the aforesaid grave summoned him. Defendant cannot deny. . . . . amerced . . .

Henry Sprigonel, surety for . . . . . . against Robert the Yongh, amerced . . . because he does not come.

[*mem.* 9 *dors.*]

SANDALE.—John, s. of Thomas, and Thomas, s. of Roger, and the other defendants have a love-day.

HIPERUM.—William de Sonderland has license to take 12 acres of land in Hiperum from Matilda, his sister, for the term of her life [being the land he was amerced for at last court]

RASTRIK.—Alexander del Briggehous gives 6s. 8d. to take a bovate in Rastrik with buildings from John, s. of Richard, for 20 years. Sureties : Matthew de Tothille and William de Sonderland.

SOURBY.—John del Gledeholte gives 40d. to take 6 acres with buildings in Werloley, the dower of Beatrice, formerly wife of Jordan de Skircotes, for the life of said Beatrice.

It is ordered that 3 acres of native land in Fikesby, which Henry, s. of Thomas de Fikesby, freely held, be seized into the lord's hands, and the aforesaid Henry is to be distrained for entering on the said land without license.

ALVIRTHORP.—William Grenehod gives 12d. to take two and half roods in the graveship of Alvirthorp from Robert Gerbode, after 2 years' term that German Swerd has therein.

Thomas, s. of Laurence, gives 2s. 6d. to take 2 acres in the graveship of Alvirthorp from Robert Gerbode, for 20 years.

HOLNE.—Twenty shillings, collected by Richard, s. of Michael, and Adam, s. of Nicholas, and others, in Holnfrith, to the use of Henry de Walda, to be levied to the use of the lord.

The grave of Holne is ordered to cause Alice, d. of Simon de Hepworth, to come and abjure her adultery with John Kenward, who comes and abjures the same under pain of deprivation and disheriture of lands and chattels. Alice afterwards abjures the same at the tourn at Birton, under the same penalty.

Thomas, s. of Richard del Rode, is amerced for a false presentment regarding the whole neighbourhood [*patria*]. The grave is ordered to confiscate all his goods and chattels, and to seize his land into the lord's hand. He afterwards comes and fines 40s. Sureties : John Kenward of Hepworth and John, s. of Adam.

NEW RENTS.—Adam del Mere gives 2s. to take an acre of new land from the waste land in Fouleston wood, at 4d.

Richard del Dene, 4s. for 2 acres of new land on Langeleye Moor, at 4d. an acre yearly, and the said 2 acres lie in the Hadeker.

Thomas, s. of Simon de Heppeworth, 2s. to take an acre of new land in Heppeworth common, at 4d.

Adam del Grene, 4s. to take 1½ acres in Cartworth, at 6d. an acre.

STANLAY.—Walter Hog, amerced 3d. for contempt in court.

H

THORNES.—Juliana, formerly wife of William the Westerne, sues Johanna Dade for her dower in 16 acres in Thornes, after her husband's death. Defendant can advance no reason against the recovery, which is accordingly ordered by view of the neighbours. Johanna amerced 3*d.* for unjust detention.

The same Juliana sues Henry de Lupesheved for her dower in a messuage in Thornes ; but he, having no claim nor interest therein, cannot be sued, and Juliana is amerced 3*d.* for false claim.

The same Juliana recovers her dower in a messuage in Thornes against Richard de Lupesheved ; he is amerced 4*d.*, and is to make satisfaction.

OSSET.—Thomas Bole of Dewesbury, elected grave of Osset on account of the villein [*nativa*] land he holds of the lord, 40*d.* for not coming when summoned by the grave of the same to receive office. The land to be seized into the lord's hand.

William Bernard, elected grave of Osset, 40*d.* for a similar offence, and his land seized.

STANLAY.—Robert, s. of Ralph de Stanlay, sues Walter Hog for an acre of land in Stanlay as his inheritance, to which Walter has no right except under a loan of the land from plaintiff, made 30 years ago, when he was a minor ; and Robert sued for the said land 6 years ago, and Walter would not give it up. Defendant says Robert surrendered the land to him 18 years ago, before John de Donecastre, then Steward ; and calls the rolls to witness. The rolls not being at hand, an inquisition is taken by the oath of Robert Pesci, Robert Ricard, Robert de Mikelfeld, John Cockespor, John, s. of Alice, William Aubray, John Poket, Richard del Ker, Philip the Siour, Robert, s. of Robert, Simon Tyting, and William, s. of . . . . . . , who find for plaintiff. Robert fines 12*d.* for admittance, and William is amerced 12*d.* for wrongful detention.

THORNES.—Philip Wolf gives 12*d.* to take ½ acre in Thornes from William, s. of Thomas, for 12 years, after the two crops that Robert, s. of Robert Goldsmith, has therein, by demise of the said William.

ALVERTHORP.—John Rate, 3*d.* for not coming when summoned to answer William de Locwode, *re* a plea of carrying away wood.

THORNES.—Nicholas de Batelay sues John Pymme, the heir of Robert Pymme, his brother, in a plea of debt, and because the said John Pymme was distrained by one horse at the house of John Dade, which the said John Dade promised to sell contrary to the Bailiff's attachment, it is ordered that the said John Pymme and John Dade be attached by the next court.

ALVERTHORPE.—John de Gairgrave sues Richard Withehoundes for having impounded the cattle of the said Richard found in his corn, and the said Richard broke the pinfold and carried away the cattle. Richard denies the charge, and an inquisition is ordered.

Robert Pegher [3*d*.] and William Dolfyn agree.

HIPERUM.—William, s. of Pel de Thorp, 6*s*. 8*d*. for planks carried away.

Henry del Rode, 12*d*.; Richard del Wro, 40*d*.; Henry Fynch, 2*s*.; the widow of Roger del Briggehous, 6*d*.; Richard Tailor [*cissor*], 6*d*.; John de Hiltone, 12*d*.; Gilbert Brid, 6*d*., and Henry Horn, 6*d*., for vert.

SANDALE.—Adam, s. of Roger, 6*d*.; Henry, s. of William s. of Alice, 6*d*.; John, s. of William de Plegwyk, 3*d*., and William the Peyntour, 3*d*., for vert, etc.

STANLEY.—John Cort, John Isabele, Adam the Hewer, Martin Ded's daughter, and Philip Isabele, 3*d*. each for dry wood.

ALVIRTHORP.—Richard Wythehoundes, 3*d*. for the same.

STANLAY.—Philip, s. of Agnes, 3*d*., and 3*d*. for his tenant, for dry wood.

Roger the Carter, 12*d*. for breaking palings.

SOURBY.—Thomas Willes' stepson del Bothem sues John de Cockcroft for security given. Surety: the grave of Sourby.

Thomas del Feld sues William de Covenhale for debt.

ALVERTHORP.—John, s. of John de Chikenlay, sues Robert, s. of Ralph de Neweton, for debt.

Sum total of this Court: 117*s*. 10*d*., and new rent, 2*s*. 1*d*.

i.e. Sourby,	3*s*. 3*d*.	Hyperum,	16*s*. ..
Rastrik,	6*s*. 8*d*.	Sandale,	2*s*. 9*d*.
Holne,	72*s*. (and new rent, [2*s*. 1*d*.])		
Stanley,	4*s*. 6*d*.	Thornes,	2*s*. 1*d*.
Osset,	.. ..	Alverthorp, [?] 7*s*. ..	

[*mem.* 10.]

COURT held at Halifax on Monday, the Morrow of the Octave of Easter, 8 Edw. II.

SOURBY.—Adam, s. of Ivo, grave of Sourby, and John the Brewster of Skirecotes, 12*d*., and 6*d*. for not coming.

The daughters and heirs of William de Stodley, who hold divers tenements from Thomas de Langfeud, whose heir is in the Earl's custody, fined 13*s*. 4*d*. to have respite of homage till Michaelmas, if homage is due on the said tenement, and are to answer for relief at the next court at Wakefeld.

Margery, formerly wife of William de Stodlay, gives 12*d*. to take an acre in Stodlay, formerly held by the said William.

John Pikeston gives 3*s*. to take 2¼ acres in Sourby from Matilda, d. of Elias Pyroneys.

John de Wadesworth, 4*s*. to take from Agnes, formerly wife of Michael de le Lum, her dower in her husband's lands.

Thomas Willes' stepson del Bothem sues John de Cokcroft for 11*s*. 9*d*. as surety for Ingelram de Eclesley in the purchase of an ox which Ingelgram bought of the said Thomas. John acknowledges half the debt, and is amerced 6*d*., and Thomas 6*d*. for claiming the whole security wrongfully, as is found by inquisition.

Ellen, formerly wife of Thomas de Langfeud, gives 13*s*. 4*d*. for the lands and tenements of her late husband, seized into the lord's hand, to be held to extent until the Earl shall have been consulted.

GRAVE.—Robert de Sourby, elected grave de Sourby, is received and sworn, because Adam, s. of Ivo, previously elected and received, is now indicted for theft, and is taken and sent to the prison of Wakefeud.

William de Wolronwall, indicted for alienating an ox, gives 13*s*. 4*d*. for having grace [*suavitas*] of prison till the next court at Wakefeld, under the mainprise of Thomas, s. of Robert de Russcheworth, Thomas, s. of John de Staynland, William de Wolronwall, Robert de Wolronwall, Robert de Saltonstall, and Adam de Coventre.

John, s. of Hanne de Skirecotes, elected one of the twelve, is amerced for not coming.

John de Haldworth gives 6*s*. 8*d*. to take a messuage and 14 acres in Werloley from William de Covenhale for 8 years.

Sum total of this Court : 57*s*. 2*d*., all from Sourby.

TOURN there the same day.

BAILIFF ; 12 Jurors.—Adam del Schagh, John Fox of Stanesfeld, William de Sothill, junior, John Colpoun, Richard de Cheswelley, Richard de Saltonstall, William, s. of Hanne de Northland, John, s. of Hugh del Toun, Thomas del Bellehous, Thomas de Wadesworth, William de Estwode, and Thomas, s. of Robert del Brigge, who say

Adam, s. of Roger de Walschedene, Henry Schorthose and John, s. of Nicholas de Warlolay, burgled Alice de Coplay's house, and carried off a robe of linen cloth [*tela*] containing 40 ells, and other goods, etc. They also broke into the house of William the Milner of Warlolay, carrying off goods worth 40s. They are to be taken.

Elias de Haderschulf met with a thief in the Southstrinede [*Southst'nede*], and took from him a russet cloth, 10s. in silver, a hood, and a sheet, without a warrant. He is to be attached.

Adam the Tornour, 6d. for not coming to the turn.

Peter de Crosseleye drew blood from Adam de Whytworth ; 12d.

Adam, s. of Isolde, stole 3 oxen from Matthew Dolfyn of Clyvache. He is to be taken.

William de Clifton drew blood from Richard the Eremite ; 12d.

Ralph, s. of the vicar of Birstall, stole an ox from Robert de Russcheworth ; 2 cows from Walter de Aderichgate, and one from a woman of Northourum. He is to be taken.

Ingelard de Eclesley and other thieves unknown broke into Margery del Wod's house. They are to be taken.

Sarah, wife of Bate of Halifax, commonly brews at 1d.; 12d.

Margaret de Ripoun, 3d.; Margaret, wife of Jordan Spyvy, 3d.; Amabilla de Sourby, 3d.; Matilda wife of John, 3d., and Aimery, d. of Ibota, 3d., for brewing at ½d.

Adam Laverok, 6d. for not coming.

Adam, s. of Ivo de Warloley, to be taken for cheating Henry, s. of William de Saltonstall, over the exchange of a sow for a pig. He is amerced 12d. for blocking up a path at Luddyngdene forth.

Roger, s. of Henry de Soland, drew blood from Oto [*Otone*] de Lyhtheseles ; 12d.; and Oto from Roger, 12d.

Custance, wife of Thomas de Haytfeld, brewed twice contrary to the assize ; 6d.

Ellen, d. of Henry del Holgate, drew blood from Alice, wife of John Sourmilk ; 12d.

William de Godelay, junior, sold an ox in town of Wakefeld, and the ox afterwards returned to William's house, and he sold it again to William the Horsknave of Soland. He is to be taken for alienating the said ox, which is the lord's waif.

Henry de Godelay took a sheep belonging to the Lady of Russcheworth, without her knowledge ; and when the neighbours reported [*defamaverunt*] him for the sheep, he went to the Lady and offered her the sheep or the price thereof, but she would not accept either, upon which Henry drove the said sheep from his fold. He is nevertheless to be attached for the abduction.

Robert de Wolrunwall sold a cow, which had been distrained by the town-constable and by the Earl's servants, for a fine owing to the Earl. To be attached.

Richard del Ker blocked up a path in Stanesfeld ; 12*d.*

William de Cokcroft stole a cow from Alexander, s. of Michael de Ratchesdale, four sheep from his father, and 2 oxen from Robert de Wolrunwall, which he sold at Pontefract fair. He is to be taken ; and is fined 6*d.* for not coming.

William del Snap, Thomas, s. of Robert, and William de Wolrunwall, jurors of the town, 3*s.* for concealing William Cokcroft's absence.

John Soughel is a forestaller of hens, pullets, eggs, and other poultry ; amerced 12*d.*

Elias Bek, Peter del Grene, Cecilia Hors of Warlolay, Sibilla de Erdelawe, John de Bateley, Eva Brounile, Tille the Pipere, Beatrice, d. of the cobbler [*sutor*], John de Bretby, 12*d.* each for the same.

Thomas de Rodelsete is a forestaller of salt ; 12*d.*

Hugh de Baliden is a forestaller of meat ; 12*d.*

Richard, s. of Jordan Spivi, took toll above what was due, to the injury of the neighbourhood and the damage of the lord's market ; 12*d.*

Richard de Ourom is a forestaller of all kinds of victuals.

Sum total of this Tourn : 28*s.* 3*d.*, all from Bailiffs.

[*mem.* 10 *dors.*]

RASTRIK.—Hugh de Tothill sues John, s. of Henry de Fikesby, for debt. Surety : William Marjoriman.

Void.—William Milner del Briggehous sues Beatrice, wife of Alexander del Briggehous, for debt. Surety : Henry, s. of John de Rastrik.

HIPERUM.—John Cobbler [*Sutor*] of Halifax sues William del Hynginderode for debt. Surety : William de Schipdene.

John, s. of Henry Smith [*faber*] of Schipdene, sues the said William for debt. Surety : Robert, s. of Alexander.

RASTRIK.—John, s. of Roger del Briggehous, sues Hugh, s. of Isabel de Lynlay, for debt. Surety : Thomas de Tothill.

HIPERUM.—Adam Forester sues Henry del Rode on an agreement.

RASTRIK.—John, s. of Henry de Fikesby, sues Alexander Milner del Briggehous for debt. Surety : Henry, s. of Moloc.

COURT held at Rastrik on Tuesday after the Octave of Easter, 8 Edw. II.

HIPERUM.—Henry de Saltonstall gives 20s. to take 18 acres with buildings in Northorum from Matthew, s. of Richard atte Wode.

Thomas de Waddesworth, clerk, gives 12d. to take an acre in the Blacker from Dom. Richard de Middelton, chaplain.

RASTRIK.—Henry, s. of Thomas de Fikesby, 6d. for entering into 3 acres of villein [nativa] land in Fikesby, without license from the court ; and he gives 2s. to take the said land from Alice, d. of Eva de Fikesby, for 12 years.

Hugh de Tothill sues John, s. of Henry de Fikesby, for 2s. 6d., which he has owed him for a year.   John acknowledges 2s.   Decision as to the disputed 6d. postponed till the next court at Wakefeld.

HIPERUM.—John, s. of Henry Smith [faber] of Schipdene, sues William del Hynginderode for 2 quarters of oats, as surety for John de Skolcotes ; the debt is acknowledged ; fine, 6d.

John Cobbler [Sutor] of Halifax sues the said William for 3s. 8d., as part security for the same, in the purchase of a cow for 11s.   An inquisition finds for plaintiff, and defendant is amerced 6d.

RASTRIK.—William del Wodehous surrenders to William, s. of Adam s. of Ivo, and Isabella, his wife, 2¾ acres in Rastrik, to hold to them and their issue, with remainder, in default, to grantor.   They pay 18d. for the recognition.

John, s. of Roger del Briggehous, and Hugh, s. of Isabella de Lynlay, agree on Hugh's paying 7s. for the ox which was stolen out of his custody ; fine, 6d.   Sureties : Robert, s. of Margery de Lynlay, and Robert, s. of Hugh de Lynlay.

HIPERUM.—Andrew Forester and Henry de la Rode [6d.] agree. Surety : William de la Rode.

William Milner, 12d. for contempt.

John Milner of Schipdene, 12d. for the same.

RASTRIK.—Richard, s. of Matilda de Rastrik, laid waste a toft in Rastrik by pulling down a house, 6 years ago, in the time of John de Donecastre, then Steward, who enjoined him to rebuild the said house, or put up a better ; this he has not done.   He is now ordered to rebuild before next term, under a penalty of 6s. 8d.

Sum total of this Court : 29s. 6d., i.e. Hyperum,   24s. 6d.

Rastrik,   5s.

TOURN there the same day.

12 JURORS.—Alexander del Frith, John Flemyng of Dalton, Thomas de Dalton, physician [*fisicus*], John, s. of Adam de Locwode, John de Hertesheved, clerk, John de la Rode of Hiperum, Henry de Coldelay, William the Squier of Hiperum, Thomas de Fikesby, Roger del Haghe, John de Nettelton, and John, s. of John de Locwode, who say that

Ralph, s. of the vicar of Birstall, stole an ox from Robert de Russcheworth, a steer from Thomas de Burgh, an ox from Thomas del Wythill, and a cow from Alice, sister of Richard the Baggere of Northorum. To be taken.

John de Scolcotes of Northorum stole a tunic, a hood, and a sheet, etc., worth 6s. 8d. To be taken.

William de Morley was an accomplice to the thefts of Ralph, s. of the vicar of Birstall, and received the hide of one of the oxen as his share of the theft.

Adam de Aldelay stole a heifer from Thomas de Aldelay, his brother. To be taken.

BAILIFF.—Alice, wife of John Fuller or Walker of Gouthelak-kerres, and Alice, wife of John Dyson of Lyntwayt, 3d. each for brewing, etc.

John, s. of Cecilia, is a forestaller of poultry ; 6d.

John de Seiville, 12d. for not coming.

HIPERUM.—Agnes, wife of Roger de Briggehous ; Amabilla, wife of Richard the Taillour, William Fonne's wife ; Agnes, wife of Thomas de Briggehous, and Alice, wife of William Milner, 3d. each for brewing, etc.

Thomas the Webestere of Hyperum drew blood from Alice, d. of Henry de la Rode.

The house of William, s. of Adam de Hyperum, was broken into by thieves, and two sheets and other things stolen, and the town of Hyperum would not raise the hue, so that the thieves escaped. They are amerced 6s. 8d.

BAILIFF.—Thomas de Tothill raised the hue justly on Richard de Aunlay, who is amerced 2s.

Richard de Avenlay drew blood from Thomas, s. of Presst of Elaund ; 12d.

Adam, s. of Henry de la Rode, from Richard de Avenlay ; 12d.

HIPERUM.—John de Schipdene, from Amabilla, wife of Thomas de Schipdene ; 12d.

BAILIFF.—Sarah de Staynland is a forestaller of poultry and eggs ; 6*d.*

John, s. of Roger del Clif of Hiperum, the lord's villein [*nativus*], purchased a tenement and 6 acres of land by charter. The land is to be taken into the lord's hand.

HIPERUM.—Magota de Scheplay, 6*d.* for brewing against the assize.

BAILIFF.—Adam Shepherd blocked up a public path at Fouleshaghe Clogĥ, at the head of Rybourne Bridge ; amerced 12*d.*

John, s. of Henry de Fikesby, John, s. of William de Dyhtone, and Adam Sparbottre, 6*d.* each for not doing suit at Rastrik mill.

Alice de Lynlay, 6*d.* for receiving William de Lynlay, her son, who was indicted 3 years ago   She is to be attached.

Richard the Pedder of Staynland, 6*d.* for not coming.

Ingelard de Ecleslay, John de Avenlay, Henry del Rydynges, and John, s. of Nicholas de Warlolay, broke into the house of Alice de . . . . . . , and took goods worth 100*s.* [?].   They are to be taken.

Henry, s. of Nalle de Northland, stole an ox from the house of William del Bothem, who was one of the cattle stealers from the Lady of [? Risscheworth].

Christiana del Wodeheved received the thieves John de Avenlay and Henry, s. of Nalle de Northland, in their flight.   To be attached.

William del Bothem received the same thieves, and also received Ingelard de Eclesley.   To be attached.

BAILIFF.—John the Pynder of Hiperum, 6*s.* 8*d.*, and to be attached, for making a rescue from the Earl's bailiffs.

Thomas del Brigge of Querneby and William, his serving-man, 6*d.* each for not coming.

Sum total of this Tourn : 27*s.* 10*d.*, *i.e.* Bailiff,   17*s.* 8*d.*
                                                   Hiperum, 10*s.* 2*d.*

[*mem.* 11.]

HOLNE.—Margaret de Scheplay sues Roger, s. of Matthew, for trespass.

Peter de Wildeborleye sues Thomas, s. of Gilbert, for trespass. Surety : John de Rilay.

He also sues Matthew, s. of Gilbert, for trespass.   The said Matthew and Gilbert de Alstanley sue the said Peter for trespass. Surety : Adam del Grene.

William and Thomas, sons of Gilbert de Alestanley, sue the said Peter for trespass.   Sureties : Alan de Alestanley and the grave.

Thomas, s. of Gilbert, sues Mariota, wife of the said Peter, for trespass.

Richard Smith of Sadelworthfrith sues Nicholas, s. of Nicholas Kenward, on an agreement. Surety: Robert de Wades.

Roger del Oldefeld sues William de Halmschire for trespass. Surety for prosecution: the grave.

COURT held at Birtone on Wednesday after the Octave of
Easter, 8 Edw. II.

HOLNE.—Margaret de Scheplay and Roger, s. of Matthew [6d.], agree. Surety: John Clerk of Scheplay.

Thomas, s. of Gilbert de Alestanley, is charged with adultery with Mariota, wife of Peter de Wildeborleye. They both acknowledge the same ; and both abjure the adultery under penalty of forfeiture of their lands, and confiscation of all their goods and chattels. Nevertheless, they are amerced 10s. and 40d. respectively.

The above suits between Peter de Wildeborleye and Gilbert de Alestanley and his sons, are terminated by agreements ; the plaintiff in each case fining for license to agree. Total of fines, 5s.

Thomas de Elewardholes, 3d. for not carrying out the Steward's order.

Richard, s. of Christiana de Birtone, gives 6d. for one cropping of 2½ acres in Wolvedale, which he took from Adam, s. of Jordan.

NEW RENTS.—John de Thowong, 18d. to take 1¼ acres of new land in the bounds of Scoles, at 4d. an acre.

Adam, s. of Jordan Milner, 40d. to take 2 acres of new land in Cartworth, at 6d. an acre.

Thomas del Clif, 40d. to take 2 acres of new land in Cartworth, which Richard Bullok, a stranger [adventitius], took from the lord, and now has left, and has retired from the neighbourhood.

Thomas, s. of Adam Shepherd, 12d. to take 2½ roods in Hepworth from Thomas, s. of Elias.

NEW RENT.—John, s. of Matilda de Cartworth, 5s. to take 1½ acres of new land in Cartworth at 6d. an acre.

Adam de Horn, 3d. for contempt in court.

NEW RENTS.—Richard de Cartworth, 3s. to take an acre of new land in Cartworth, at 6d.

Peter de Gouthelakkerres, 6s. 8d. to take 2½ acres of new land in Cartworth, at 6d.

Adam de Gortone, 12d. to take 4 acres in Fouleston from Richard de Derneschagh, in exchange for 4 acres in Holne; for which Richard likewise pays 12*d.* Adam pays 2*s.* to take another 2 acres with buildings in Foulestone from the same Richard de Derneschagh.

Mariota, formerly wife of Thomas, s. of John, has free license to marry because she is poor.

Thomas, s. of Matthew de Hepworth, gives 2*s.* to take 2¾ acres in Wolvedale from John del Bothe.

Thomas, s. of Matthew, surrenders 16 acres with buildings in Schaveley, which remain in the lord's hand till the next court at Wakefeld.

An inquisition finds that William de Halmschire drove a certain foal [*pultrellum*] belonging to Roger del Oldefeld from his common, with such violence that he broke its leg. It is valued at 20*d.*, besides the price of the hide. Amerced 6*d.*, with an order for damages. Sureties : William, s. of Wilkes, and Thomas Brid.

An inquisition finds that William Brid broke an agreement with Richard de Thornotlay concerning an ox. Damages taxed at 12*d.*; amerced 12*d.*

Sum total of this Court : 51*s.* 8*d.*, and new rent, 3*s.* 11*d.*—all
from Holne.

TOURN there the same day.

12 JURORS.—Henry de Schellay, Adam de Helay, Richard de Thornotlay, Robert de Wolwro, John Wyther, Henry de Birtone, Richard de Birtone, John, s. of Adam, ——, s. of Adam, Adam de la Grene, Hugh del Hole, and Richard del Dene ; who say that

HOLNE.—Thomas, s. of Richard de Cartworth, drew blood from Richard, s. of Juliana, 12*d.*

The wife of Robert del Scoles, and Cecilia del Witstones, 3*d.* each for brewing against the assize.

Richard, s. of the chaplain of Bradefeld, who is called Charthers, brought a calf to Heppeworth and sold it to William, s. of Wilks, and afterwards the same Richard brought two stirks, which the said Richard and William sold at Wakefeld fair, and Richard is suspected of being a cattle stealer. He is to be taken, when found ; and William to be attached.

BAILIFF.—The wife of Robert Clerk of Birton, Christiana de Schellay and Amabilla the Baggere, 12*d.* each for brewing at 1*d.*

HOLNE.—Henry Wade of Wolvedale is a common forestaller of poultry, butter, eggs and cheese, and other victuals ; amerced 12*d.*

BAILIFF.—William de Sandale of Wakefeud, and Robert his son, are also forestallers ; amerced 12*d.*

HOLNE.—Thomas, s. of Elyas, drew blood from Alice, wife of Thomas the Coupere, 12*d*.; and Alice from Thomas, 6*d*.

Margery del Storthes and Alice, d. of Jordan, 3*d*. each for brewing at ½*d*.

William the Seger's wife is pardoned for the same because she is poor.

BAILIFF.—Robert Silver [*argent*] drew blood from Roger del Flosch ; 12*d*.

Margery de Todeholm brews ale and sells for ½*d*.; amerced 3*d*.

HOLNE.—William Strekeys advanced 4*s*. to Richard de Holme, for which he receives interest 1*d*. a week ; amerced 40*d*.

BAILIFF.—Margery, d. of John Smith of Scheplay, brews and sells for ½*d*.; amerced 3*d*.

Sum total of this Tourn : 13*s*. 4*d*., *i.e.* Bailiff, 5*s*. 3*d*.
Holne, 8*s*. 1*d*.

TOURN at Wakefeld the Thursday following.

12 JURORS.—Robert de Wynrumthorp, William de Dewesburi, Thomas de Wytlay, Henry de Chivet, John Patrik, Richard de Salsamara, William Alayn . . . . . , Robert the Walker of Wakefeud, German Filcokes of Wakefeld, John Tasche of Wakefeld, Robert the Roller of Wakefeld, and John de la More, who say that

BAILIFF.—Beatrix, wife of Adam de Wodesum, brews contrary to assize ; 6*d*.

Henry, s. of Robert de Flokton, assaulted Alice, d. of Michael de Overhall, so that she raised the hue on him. He is amerced 12*d*.

Alice Tagun of Floketone sold ale without its being tasted by the tasters ; 6*d*.

[*mem.* 11 *dors.*]

Beatrix, living in Westbrettone, 3*d*.; Margery, wife of John, s. of Derkyn, 3*d*.; Agnes, formerly wife of Robert Clerk of Dewesburi, 3*d*., and Ellen, wife of Richard Litster [*tinctor*] of Dewesburi, amerced 6*d*., for brewing contrary to assize.

Ralph the Colier and William Cokewald, of the same, amerced 12*d*. each for opening the King's highway in Dewesburi, in digging for coals, because it was to the injury of all travellers.

SANDALE.—Alice, wife of John Hancok of Sandale, and Mabel, wife of John Plouman, 6*d*. each for selling ale untasted by the tasters.

Amabilla, d. of Geoffrey, 6*d*. for brewing.

ALVIRTHORP.—Richard de Collay's wife for the same, 6*d*.

BAILIFF.—Richard, servant of the parson of Wakefeld, drew blood from Magota, d. of Richard Broun of Alvirthorp, 12*d*., and she raised the hue upon him.

Robert Marescall of Wakefeld blocked up a way between Snaype-thorp and Alvirthorp ; 12*d*.

HORBIRY.—Margaret, wife of John de Horburi, and Alice, wife of Thomas Gige, 3*d*. each for brewing, etc.

ERROR.—John de Mora blocked up a certain path beyond Lopis-hevedfeld, where a common footpath is wont and ought to be.

BAILIFF.—Agnes, wife of John Tylly of Normanton, and Ellen del Wodehous, 6*d*. each for brewing contrary to the assize.

William the Hyne, 12*d*.; and John, s. of Nelle, and Adam Pogge, 6*d*. each, for not coming to the Tourn.

THORNES.—Richard Proudfot and William de la Rode do not come ; because they are burying their mother at Birstall.

John del Hagh blocked up a common path in Snaypthorp with the paling of his plantation ; amerced 12*d*.

The wife of Ivo de Snaypthorp, 3*d*. for brewing, etc.

SANDALE.—Adam Schakelokes of Holinthorp enclosed 6 feet by 4 of the common street in Holinthorp by a bank ; 12*d*.

John Goldhor appropriated to himself waste land in the commons in Westwodside ; he says it is in the Steward's roll. The rolls are to be examined at the next court.

Magota, wife of Henry Sprigonel, 3*d*. for brewing, etc.

BAILIFF.—John Hancokes drew blood from Thomas de Thyng-lawe, and is amerced 6*d*.

Robert de Mikelfeld, the Earl's villein [*nativus*], purchased an acre of free land from John Dade in Stanlay fields, which he did not previously present in court. The land is to be taken into the lord's hand.

STANLEY.—Agnes, wife of Nicholas de Bateley, 6*d*. for brewing twice against the assize ; Johanna, wife of Hugh Forester of Stanley, 3*d*. for brewing once ; Juliana, wife of Robert de Stanlay, 6*d*., and the wife of Richard Isabell, 3*d*. for the same.

BAILIFF.—Henry Sprigonel, warenner, raised the hue on Robert Tailor [*cissor*] of Wakefeld for going over the corn in Crigelestone carrying dung, and Robert would not attach himself ; 6*d*. He is to be attached.

[?] SANDALE.—Adam Sprigonel's wife, 3*d*. for not sending for the wardens of assize.

The wife of Robert Isaud, 3*d*. for brewing at $\frac{1}{2}d$.

. . . . . —John Bullokes and Richard, his son, dug coal on the Earl's villein [*nativa*] land, and sold part and burned part ; amerced 12*d*.

. . . . . .—Reginald Snart, Richard Snart and William Graffard, 12*d*. each for assaulting one another.

[SANDALE.]—William de Collay of Crigelestone, 12*d*. for digging coal on the lord's land, and selling it.

Margery Carpenter [*Carpentatrix*] of Crigelstone for doing the same on villein [*nativa*] land, 6*d*.

Henry the Nonne dug a pit for a coal mine [*fossura Carbonum*], and took part of the coal out, and sold it. The lower part of the pit is stopped by water ; amerced, 12*d*.

. . . . . .—William Tyrsi drew blood from Robert Fynger ; 12*d*.

Henry Fauconberge, 12*d*. for contempt in refusing to swear.

Margery Peger and her daughter raised the hue on John Wolmer for beating them. John amerced 12*d*.

William, s. of Hugh, [?] 12*d*. for obstructing the common way in Wrengate by his tanning [*tannum*].

John, s. of Juliana, drew blood from Geoffrey the Chapman ; 12*d*.

Jordan the Littester from Thomas the Taverner ; 12*d*.

Richard the Wayte from John de Thwong ; 12*d*.

Robert Dodeman's wife stole a " broddisch," worth 2*d*., a ℔. of wool worth 4*d*., etc., from the houses of Robert the Yongh, Hugh Mercer [*mercenarius*], and John, s. of John Levediman. She is to be taken.

Hugh, s. of Katherine, drew blood from William de Sandale ; 12*d*.

Robert Dodeman from Philip Damoisele ; 12*d*.

Philip Damoisele from Robert Dampson ; 12*d*.

The wife of Adam Torkatro, 3*d*. for raising the hue unjustly on William Nelot.

Matilda, wife of Henry Clerk, stole a goose from Robert the Yongh, of the value of 3*d*. She is to be attached.

John de Kendale, 3*d*. for obstructing the common way in Wrengate ; 3*d*.

John Dun, for making a way for entrance and exit, to which he was not entitled beyond [*ultra ; Quære* against] the lord's villein [*nativa*] land, and beyond the land of his neighbours, to the head of his garden, is amerced

Alexander de Mora, 6*d*. for not coming to the Tourn.

John Damyas, 2*s*. for making an unlawful enclosure with walls in the common of the town of Wakefeld in the Millerodes ; and 12*d*.

for obstructing the common way to the common ford over the Keldre, by two weirs wrongfully raised, so that Wakefield Bridge as well as the lord's mill is injured [?]. The weirs are to be cast down, and he is amerced —

Sum total of this Tourn : 40s. 6d., i.e. Bailiff,   27s. 6d.

Alvirthorp,	9d.	Thornes,	15d.
Sandale,	5s.	Stanley,	2s. 6d.
Horbiry,	6d.	Ossete,	3s.

[mem. 12.]

COURT held at Wakefeld on Friday after the Octave of Easter, 8 Edw. II.

SANDALE.—Thomas de Holgate, grave of Sandale, 6d. for not carrying out the Steward's command.

ALVERTHORP.—Henry del Bothem, grave of Alverthorp, 6d. for the same.

HORBURI.—Adam, s. of William, grave of Horburi, 6d. for the same.

OSSETE.—William de Hetone, grave of Osset, 6d. for the same.

STANLAY.—Robert, s. of Walter, grave of Stanlay, 6d. for the same.

BAILIFF.—Richard Tilli [6d.] and Richard Birstall of Normantone agree.

SANDALE.—John, s. of Thomas [3d.], and Thomas, s. of Roger, agree.

HOLNE.—William, s. of Wilkes, indicted at Birton Tourn for receiving a thief from the Earl of Lancaster's fee, fines 20s. for that trespass. Sureties : John, s. of Adam de Hepworth, and Richard, s. of John s. of Gilbert.

SANDALE.—An inquisition finds that Henry Sprigonel encroached upon Thomas del Holgate's land at Crigeleston ; he is to satisfy him, and is amerced 6d.

John, s. of Thomas, agrees with Alexander Shepherd [bercarius], Alexander de Dritker, and John, his son ; the three defendants paying 6d. each for license to agree. Sureties : Thomas, s. of Roger, and Thomas del Holgate.

Robert, s. of Hugh, charges with divers trespasses, left the bar contemptuously, and was amerced 6d.

BAILIFF.—William de Godelay, indicted at the Halifax Tourn for alienating an ox, fines 26s. 8d. Sureties : Thomas, s. of Robert de Russcheworth, Thomas, s. of John de Staynland, William de

Wolrunwall, Robert de Wolrunwall, Robert de Saltonstall, and Adam de Coventre.

Henry de Godelay, taken for alienating a stray sheep, fines 50s. Sureties : William de Sonderland and William de Godelay, senior.

SOURBY.—Adam, s. of Ivo de Warlolay, indicted for alienating a sow in Warlolay wood without licence, fines £4 for that trespass, and for the amercements of four townships, which kept him out of Wakefeld prison at Halifax for one night.   Sureties : Thomas de Aula, Robert de Saltonstall, and Adam at Townend de Megeley.

WAKEFEUD.—John Cay essoins against Henry Tyting, by German Cay.   Surety : William Marjoriman.   The defendant to be attached.

SANDALE.—An inquisition finds that Robert, s. of Hugh de Chapel-thorp, committed waste on a messuage held in villeinage [*de nativi-tate*] and 4 acres of villein [*nativa*] land he has in Crigelestone, as guardian of Agnes, d. of Henry de Vallibus, a minor, by cutting down ashes and apple-trees worth 8d., and making a ditch in seeking for coals ; and carrying the earth away from this land as a compost for his free land.   The land is taken into the lord's hand.   Amerced 12d.

ALVERTHORP.—William, s. of Thomas de Alverthorp, gives 12d. to take a messuage, a toft and ½ rood of land in Alverthorp from Alice, d. of Richard Brounesone, in exchange for a similar tenement, for which Alice pays 12d.

Thomas Bonny, 2s. to take ½ acre in Neweton from John, s. of Henry the Nonne.

ALVIRTHORP.—Richard Wythehoundes is made taster of ale in Alverthorp, and sworn.

STANLAY.—Robert Richard in Stanlay.

THORNES.—John Graffard in Thorne.

SANDALE.—William del Overhall in Sandale.

CRIGELESTON.—Thomas, s. of Pelle, in Crigelestone.

HORBURI.—Richard, s. of the grave in Horburi.

NORMANTONE.—Thomas the Leper and Ralph Shepherd in Nor-mantone.

EMELAY.—Richard Cosyn in Emelay.

WALTONE.—John de Wodekirke and William, the grave, in Waltone.

WESTBRETTONE.—Thomas Erl in Westbrettone.

DEWESBURI.—Thomas Bythebrok and Ralph de Karlinghagh in Dewesburi.

ERDESLAWE.—William del Haghe in Erdeslawe.

OSSET.—Swayn de Osset in Osset.

BAILIFF.—William, s. of Nalle of Northland, indicted for an ox, fines 26s. 8d. for an aid to have deliverance at this court.   Surety : Thomas de Aula.

William del Bothem, indicted for receiving thieves, viz. John de Wodeheved and Ingelard de Ecclesley, none of whom are attached or convicted, fines 26s. 8d. and to be acquitted.   Sureties : Thomas de Aula and Henry Clerk de Aula.

Christiana del Wodeheved, indicted for a similar offence, fines 6s. 8d. for an aid to prevent her being attached.   Surety : John the Flemyng of Cliftone.

Elyas de Hadereschulf, indicted for meeting a thief in the South-strenede, on his way from a robbery, and taking goods from him, fines 20s. for that trespass.   Sureties : Roger Rotel, Robert de Saltonstall, Adam Townend, and Jordan del Hirst.

William de Cokcroft, indicted in Halifax Tourn for divers thefts, fines 40s. for an aid to have deliverance at this court.   Sureties : John de Cokcroft and Henry de Warlolay, clerk.

SOURBY.—Robert de Saltonstall, elected grave in the room of Adam, s. of Ivo, gives 2s. to retire till Michaelmas, and the said Adam is restored to office.

Matthew, s. of Thomas de Fouleston, and Alice, his wife, give 16s. to take 16 acres with buildings in Schagheley from Thomas, s. of Matthew.

The said Matthew gives 2s. to take 2½ acres in Schagheley from Adam, s. of Elyas, and Alice, his wife.

ESSOINS.—William de Rastrik, by Thomas de Wytlay.   Surety : Thomas de Bellehous.

Richard de Crosseland, by William Marjoriman.   Surety : William Wildebor.

ALVERTHORPE.—William de Locwode and John Broun [2d.] agree.

SANDALE.—John del Holyns, indicted for raising a bank on Crigeleston common, fines 2s. for mercy, and for license to retain the said bank, so that it may not be destroyed.

HOLNE.—Robert Smith [faber] of Sadelworthfrith gives 4s. to take 3 acres and a half and the sixth of an acre in Wolvedale from Nicholas, s. of Nicholas Kenward.

SANDALE.—Robert the Yonghe and John, s. of Margery de Crigelestone [3d.], agree.

I

THORNES.—Philip de Mora of Thornes surrenders ½ bovate in a place called Willefeld, and afterwards takes it again for his life, with remainder to William, his son ; who fines 6s. 8d. for the recognition.

SANDALE.—Johanna, d. of Adam the Roper, pays 2s. for license to marry John, s. of Geoffrey de Sandale, who pays 2s. for license to enter ½ bovate of land in Sandale with the said Johanna, who holds it in bondage.

ALVERTHORP.—John de Gayrgrave and Richard Wythehoundes [6d.] agree.

John, s. of John de Chikynlay, and Robert, s. of Ralph de Neutone, have a love-day.

Thomas, s. of Laurence, gives 3s. to take 2 acres in a croft at Flansawe from Richard Wythehoundes, for 12 years.

WAKEFELD.—Elyas the Couper's wife, 4d.; Richard Fegald, 2d.; Thomas Chude's wife, 2d.; the handmaids of Robert Hodde and Adam Halfmark, 2d. each, for dry wood.

Adam de Castilford's maid, 3d. for vert.

STANLAY.—Philip the Syour, 3d. for vert.

WAKEFELD.—Robert Liftfast, 3d.; the handmaids of Walter Hogge and John Clement, 2d. each ; Mannolstygh, 3d., and Spirhard, 1d., for dry wood, vert, and underwood.

OSSET.—Richard de Gaukthorp, 3d.; Robert Sonneman, 3d.; Richard, s. of John, 2d.; Alot, wife of Thomas the Pynder, 6d.; Richard Snart's son, 2d.; Amabilla Hirnyng, 6d.; Agnes the Colyer, 2d.; Richard the Barler [?], 2d.; William the Louth, 2d., and Hugh Litster [tinctor], 2d., for escapes and dry wood.

HORDBURY.—Adam Schilyng, 2s. for vert.

WAKEFELD.—Idonea Pollard ; Agnes Broun ; John Dun ; Roger Wasse ; Robert de Feri ; the son of German the Gardiner ; William the Gardiner's handmaid ; Emma Godith ; John de Feri ; William Dun ; Reginald de Swylington's son, and Thomas Cate, 2d. each for dry wood.

THORNES.—Alice Graffard, 2d. for the same.

WAKEFELD.—John de Grenegate, 3d. for vert.

ALVERTHORP.—Richard Wythehoundes, 12d. for ivy.

STANLAY.—John and Philip Isabel, 6d. each ; William Harkill, 12d.; Robert de Schellay, 6d., and William Chekes, 6d., for the same. [mem. 12 dors.]

STANLAY.—Geoffrey Fonne, and a strange woman, 3d. each for ivy. Surety : Robert the Yonghe.

ALVERTHORP.—Richard Wythehoundes' wife, 2d. for dry wood.

STANLEY.—John Isabel, 1d. for the same.

WAKEFELD.—Cecilia Bucke, 3d. for the same.

STANLAY.—The servant of Peter the Pynder, for the same, 6d. Surety : P. the Pynder.

Thomas Bele, 2d. for mendacity [mendacio].

RASTRIK.—Henry, s. of John de Rastrik, sues Richard, s. of Jordan de Northorum, and John the Couherd of Rastrik for trespass. Surety : Matthew de Tothill.

Hugh de Tothill sues John, s of Henry de Fikesby ; they were ordered to be at this court, when a love-day was granted them.

SOURBY.—Henry de Saltonstall, 6s. 8d. for taking the redemption money he received from Adam, s. of Ivo, 2s., for one sow sold by Adam. Surety : Robert de Saltonstall.

BAILIFF.—Robert, s. of William Layron ; John the Couper ; Adam Wytbelt ; William, s. of Richard Saucemer ; Peter, s. of Ellen ; Thomas, s. of Elyas de Thorp ; William, s. of Walter de Toftclif ; John Baker of Wodekirke ; Robert the Spencer ; Thomas Curtays ; William de Middeltone ; William de Wyrkelay ; John Passemer ; Henry Crogel ; John Carter ; William Cowhird ; Richard the Boner ; Adam Almoc ; William Thirse ; Roger Porker ; William Smith [faber], and Elias Milner, 2d. each for not coming to the court.

SANDALE.—Thomas Drille of Crigeleston ; William the Payntour ; John, s. of Margery ; Thomas, s. of William ; Thomas, s. of Nelle ; William Pykenot ; Hugh, s. of Elias Milner ; Robert, s. of Elias Milner ; Richard, s. of Roger ; Thomas Felice ; Adam Tubbing; John, s. of Hugh Tubbing ; William Elyot ; Hugh de Sevile [or Senile] ; Henry, s. of Roger ; Adam Trubbe ; Adam, s. of Peter ; John, s. of Beatrix ; Matthew, servant of William de Stodley, and William, serving-man of Edith, 2d. each for the same.

Thomas, s. of Robert de Sandale ; William Fox ; and John Page, 2d. each for the same.

STANLEY.—Thomas del Bothem ; Robert, s. of Walter del Spen, and Henry, s. of Hugh, 2d. each for the same.

ALVIRTHORP.—Robert Cay of Alvirthorp, 2d. for the same.

STANLEY.—Richard Mariot, 2d. for the same.

HORBIRY.—John, s. of Thomas Smith, and Jordan Sir, 2d. for the same.

THORNES.—Robert, s. of Ivo de Thornes, and Henry Bulneys, 2d. each for the same.

BAILIFF.—Roger Baker of Normanton ; Adam the Couper ; Adam Marmioun ; Ralph Pykard ; John Allerun ; Adam, s. of Hayne of Dewesburi ; Ralph the Colier ; Robert Trubbe ; William de Howorth ; Walter, s. of Richard de Armerawe ; William de Morlay ; Ralph de Wik of Bretton ; John Malle ; John Batty ; Robert Milner ; Robert, s. of John ; William Batti ; John, s. of Henry ; John del Clay ; John Campe ; John, s. of John Batti ; Adam Pogge of Emeley ; Adam, s. of Dyonisia ; Peter de Wortlay ; William, s. of Til ; Robert, s. of Hugh ; Thomas Stedman ; Henry, s. of William ; Adam, servant of Robert Carpenter ; Adam Ingoys ; Henry de Flokton ; John, s. of Juliana ; William de Grenegate ; Thomas, s. of William the Gardiner ; William, s. of Richard Mille ; Richard, s. of Adam the Couper ; Richard Danyel ; Robert Alayn ; Robert de Abathia ; Alexander de Mora ; Simon Thrombald ; John, s. of Scolicia ; Richard Anoc ; John de Scharneston ; Thomas the Machoun ; John, s. of Agnes ; Richard de Stel ; Adam the Wayte ; Thomas Forester ; Thomas, s. of Joseph ; William Takel ; John Swayn ; John de Methelay ; Thomas Tailor ; Robert Pollard ; German Herward ; Henry de Adyngham ; John the Rased, junior ; John, s. of Hugh Chapman ; Robert, s. of William de Sandale ; Thomas, his son ; John Wolmer ; Roger Preest ; John Wayteskath ; John Beek ; John Hood ; Robert Tailor, and Richard Wheelwright [*carpentar rotarum*], 2*d*. each for the same.

Sum total of this Court : £19 9*s*. 8*d*., *i.e.* Holne,   42*s*.

Thornes,	7*s*. 2*d*.	Wakefeld,	4*s*. 6*d*.
Sourby,	£4 8*s*. 8*d*.	Bailiff,	£10 12*s*. 2*d*.
Stanley,	5*s*. 9*d*.	Alvirthorp,	9*s*. 3*d*.
Sandale,	14*s*. 4*d*.	Horbury,	2*s*. 10*d*.
Osset,	3*s*.		

SOURBY.—John Sourmilk sues Henry Holgate for trespass.

ALVERTHORP.—John Turoud sues Henry the Nonne for land.

Nalle Gerbode sues Robert Gerbode and John Gerbode for dower.

Robert, s. of Adam, sues Robert, s. of Pelle, for trespass.

John Leche sues Hugh the Carter of Pountfrett for detention.

Vaccaries.

SOURBY, SALTONSTALL.—Saltonstall dairy is farmed this year to Thomas de Saltonstall, for £4 6*s*. 8*d*. Sureties : John del Dene ; John de Chesewelley ; Thomas de Routheleset , Hugh, s. of Eva ; Richard Smith, and Hugh, s. of Reginald.

FERNESHIDE.—Ferneshide dairy, to John, s. of Ivo Smith, for £4 13*s*. 4*d*. It is to be kept up under a penalty. Sureties : William de Heptonstall, clerk ; William, s. of Adam de Heptonstall ; William del Foldes ; Henry del Schaghe ; Adam, s. of Ivo, and Jordan del Hirst ; and moreover 4 heifers are farmed for the year to the said John Smith for 8s.

CROMTONSTALL.—Cromtonstall dairy is leased to Adam de Routonstall for £4. Sureties : John, his father ; Henry del Schaghe ; Thomas del Brigge; William, s. of Adam de Heptonstall, and William del Foldes ; and four heifers besides are farmed to him for 6s.

WYTHENES.—William Milner took the cattle not in calf [steriles] into his custody. Sureties : John de Chesewelley ; Hugh, s. of Eva ; Richard de Saltonstall ; Thomas de Saltonstall ; Richard, s. of Nalle, and Richard [sic] de Saltonstall.

[mem. 13.]

COURT held at Wakefeud on Friday after the Feast of SS. Tiburtius and Valerian [April 14], 8 Edw. II.

ESSOINS.—Hugh the Nodder, attorney of Margaret de Neyvile, by William Margeriman. Surety : Hugh de Tothille.

John de Leptone, by Thomas de Wytlay. Surety : John de Mora.

Thomas de Thorntone, by Adam de Oxnop. Surety : John de Toftclif.

John Hood, by Adam de Staynclif. Surety : Richard de Birstall.

William de Rastrik, by Thomas de Tothille. Surety : Hugh de Tothill.

ALVERTHORP.—Robert, s. of Ralph de Neutone, amerced 2d. for withholding 4d. from John, s. of John de Chikenlay.

BAILIFF.—William Cobbler [Sutor] of Morlay, taken for stealing an ox stolen from Robert de Ruscheworth, pleads not guilty ; John de Batelay sues him for the same in due form, the ox being his, in the custody of Robert de Russcheworth. An inquisition taken by the oath of Richard de Salsa-mara, Robert de Heyrode, Richard de Birstall, John de Toftclif, Walter de Toftclif, John de Mora, Michael Dodeman, William de Haya, Richard de Crosseland, Thomas del Bellehous, William del Okes, and William Bernard find him not guilty. John de Batelay is therefore committed to prison.

PRISON.—Adam Wardelyn of Thornhill attaches himself by his pledges, Adam Cosyn of Floketone and Adam Cappe, against Custance Morre of Pontefract, saying that his house at Thornhill was broken into, and an overtunic, amongst other things, taken ; and this was found in possession of Custance Murre. Defendant says she bought the overtunic honestly last Sunday in Pontefract, from two women who were carrying it about for sale. She is remanded [*reposita*] to prison, and ordered to have her warranty at the next court.

HIPERUM ; new rent.—Andrew Forester of Hiperum gives 12*d*. to take 2 acres of new land in Heckedene, in the graveship of Hiperum, at 6*d*. an acre, for term of three years.

BAILIFF.—Hugh de Tothill sues John, s. of Henry de Fikesby, for 5*s*., part of a tithe purchased from him, 5 Edw. II. Defendant comes and makes no defence, but leaves the bar with contempt ; he is therefore convicted, and is amerced 12*d*.

RASTRIK.—Henry, s. of Richard de Tothill, gives 6*s*. 8*d*. to take 7 acres in Rastrik from Beatrix, formerly wife of Alexander del Wodehous.

ALVERTHORP.—John de Gairgrave, 6*d*. to take ½ acre in Alverthorp from Robert Gerbode, for 12 years.

SOURBY.—John Sourmilk and his pledge [surety] are amerced 6*d*. for not prosecuting his suit against Henry del Holgate.

SANDALE.—An inquisition finds that Robert, s. of Pelle, had a horse stopped in Pontefract, which was being taken by Robert, s. of Adam, to sell at Pontefract market, for part of his arrears ; damages, 2*s*., which he is to pay, and he is amerced 2*s*.

BAILIFF.—William Cobbler [*Sutor*] of Morley gives 6*s*. 8*d*. for an aid to have deliverance of the charge on which he was indicted at Rastrik Tourn.

William Tyrsi for contempt in Court of the Burgesses, by an assault made by himself and his wife on a certain strange man, 6*s*. 8*d*.; and if he or his wife offend again, they are to pay the lord 40*s*.

ALVERTHORP.—John atte Barre surrenders an acre of land which remains in the lord's hands.

WAKEFELD.—Thomas Molle, 2*d*. for broken wood.

Eva, wife of William, s. of Ralph, 3*d*. for ivy.

STANLEY.—William, s. of Thomas del Wodehall, for the same, 3*d*.

WAKEFELD.—William Peger, 12*d*. for carrying off a paling.

John Wolmer, 3*d*. for vert.

ALVERTHORP.—The wives of John Bonny and Thomas Bunny, 2*d*. each for dry wood.

STANLEY.—John Flockard, for the same, 2*d*.

ALVERTHORP.—William, s. of Walter, for the same, 2*d*.

STANLEY.—Richard del Ker, 6*d.* for an escape.

John Page, 6*d.* for rods.

WAKEFELD.—John Dun of Keregate ; Roger Wasche ; John Leuet's wife ; Robert Gurdon ; Thomas Cat, and Henry, s. of Idonea, 2*d.* each ; and Ralph, s. of Henry, 4*d.*, for dry wood.

THORNES.—John Graffard, 3*d.* for an escape.

WAKEFELD.—William Tyrsi, 3*d.*; Richard, s. of Mille ; Matilda Gunne, and John Pollard, junior, 1*d.* each ; William the Glover ; Robert de Chedel, and John Cokspor, 2*d.* each, for dry wood, etc.

STANLEY.—Robert, s. of Geoffrey, 1*d.* for breaking the paling of the new coppice.

John Flachard, 4*d.*; Emma Gundy, 4*d.*; Thomas Hancok, 2*d.*; John Hancok, 4*d.*; William, s. of Thomas, 4*d.*; Roger the Turnur's wife, 2*d.*; William, s. of Walter, 4*d.*, and Isolda Danays, 2*d.*, for escapes.

SANDALE.—Henry, s. of Ralph, 4*d.*; Isabel Lambe, 3*d.*; Robert de Ketelthorp's handmaid, 3*d.*, and William, s. of Alot, 3*d.*, for vert.

Sum total of this Court : 34*s.* 8*d.*, and new rent, 12*d.*

i.e. Bailiff,	14*s.* 4*d.*	Alverthorp,	14*d.*
Hiperum,	12*d.* (and new rent, 12*d.*)		
Rastrik,	6*s.* 8*d.*	Sourby,	6*d.*
Sandale,	3*s.* 1*d.*	Thornes,	3*d.*
Wakefeld,	4*s.*	Stanlay,	3*s.* 8*d.*

THORNES.—Agnes Pymme sues John Dade of Wakefeld for land. Surety : Richard Proudfot.

HOLNE.—William, s. of Wilkes, sues Elyas, s. of Henry, for trespass. Surety : William, his brother.

RASTRIK.—William Milner of Rastrik sues Henry Milner for debt. Surety : Adam Milner. Henry is attached by Alexander the Taillour.

BAILIFF.—Henry de Court [*de Cur'*] of Osset sues Hugh, s. of William de Disforthe, for trespass. Surety : William Carpenter of Osset.

OSSET.—Thomas de Schellay of Osset and Margaret, his wife, sue Robert Stute and Juliana, his mother, for land. Surety : Jordan Elyot.

HIPERUM.—Richard, s. of Jordan de Northorum, sues Thomas, s. of Thomas de Hiperum, for trespass. Surety : Roger de Cliftone.

Adam del Wode is dead. His land, therefore, to be taken into the lord's hand.

[*mem.* 13 *dors.*]

COURT held at Wakefeud on Friday in Whitsunweek, 8 Edw. II.

ESSOINS.—Thomas de Thorntone, by John de Thorntone. Surety: Robert de Heyrode.

Thomas del Belhous, by Thomas de Witlay. Surety: Richard de Birstall.

Robert, s. of Geoffrey de Stanlay, by William Marjoriman. Surety: Robert de Wyuerumthorp.

Richard de Salsa-mara, attorney of Sir Adam de Everingham, by Robert, s. of John. Surety: William del Okes.

Thomas de Tothill, attorney of William de Tothill, by John Patrikes.

John de Mora, by William, his son.

John de Blakhoumore, taken at the suit of Roger Walgar of Almanbury, for breaking into his house at Almanbury, and stealing goods and chattels, value 10s., which goods were found in his possession and are brought into court, is asked what defence he can make for the said burglary and theft ; he pleads not guilty. An inquisition taken by the oath of Thomas de Seyuile, John de Leptone, Richard de Birstall, Robert de Heyrode, William del Okes, Richard de Crosseland, Adam Sprigonel, John Patrikes, John Hood, John de Megeley, Robert de la Grene of Osset, and Robert de Saltonstall, finds him guilty. He is ordered to be hanged. He has no goods.

RASTRIK.—John, s. of Henry de Fikesby, sues Alexander del Briggehous for 4s. 6d., for which he was surety, and became principal debtor for Alexander del Wodehous in 5 Edw. II, re the purchase of a bay horse bought from plaintiff. Defendant says the money was paid by Alexander del Wodehous. An inquisition to be taken.

HOLNE.—William, s. of Wilkes, and Elyas, s. of Henry [6d.], agree, re a plea of trespass.

RASTRIK.—William Milner of Rastrik is sick ; his suit against Henry Milner postponed till next court.

OSSETE.—Henry del Court [6d.] and Hugh, s. of William de Disforde, agree, 6d.

HIPERUM.—Richard, s. of Jordan de Northourum, and Thomas, s. of Thomas de Hiperum [6d.], agree, re a plea of trespass.

John de Withill of Northorum gives 4s. as a heriot on 8 acres of land in Northorum after the death of Adam del Withill, his father.

Thomas Bokerel is dead ; his land to be taken into the lord's hand.

John de Sonderland, grave of Hiperum, amerced 12d. for false presentment and concealment.

SANDALE.—The land of Adam Painter of Crigelestone to be taken into the lord's hand, because he is dead.

HOLNE.—Richard, s. of William de Foulestone, gives 5s. to take 6½ acres in Foulestone from Thomas Brid.

SANDALE.—William Pikenote gives 12d. to take a piece of land in a toft in Crigelestone, 30 feet by 10 feet, from John, s. of Thomas.

ALVIRTHORP.—Henry Nonne amerced 2d. for not coming when summoned to answer John Thorold.

THORNES.—An inquisition finds that Juliana formerly wife of William the Westerne, broke an agreement made with John Dade, concerning her dower out of the land which her late husband formerly sold to her. She is to pay damages, taxed at —. Her amercement is pardoned, because she is poor.

[? WAKEFELD.]—2¾ acres held by William Nelot to be taken into the lord's hand.

RASTRIK.—Henry, s. of John de Rastrik, 6d. for false claim against Richard, s. of Jordan de Northorum, and John le Couhirde.

ALVIRTHORP.—Alice, formerly wife of Gerbode de Alvirthorp, 3d. for not prosecuting her suit against Robert Gerbode.

THORNES.—Agnes Pymme has license to withdraw her suit against John Dade of Wakefeld.

[OSSET.]—Thomas de Schellay and Margery, his wife, sue Robert Stute and Juliana, his mother, for 1½d. annual rent out of two heads [capit'] [i.e. headlands] of 2 selions belonging to defendants' land, which rent was formerly received by Adam de Wytwode, former husband of the plaintiff Margaret. An inquisition is to be summoned from the graveships of Osset and Horbury.

BAILIFF.—Ellen, formerly wife of Thomas de Langfeld, gives 20s. to have an inquisition as to whether William, her [? son], should be in the lord's custody for his lands and tenements, or not.

Adam the Crouder gives 3s. for an aid to recover 14s. from Robert the Yonghe.

PRISON.—Custance Murre of Pontefract is found not guilty, and is acquitted of theft by an inquisition ; and she gives 3s. for an aid against Adam Wardelein of Thornhill for false accusation. Surety : John, s. of Robert Pollard.

John Wilcokes and John Richard made themselves bailiffs, and took and bound Henry, s. of Richard Broun. They are, therefore, attached, viz. John Wilcokes by William Goldsmith and Robert the Roller, and John Richard by William de Hetheneshale and John Wilcokes.

[*mem.* 14.]

SOURBY.—Richard del Dene, 2*d.*; Henry, s. of Beatrix, 3*d.*; William Mohoud, 3*d.*; Nicholas Milner, 12*d.*; Thomas de Stodlay, 3*d.*; John del Bothe, 3*d.*; Jordan del Hirst, 2*d.*; Roger Gildyn-ballokes, 3*d.*; Robert, s. of Roger de Sourby, 2*d.*; Thomas, s. of John de Migelay, 2*d.*; John del Redyker, 21*d.*; Jordan del Hirst, 6*d.*; Robert, s. of John, 2*d.*; Robert, his brother, 2*d.*; John de Cokcroft, 2*d.*; Thomas del Feld, 3*d.*; Adam the Crouther, 4*d.*; John Swyft's son, 1*d.*; John de Megelay, 1*d.*; Robert, s. of John, 3*d.*; Robert, s. of William, 3*d.*; John de Megelay's son, 1*d.*; Eva de Godelay, 4*d.*; Thomas, s. of Sabyna, 6*d.*; Richard, s. of Matilda de Rastrik, 2*d.*; Richard, s. of Peter, 2*d.*, and Richard del Dene, 2*d.*, for escapes in Luddenden and the Firth, etc.

STANLAY.—Peter the Pynder, 6*d.*; Robert the Yonghe 2*d.*; Robert Gunne, 2*d.*; Walter de Odam's son, 3*d.*; William Albray's son, 3*d.*; Simon Tyting, 3*d.*

WAKEFELD.—Philip Damosele, 3*d.*; William the Gardiner's wife, 2*d.*; the handmaid of Robert de Feri ; Reginald de Swylingtone ; Matilda de Sourby ; the wife of Ralph, s. of Henry, 2*d.* each, for dry wood.

ALVERTHORPE.—Adam de Flansowe, the same.

OSSET.—John, s. of Richard, 3*d.*; Richard, s. of John ; Robert Scut's [*or* Stut's] wife ; John, s. of William ; Richard, s. of John, and Adam de Gaukthorp, 2*d.* each, for dry wood.

STANLAY.—Simon the Warde, 6*d.*; Ellen atte Kirk, 12*d.*, for escapes. Surety : Richard del Bothem.

WAKEFELD.—Robert Liftfast, 3*d.*; Adam Halfmarkes, 3*d.*, and Alice Withehoundes, 2*d.*, for dry wood.

ALVIRTHORP.—William Culle's wife, 2*d.* for the same.

STANLAY.—John Bernard, 4*d.* for an escape. Surety : William Tagge.

ALVIRTHORP.—Walter del Bothem, 6*d.* for vert.

Henry del Bothem, 3*d.* for dry wood.

STANLEY.—William, s. of Thomas, 6*d.* for an escape.

William Tagge, 2*d.*; and Henry the Dyker, 2*d.* for dry wood.

SANDALE.—Magota de Ketelthorp, 6*d.*; Robert Lorimer, 4*d.*; John Monykes, 4*d.*, and William Peti, 4*d.*, for vert.

WAKEFELD.—John Clement, 2*d.* for dry wood.

ALVIRTHORP.—Henry Nonne, for the same, 2d.

WAKEFELD.—Richard Fegald, 2d.; Agnes Clerk, 1d.; William Wolmer's son, 1d.; Robert de Stanlay, 1d.; Philip Pickestulle, 2d., and Agnes de Bramlay, 2d., for dry wood and vert.

STANLEY.—Richard Long's wife, 2d.; John Fegald, 2d., and John Flachard, 2d., for vert, etc.

HOLNE.—Peter de Wildeborley and Adam del Grene, 4d. each for vert.

Robert Chopard, 4d. for 2 stirks found in the hollyn.

John, s. of Magota, and Henry de Litlewode, 9d. each for the same.

Thomas del Hole, 6d.; Richard de Cartworth, 6d.; Thomas de Fonte, 4d.; William, s. of William, 3d., for vert, etc.

Elyas Abraham of Marcheden and Thomas de Ploulay, 2s. for 13 stirks.

OSSET.—Henry Cobbler [sutor] of Gaukthorp ; William the Longe and Richard de Blakebourne, 2d. each for dry wood.

Alice Gerbode, 3d. for an escape in the Hagge.

THORNES.—Ivo Smith, 6d.; Margery Hawe, 3d.; Philip Smith of Snaypthorp, 6d.; John Graffard, 6d.; John, s. of Magota, 3d.; Agnes de Snaypthorp, 3d., and William, s. of Agnes, 3d., for the same.

Sum total of this Court : 68s. 7d., i.e. Bailiff,   26s.

Sourby,	8s. 5d.	Osset,	2s. 4d.
Holne,	11s. 6d.	Sandale,	2s. 6d.
Hiperum,	2s. 6d.	Rastrik,	6d.
Stanlay,	4s. 9d.	Alverthorp,	23d.
Thornes,	2s. 6d.	Wakefeld,	2s. 8d.

BAILIFF.—Henry Fletcher of Osset sues Robert Pees for trespass. Surety : Thomas Alayn.

Robert de Russcheworth sues John de Withill on an agreement. Surety : Thomas de Wytlay.

ALVIRTHORP.—Gilbert Gayrough sues Robert Gerbode for debt. Surety : Henry del Bothem.

HOLNE.—Gilbert de Alstanlay sues Robert, s. of John de Scheplay, Robert, s. of Sarah de Foulestone, and Thomas Smith, of Scheplay. Surety : William Wether of Wolvedale.

WAKEFELD.—Robert Preest sues Robert Estrild for land. Surety: John Nelot.

SANDALE.—John, s. of Beatrix, sues Robert Tailor [cissor] of Waltone for assault. He is attached by Thomas de Cheet.

COURT held at Wakefeld on Friday after the Feast of St. Boniface the Pope [May 26], 8 Edw. II.

ESSOINS.—Richard de Crosseland, by John de Crosseland. Surety : Thomas del Bellehous.

Adam Sprigonel, by William Marjoriman. Surety : Richard de Salsa-mara.

Hugh the Nodder, attorney of Lady Margaret de Neyvile, by John de Brerlay. Surety : William Wildebore.

John de Leptone, by Thomas de Wytlay. Surety : Richard de Birstall.

BAILIFF.—John Wilcokes attached by pledges of William Goldsmith and of Robert the Roller, and John Richard attached by pledges of William de Hetheneshale and John Wilcokes, are amerced 6s. 8d. for not having them in court to answer.

John de Bollyng and Alice, his wife, have license to withdraw their suit against Ingelard, vicar of Halifax, because he is dead.

RASTRIK.—William Milner of Rastrik and Henry Milner [6d.] agree.

BAILIFF.—Hugh Carter of Pontefract, 6d. for sundry defaults.

Robert de Risscheworth and John Withill agree, fine . . . . .

[*One line illegible at the end of the membrane.*]

[*mem.* 14 *dors.*]

HOLNE.—Robert Witkirtel of Marchesdene gives 5s. to take 3¾ acres in Wolvedale from Robert Smith of Sadelworthfrith.

William, s. of Wilkes, gives 6s. 8d. to take 5¼ acres with a toft in Hepworth from William de Halomschire.

SOURBY.—Reginald, s. of John Chater, gives 10s. to take 18 acres in Warloulay from Henry de Saltonstall for 20 years ; and ½ acre in perpetuity.

BAILIFF.—John de Leptone, 3d. for not coming when summoned on the inquisition regarding the lands, etc., formerly held by Thomas de Langfeld.

HIPERUM.—Richard, s. of Thomas Bokerel, gives 4s. as a heriot on 4 acres in Hiperum after his father's death.

THORNES.—John, s. of Margery, gives 10s. to take a bovate of land with a toft in Snaypthorp, from John Rate.

SANDALE.—Adam, s. of Roger s. of Gilbert, gives 2s. to take 1½ acres in Holynthorp from Elyas de Doncastre.

John, s. of Henry de Sandale, gives 40d. to take 3¼ acres in the Newebyggyng from Peter Strekelevedy.

ALVERTHORP.—John de Grenegate gives 2s. to take an acre in the Morcroft and in the Halkes from Robert Gerbode for 12 years.

OSSET.—Thomas de Schellay and Margery, his wife, fined 6d. under an inquisition for false claim against Robert Stute and Juliana, his mother.

SOURBY.—An inquisition taken concerning the lands and tenements formerly held by Thomas de Langfeud in Sourbyschir, as to whether the Earl ought to have the custody and marriage of the heir of the said Thomas, a minor, by the oaths of John de Stanesfeld, Richard de Wadesworth, William de Sothill, John, s. of Hugh de Northland, John the Harpour of Stodlay, John del Asschenhirst, John de Crosseleye, John del Ker, Peter Swerd, Matthew del Wode, William del Estwode, and Henry de Coldelay ; the jurors say Thomas held all his tenements in soccage and not by military service , and the Earl ought not, and has not been accustomed, to have anything from the said tenements except fealty and double farm [*firmam duplicatam*].

SANDALE.—The land held by Adam Painter of Crigeleston to remain in the custody of Eva, his widow, until the coming of his heir.

John Torold sues Henry the Nonne for not giving him possession of a rood of land bought from him 3 years ago, for 3s. 6d. Henry acknowledges the agreement, is amerced 2d., and is to make satisfaction.

Gilbert Gayrok, 3d. for not prosecuting his suit against Robert Gerbod.

SOURBY.—William, s. of Adam s. of Nalk, 3d.; Henry del Foldes, 2d.; Henry de Holgate, 3d.; John de Langeley, 2d.; William del Bothem, 1d., and Adam Cappe, 6d., surety, Henry de Sothill,—for escapes in Ayrikdene.

Hugh de Lyghtheseles, 4d.; John Milner, 2d.; Adam Migge of Saltonstall, 2d.; Richard del Feld, 2d.; Richard, s. of Alot, 2d.; John de Cokcroft, 1d.; John Therys, 2d.; William de Wolrunwall, 2d.; Eva de Godelay, 2d., and John Godheyr, 2d., for escapes in the Marschagh and the Baytinges.

ALVIRTHORP.—Henry Wolf, 12d. for throwing down an oak with another oak.

WAKEFELD —Philip Pikescolle, 2d.; John Tassche, 2d.; Philip Damoisele, 2d.; Thomas Forester's wife, 2d., and Alan le Mercer's wife, 1d., for vert.

STANLEY.—Thomas de Wollehouse, for an escape in Stanley Coppice, 12d. Surety : Richard Poket.

ALVIRTHORP.—Robert Campion, 6*d*., and Richard Bonny and Thomas, his brother, 4*d*., for the same.

HOLNE.—Adam Stirk, 3*d*.; Robert, s. of Sara, 4*d*.; John Broke, 3*d*.; Adam de Botirlay, 4*d*.; Robert de Smalschagh, 12*d*.; Robert de Nonnys, 4*d*., and Sir William de Felton, 8*d*., for escapes and vert.

STANLEY.—William, s. of Thomas, and Robert the Yongh, 3*d*. each for escapes in the new coppice.

Peter the Pynder's servant, for cutting vert prohibited, 3*d*.

WAKEFELD.—Hugh the Chapman's son, and Agnes, d. of John Molle, 3*d*. each for dry wood.

STANLEY.—William Tagge, 2*d*.; Peter the Pynder, 3*d*.; Robert the Yonghe, 3*d*., and William de Erdslow, 6*d*., surety, William Isabel, —for escapes.

HIPERUM.—William, s. of Robert, 2*d*.; John, s. of Walter, 2*d*.; John, s. of William del Hayleye, 2*d*.; John del Lache, 2*d*.; John del Holewey, 3*d*.; Thomas Poyde, 3*d*.; John, s. of Walter, 3*d*.; Richard the Baggere, 2*d*.; Richard Warout's son, 1*d*.; John the Pynder, 2*d*.; John, s. of Alexander, 2*d*.; John Milner, 1*d*.; Michael Aggreve, 2*d*.; Thomas, s. of Thomas, 2*d*.; Alexander the Waynwright, 3*d*.; William Scharp, 2*d*.; Henry de Northclif, 2*d*.; Thomas de Hemmingwey, 2*d*., and John del Wythill, 2*d*., for vert and escapes.

SOURBY.—John de Megeley holds 2¼ acres from Matilda, d. of Elyas, without license.

Henry de Saltonstall, 5 acres from Beatrix, wife of Jordan de Skircotes, without leave of the court.

John de Routonstall, 3 acres in Werloley wood from Richard del Dene, without leave.

Richard de Covenhale, 3 acres from Alice de Russcheworth, without leave.

HOLNE.—Henry Bridmonth[orp ?] bought 3 acres in Hepworth from William Pyntel without license, and afterwards sold the same to Robert de Langelay, and William Pyntel came into court and surrendered the land to said Robert, so as to conceal Henry's fine and amercement.

Elyas, s. of Henry de Hepworth, took a rood of land from the lord's unoccupied land, and held it for a year, afterwards coming and fining for it.

[Matilda], d. of Nicholas, took an acre of land from Peter Pede three years ago without license, because Peter died before a court was held.

Sum total of this Court :	76s. 4d., i.e.	Bailiff,	7s. 8d,
	Rastrik, 6d.	Hiperum,	15s. 1d.
	Holne, 14s. 10d.	Sourby,	13s. 5d.
	Thornes, 10s.	Sandale,	5s. 10d.
	Alverthorp, 4s.	Osset,	6d.
	Wakefeld, 19d.	Stanlay,	2s. 11d.

[*The entries of suits brought at the end of the membrane are too mutilated to be satisfactorily copied.*]

[*mem.* 15.]

COURT held at Wakefeld on Friday after the Nativity of St. John the Baptist [June 24], 8 Edw. II.

ESSOINS.—Thomas del Belhous, by Roger de Horburi, clerk. Surety : John de Leptone.

Thomas de Thorneton, by Thomas de Witlay. Surety : Robert de Heyrode.

Richard de Birstall, by John de Normanton. Surety : Richard de Salsa-mara.

Hugh the Nodder, attorney of Lady Margaret de Neyvile, by Robert de la Grene. Surety : John Patrikes.

Richard de Crosseland, by John de Crosseland. Surety : Thomas de Wytlay.

William de Rastrik, by Thomas de Tothill. Surety : Hugh de Tothill.

SANDALE.—John, s. of Thomas [6d.], and John, s. of Hugh de Holgate, agree.

HIPERUM.—William de Bothes withdraws his suit against Richard, s. of Ivo, because said Richard has no goods and cannot be attached ; fine, 2d.

BAILIFF.—Robert Beausir of Crigeleston, who appealed John de Byngelay and John, s. of Hugh de Ledes, for theft of a horse, came and acknowledged himself wrong in his appeal [*et recognovit se de appello suo*] ; he is sent to prison ; and Adam Sprigonel and Henry de Goutoun, his sureties, are amerced 40d.

The defendants to the suit of Gilbert de Alstanlay acknowledge 6s. of the 11s. 6d. sued for as the price of an ox bought from plaintiff ; an inquisition to be taken with regard to the remainder.

OSSET.—Avice, formerly wife of Adam del Dene [4d.], and William Milner agree.

HOLNE.—Adam Strekeys sues Agnes, formerly wife of John, s. of Hugh, for 25s. as surety for Thomas Bole of Boudrode, in the purchase of 2 oxen. Agnes says she was neither present at the transaction, nor agreed to find surety. An inquisition is to be taken.

Thomas del Holme [6*d*.] and Isabel del Dam agree.

ALVERTHORP.—Henry del Bothem, grave of Alverthorp, 6*d*. for contempt in court.

SOURBY.—Wymarka, d. of Seyer of Sourby, 6*d*., and her surety, Richard del Feld, for not prosecuting her suit against John Pykeston.

RASTRIK.—Alexander del Briggehous, convicted by the jury and amerced 6*d*. for withholding 18*d*. from John, s. of Henry de Fikesby, as surety for Alexander del Wodehous. John is amerced 6*d*. for false claim for 2*s*. 3*d*. [*sic*] against the said Alexander.

SOURBY.—Elyas the Couper of Sourby and Thomas, s. of John de Megelay [4*d*.], agree.

BAILIFF.—Nicholas de Cayly, plaintiff [12*d*.], William Jordan, John Pycard, John, his brother, and Ellen del Wodehous agree.

WAKEFELD.—Master Robert Carpenter gives 6*s*. 8*d*. to take a messuage and 25 acres of land and meadow in Wakefeld from William Nelot and Margery his wife.

Thomas the Roller, 12*d*. to take an acre in Wakefeld, called Codlyngcroft, from Roger Preest and Rosa, his wife, for 16 years.

HOLNE.—Agnes, formerly wife of John, s. of Hugh de Litlewode, gives 5*s*. to take 6 acres in the bounds of Thwong from Jordan Milner.

William, s. of Thomas Kenward, is dead. His land to be taken into the lord's hand.

SOURBY.—Roger, s. of Amabilla of Sourby, 6*s*. 8*d*. for putting several beasts to graze in the Earl's garden, on his own authority.

WAKEFELD.—Reginald de Swylington's handmaid ; Geoffrey, s. of Robert, and Ralph Bate, 4*d*. each for vert.

ALVERTHORP.—Richard, s. of Broun, the same.

Jordan de Thorp, 6*d*. for going beyond the paling. Surety : Robert the Yongh.

WAKEFELD.—Hugh the Chapman's handmaid, 3*d*. for rushes (*cirpis*).

ALVERTHORP.—William, s. of Geppe de Erdeslawe, 6*d*., and Ellen atte Kirke, 3*d*., for escapes.

STANLAY.—Robert the Yonghe, for a trespass against the lord, 6*s*. 8*d*.

Geoffrey Fonne, 2*d*.; Robert the Yonghe, 4*d*.; Isabel, sister of John s. of Gelle, 4*d*.; Robert de Mikelfeld, 3*d*.; and a certain man of Lofthous, 6*d*., surety, Richard del Ker,—for escapes.

From a turner [*turnarius*] at Lofthous, for vert, 3*d*.

John, s. of Philip, William de Chellay, and Hugh, s. of Philip, 2*d*. each for cutting down wood.

WAKEFELD.—Adam de Wolvelay, 4*d.*; Henry de Ayketon, 2*d.*, and Roger de Silkeston, 6*d.*, for vert, pailings carried away, etc.

OSSET.—Thomas de Holay, 4*d.* for vert.

THORNES.—Alice Graffard, 4*d.* for escape of pigs.

OSSET.—Thomas the Pynder, 3*d.* for escape of a horse.

SANDALE.—Adam de la Grene, amerced 9*d.* for not prosecuting his suits against Thomas, s. of Pelle,William de Collay, and Thomas, s. of Roger. His surety, the grave, also amerced.

ALVERTHORP.—Robert Gerbode is ill, therefore Alice Gerbode's suit against him is postponed till next court.

The said Alice agrees with John Gerbode, on condition that she quitclaims and releases all right to dower in a bovate and 2 acres in Alvirthorp, and the said Robert [*sic*] fines 2*s.* for the recognitioñ.

SANDALE.—Warenner de Karlton, guardian of Thomas and Agnes, children of Richard Beausir, on behalf of his said wards, sues Thomas, s. of Roger, for 4 quarters of oats, worth [?], and two sheep, worth 3*s.* 4*d.*, which property was given by their parents to be appropriated to their use. Defendant acknowledges the two sheep, but says they were taken for the Earl's expenses, and he will make satisfaction therefor as soon as he is paid by the Earl's servants. The oats he denies, and prays that an inquisition be ordered.

The said Warenner sues Robert, s. of Richard Beausir, for debt. An inquisition is to be taken.

Thomas, s. of Roger, sues Warenner de Karlton for trespass. Surety : William [the] Bailiff.

Adam de la Grene sues William de Collay on a security, and Thomas, s of Roger, for trespass.

Margery the Wryhte sues Agnes, d. of Geoffrey de Newebyggyng, for assaulting her in Crigeleston Chapel on St. James' day, and breaking her head with a shingle. Agnes says she has already made terms and reparation for the said assault. [Nothing further recorded.]

The town of Crigeleston, 40*d.* for concealing this shedding of blood.

Sum total of this Court : [?] 47*s.*, *i.e.*

		Sandale,	4*s.* 7*d.*
Hiperum,	2*d.*	Bailiffs,	4*s.* 4*d.*
Osset,	11*d.*	Holne, [?]	10*s.* 6*d.*
Alvirthorp,	3*s.* 9*d.*	Sourby,	4*s.* 6*d*
Sourby,	7*s.* 6*d.*	Rastrik,	12*d.*
Wakefeld, [?]	10*s.* 2*d.*	Stanley,	9*s.*
Thornes,	4*d.*		

J

[The totals are all much faded, and one or two so much rubbed as to be only conjecturable. I have put what the figures look like, though they do not add up correctly. The fines are all set forth in the abstract above.]

[mem. 15 dors.]

SANDALE.—William de la Grene sues John, s. of Nalk de Crigeleston, on an agreement. Surety: William de Lokwode.

THORNES.—William Grenehod sues John, s. of Margery, and Ivo Smith [*Faber*], for debt. Surety: William Marjoriman.

HIPERUM.—Hugh de Rachesdale sues William de Haylay for taking a horse. Surety: Simon de Tothill.

Henry, s. of Richard de Hide of Rachesdale, sues Robert the Harpour for trespass. Surety: John Pollard, baker.

BAILIFF.—John Scharp sues Richard de Bretton for debt. Surety: Thomas de Wyttelay.

HOLNE.—Henry de Hotoun sues Richard, s. of Michael, for debt. Surety: Gilbert de Alestanlay.

ALVERTHORP.—Robert de Wyverumthorp sues John Broun for debt.

SANDALE.—Robert Carpenter of Wakefeld sues John, s. of Ralph Smith [*Faber*]. for trespass.

John Thorold sues John, s. of Margery de Holins, for debt. Surety: Thomas de Holgate.

STANLAY.—Robert Gunne sues Richard Isabel for debt. Surety: Thomas Alayn.

ALVIRTHORP.—Robert, s. of Simon de Flansowe, sues Philip, s. of Thomas de Stanlay, for debt.

FORGES [*sic*].—Memorandum that on Wednesday, on the Morrow of St. John the Baptist, 8 Edw. II, John, s. of Robert, began to work and burn [*cremare*] in the great wood of Wakefeld, and will pay 14s. a week for his forge.

Memorandum that on Monday next before the Feast of St. Margaret, in the beginning of the 9th year, John Culpon began to work and burn in Twyseldene, and will pay 5s. a week for his forge.

COURT held at Wakefeld on Friday, the Feast of St. James the Apostle [July 25], in the beginning of the 9th year of Edw. II.

ESSOINS.—John de Lepton, by Thomas de Wittelay. Surety: William del Okes.

Robert, s. of Geoffrey de Stanlay, by Robert Pees. Surety: Thomas del Belhous.

Thomas de Seyvile, by John Patrikes. Surety: Thomas de Thornton.

Adam Sprigonel, by William Marjoriman.

William Wildebor, by Thomas de Waddesworth. Surety: John de Mora.

BAILIFF.—Matilda de Newmarket [de Novo Mercato] sues John, s. of Robert Mercer [mercenarius] of Wakefeld, and Gregory Mercer, for detention of cattle. Surety: John Curzoun. She appoints John de Kellesley her attorney. The defendants to be attached.

Henry Fletcher of Osset, 2d. for not prosecuting his suit against Robert Pees of Osset.

Henry, s. of Richard del Hyde, essoins against Robert the Harpur, by Richard de Hyde. Surety: John Pollard.

HOLNE.—Gilbert de Alestanlay [6d.] agrees with Robert, s. of Sarah de Fouleston, and Thomas Smith [Faber] of Scheplay.

BAILIFF.—Alice de Skrevyn, Prioress of Kirkley, sues Richard Chaplain of Hertesheved on a plea of taking cattle, by Henry de Wakfeld. Surety: Thomas de Wittelay. And John de Hertesheved, clerk, surety for the attaching of the said Richard, is fined 6d. for not having him in court.

HIPERUM.—Hugh de Rachesdale and William de Hailay [6d.] agree.

HOLNE.—Adam Strekeys and Agnes, formerly wife of John, s. of Hugh de Litlewode [4d.], agree.

SANDALE.—John, s. of Beatrix, and Robert Tailor [cissor] of Walton [6d.] agree.

HOLNE.—Henry de Hotoun [6d.] and Richard, s. of Michael, agree.

SANDALE.—John, s. of Margery del Holins, 3d. for not coming when summoned to answer John Torold.

ALVERTHORP.—John Broun of Alverthorp, the same against Robert de Wyverumthorp.

THORNES.—William Grenehod sues John, s. of Margery, and Ivo Smith [faber], for 10s., which they acknowledge; amerced 6d.

SOURBY.—John, s. of John de Megelay, 2d.; Henry de Saltonstall, 3d., and Roger, s. of Amabilla, 3d., for enclosing lands without license. John de Routonstall did not enclose land as presented.

SANDALE.—Roger, s. of Roger Tropynel, gives 6s. 8d. to take 9½ acres in Crigelestone from Roger Tubbyng.

THORNES.—Robert, s. of Ivo Smith [*faber*], gives 10s. to take 14 acres in Snaýpthorp from his father.

SOURBY.—Richard, s. of Richard de Saltonstall, 20s. to take 2½ bovates with buildings in Saltonstall from his father, and he afterwards surrenders half of the land to his father for his life ; and fines 6s. 8d. for admittance.

[?] HOLNE.—William Wether gives 2s. to take 1⅝ acres of land (with right of ingress and egress for his manure and corn) in Wolvedale from Adam, s. of Elyas.

Agnes, formerly wife of John, s. of Hugh de Litlewode, gives 18d. to take 1¼ acres in Thwong from Thomas the . . . . . .

Emma, d. of William Kenward, heir-apparent, fines 4s. as a heriot on 8½ acres with buildings in Hepworth, after her father's death, to hold to herself and her heirs, if no male heir is forthcoming.

John, s. of Henry de Heppeworth, gives 8s. to take 3¼ acres, with the reversion of 6¼ acres after the death of Nicholas del Clif, from Simon, s. of the said Nicholas.

[HIPERUM].—Jordan de Hiperum, 3s. to take 6 acres with buildings in Hiperum from William, s. of John de Hiperum.

Richard del Wyndhill—taken as a suspected thief, because he came with a message from several thieves to the wife of the late William de Stodlay [? begging] victuals for the said thieves, and because he threatened the woman to burn her unless she sent food and money by him, and fled when the Earl's foresters tried to attach him for this, and shot at the said foresters with arrows— being asked what he has to say, denies the charges, and refers himself to the court. An inquisition is taken by the oaths of . . . . . . Thorneton, John de la More, William del Okes, Thomas del Bellehous, Richard de Salsa-mara, Richard de Birstall, Robert de Heyrode, Robert de la Grene, Richard de Crosseland, John Hood of Wakefeld, John, s. of Hugh de Northland, and Richard de Counhale—by whom he is found not guilty of frequenting the company of thieves, etc.

Richard de Covenhale, [?] 6d. for entering into 3 acres by the demise of Alice de Russcheworth, without license.

[A list of the usual amercements follows, which is much rubbed ; some names are quite illegible, and others torn away ; as the names occur so frequently, and the list must be incomplete, I have omitted it.]

[*mem.* 16.]

ALVERTHORP.—Alice, formerly wife of Gerbode de Alverthorp, sues Robert Gerbode of Alverthorp for her dower in 21 acres of land in Alverthorp, of which her husband died seised. Defendant says plaintiff cannot claim dower in the land, because her husband only had a life interest therein from Richard Gerbode, defendant's father, granted him before Alexander Lucas, steward, after his previously surrendering the land in court to the aforesaid Richard. Robert, the defendant, is to have an extract from the rolls at the next court.

The said Alice sues Robert, s. of John Schirlock, for her dower in 13½ acres. Defendant denies her right, and calls the rolls to witness. He is to have an extract as above.

WAKEFELD.—The inquisition between Roger Preest and Robert Estrild for a rood of land which Roger says has been encroached on by Robert for the past eleven years, is taken by the oath of John Pollard, Henry, s. of Ellen, Robert Gonne, John Poket, Richard Poket, and Robert, s. of Walter, who say that Gerard Cussing, uncle of Rose, wife of Roger Preest, demised 3 butts [*buttas*] of land in the Rodes to defendant for his (Gerard's) life, with remainder after his death to his niece Rose ; and after Gerard's death defendant took a lease thereof for 20 years from Roger Preest and his wife. Roger is therefore amerced 3*d.* for false claim.

Robert Estrild gives 12*d.* to take ½ acre in Wakefeld by the Parsones flat from John Tenet.

Margery the Wythere and Agnes, d. of Geoffrey del Newebigging [6*d.*], agree. Surety: John, s. of William de Plegwyk.

William de Carltoun and Robert, s. of Richard Beausir [6*d.*], agree.

Adam de la Grene sues William de Collay for ½ quarter of oats, price 18*d.*, as surety for Henry, s. of Agnes. Defendant acknowledges the debt; fine, 6*d.*

An inquisition finds that Thomas, s. of Roger, is withholding from Thomas and Agnes, children of Richard Beausir, 8*s.* for 4 quarters of oats, a sheep, and the fleece of a diseased sheep [*bident' de morina*], delivered to him by Wariner de Carltoun, their guardian. He is to make satisfaction, and is amerced 6*d.*

Thomas, s. of Roger, sues Warenner de Carltoun, saying that in 7 Edw. II plaintiff took from him 3 roods of land in Crigeleston for 6 years ; and, after he had ploughed and manured the land,

and had spent on it altogether 40s., the said Warenner made default of the service due on the said land to the Earl, whose servants entered the said land sown with corn, and ejected plaintiff , damages, 40s. Warenner makes no defence ; amerced 6d. Damages to be taxed at next court.

William de la Grene and John, s. of Nalk [6d.], agree.

SANDALE.—John Goldehor is dead ; his land to be taken into the Earl's hand.

SOURBY.—John, s. of Robert, 2d.; Amabilla, his mother, 2d.; Oto Smith [faber], 1d.; John de Birstall, 2d.; William del Ryding, 1d.; Robert del Grenehirst, 2d.; Richard, s. of Nalle, 1d.; John Webster, 2d.; Adam de Olderode, 1d.; Richard de Wyndhill, 3d.; John del Hole, 4d.; Adam the Crouther, 6d.; Henry, s. of Roger, 12d.; William, servant of John Culpon, 6d.; William Wynter, 3d.; John de Langelay, 1d.; Thomas de Wadworth, 1d.; Richard del Bredinsikes, 1d.; William de Wolrunwalle, 2d.; Adam de Routon-stall, 6d., for escapes of stirks and pigs.

HOLNE.—John de Turton, 6d.; Roger Smalchaghe, 6d.; Gilbert del Hole, 3d.; Thomas de Brokholes, 3d.; Thomas Besse, 3d., and John, s. of Matilda, 2d., for escapes and vert.

HIPERUM.—Cissota, widow, del Briggehous, 4d.; Roger del Briggehous, 2d.; Gilbert Brid, 1d.; Thomas Baude, 2d.; Richard Tailor [cissor], 2d.; Alexander Tailor [cissor], 2d.; William Milner, 2d.; Roger de Clifton, 2d.; Thomas de Wolfker, 3d.; Thomas del Clif, 3d.; John del Rode, 2d.; Thomas, his son, 2d.; William, his son, 2d.; Alexander the Waynwryht, 2d.; Roger Drabel of Prestlay, 3d.; Thomas, s. of Thomas, 3d.; John the Pynder, 2d.; John the Pynder of Northorum, 1d.; Peter del Barne, 1d.; John, s. of Walter, 2d.; the wife of Richard, s. of Walter, 2d.; John, s. of Alexander, 2d.; Michael Addegreves, 3d.; Hugh de Northorum, 2d.; John del Withill, 2d., for vert, dry wood, and escapes.

ALVERTHORP.—John Torold sues John de Flansowe for debt. Surety : Richard Wythehoundes. He also sues William Carpenter of Alverthorp for debt.

Richard de Bretton sues Dyonisia, d. of Cecilia de la Wro, for debt. Surety : Thomas de Wittelay.

SANDALE.—Thomas, s. of Pelle, sues Margery the Wrythe for trespass. Surety : Elias de Donecastre.

Robert, s. of Pelle, sues John, s. of Margery, for debt. Surety : William de Donecastre.

Total of this Court : £4　8s. 2d.,　i.e. Sandale,　10s.　5d.
　　　　Bailiff,　　　　8d.　　　　Hiperum, 8s.
　　　　Alverthorp,　12d.　　　　Sourby,　32s. 10d.
　　　　Osset,　　　　2s.　　　　Holne,　18s. 10d.
　　　　Wakefeld,　15d.　　　　Stanlay,　　　21d.
　　　　Thornes,　11s. 5d.

COURT held at Wakefeld on Friday after the Feast of
St. Oswald the King [Aug. 5], 9 Edw. II.

ESSOINS.—John de Mora, by John Patrikes.　Surety : William
Marjoriman.

William de Rastrik, by Thomas de Tothill.　Surety : Thomas
de Seyvile.

Hugh the Nodder, attorney of Lady Margaret de Nevile, by
William Marjoriman.　Surety : William del Okes.

Richard de Birstall, by John de Woderoue.　Surety : Robert
Heyrode.

William Wildebor, by Thomas de Wittelay.　Surety : Robert
de la Grene.

Thomas de Thornton, by John de Thornton.　Surety : John
Hod.

[*Several lines at the bottom of the membrane are much rubbed. They
are, apparently, all essoins in various suits, and orders for attachment and distraint only.*]

[*mem. 16 dors.*]

HOLNE.—Henry Bridmouth, 6d. for entering into 3 acres of land
by lease from William Pyntel without license ; William amerced 2d.

Inquisition from Holnefrith as to lands taken and demised out
of court : Adam Shepherd, Thomas de Billeclyf, Richard, s. of
John, Nicholas, s. of John, Simon del Clif, and Richard, s. of Richard
s. of Elcok.

The land taken by Matilda, d. of Nicholas, 3 years ago from
Peter Pede, deceased, to be taken into the lord's hand.

SANDALE.—Margery and Matilda, daughters of John Goldhor,
give 12d. to take 7 acres of land with buildings in Holinthorp from
Margery del Holyns.　As they are children, the custody of them
and of the land is given to Agnes, their mother, until they come
of age.　Sureties : Thomas, s. of Pelle, and Elyas de Donecastre.

Elyas de Donecastre gives 2s. to take 3 acres in Crigeleston
from Roger Tubbing.

Robert Mayden is dead ; his land to be taken into the lord's hand.

HOLNE.—Elyas, s. of Henry de Heppeworth, amerced 6*d*. for enclosing unoccupied land without license.

ALVERTHORP.—Two acres held by John the Rased, and ½ acre held by William Wolmer, to be taken into the lord's hand because they are dead.

SANDALE.—John, s. of Margery del Holyns, to be attached to answer John Torold by the corn growing on his land, because no other distraint can be found.

ALVERTHORP.—In the suit between Alice Gerbode and Robert Gerbode of Alverthorp for her dower, the rolls of Alexander Lucas, formerly steward, show that in 7 acres thereof Gerbode, her husband, had only a life interest from Richard Gerbode, father of defendant. She is therefore amerced 6*d*. for false claim in this matter. Of the 14 acres remaining, defendant says he holds only 2½ acres as heir of his uncle, Adam Gerbode, deceased, in which she can claim dower. He is therefore amerced 3*d*. for wrongful detention, and Alice is to recover dower therein. The other 11½ acres, Robert says, were bought by Richard, his father, from the said Gerbode about 50 years ago, and afterwards surrendered to Gerbode for the term of his life ; and he appeals to the rolls, if they can be found, or else to an inquisition of the neighbours.

The rolls of Alexander Lucas, steward, show that Gerbode of Alverthorp had no rights in 13½ acres in Alverthorp, whereof Alice claims her dower, against Robert, s. of John Schirlok, having only a life interest therein from the said John Schirlok. Alice is amerced 3*d*. for false claim.

STANLEY.—Robert Gonne sues Richard Isabel for 3½ bushels of corn lent him 3 years ago ; defendant acknowledges it ; amerced 2*d*.

ALVERTHORP.—Robert, s. of Simon de Flansowe, and Philip, s. of Thomas de Stanlay [3*d*.], agree.

John de Flansowe amerced 2*d*. for not coming, when summoned, to answer John Torold.

William Carpenter of Alverthorp, the same.

SANDALE.—John, s. of Margery, 3*d*. for the same against Robert, s. of Pelle.

ALVERTHORP.—William the Templer gives 6*d*. to take a rood of land from Henry the Nonne in Neuton.

OSSET.—Robert Peny, John, his brother, Hugh de Chedeshill, and Adam Lovelevedi, 3d. each ; Richard, s. of Jouet, 'Amabilla Hornyng, and Richard, s. of John, 2d. each, for dry wood.

ALVERTHORP.—Richard Withehoundes, 3d., and Amabilla, d. of Richard Broun, 2d., for vert and dry wood.

WAKEFELD.—Richard, s. of Robert, 3d.; German Hodelyn, 2d.; the maid of John the Rased's widow, 3d.; Emayn, 2d.; and William the Theker, 2d., for dry wood.

[?] STANLEY.—William, s. of Adam s. of Cote, 6d.; the wife of Thomas, s. of Stephen, 2d.; Thomas del Hayley, 3d.; Robert de Mikelfeld, 3d.; Hugh Tagge, 2d.; William de Schellay, 3d.; Peter the Pynder, 2d.; Philip Sawyer [sarrator], 6d.; the turner of Lofthous, 3d., for dry wood, etc.

WAKEFELD.—William Lenton, 2d.; Adam Torcatro, 2d.; Twentipair, 1d.; Johanna Legat, 2d.; Robert Gurdon, 2d.; Richard Fegald, 1d.; Alice, d. of Alexander, 3d.; Richard Avot, 2d.; John Dun's son, 1d.; the wife of Richard the Long, 1d.; William Wiles' son, 2d.; and John, s. of Swayn, 2d., for vert, dry wood, and palings broken.

STANLEY.—John Rigway's wife, 6d.; Hugh Fyndyren, 3d.; Robert de Schellay, 6d., for vert, palings broken, and escape.

BAILIFF.—Johanna, d. of William the Taillour, 2s. for an aid to maintain her in her inheritance.

Sum total of this Court : 17s.   8d., i.e. Holne,   15d.

Alverthorp,	3s.		Sandale,	3s. 3d.
Wakefeld,	2s. 9d.		Osset,	18d.
Stanley,	3s. 11d.		Bailiff,	2s.

. . . . . .—Matilda del Clif sues Henry, servant of William de Sonderland, Adam, brother of the said Henry, and Thomas del Bothes, for trespass.   Surety : . . . . . . Russcheworth.

. . . . . .—Thomas de Schellay sues William the Wyte for land.

. . . . . .—Two acres of villein [nativa] land held by Hugh Pees, who died 2 years ago, to be taken into the lord's hand.

ALVERTHORP.—Robert Goldsmith of Wakefeld sues Richard Wythehoundes for debt.   Surety : Thomas Alayn.

[There are twelve lines more at the end of the membrane recording pleas put in, in some of which some words are legible, others are altogether rubbed away.]

[*mem.* 17.]

COURT held at Wakefeld on Friday, the Feast of the Decollation of St. John the Baptist [Aug. 29], 9 Edw. II.

ESSOINS.—William de Rastrik, by Thomas de Tothill.   Surety : Thomas de Thornton.

Richard de Crosseland, by William Marjoriman.   Surety : Thomas del Bellehous.

Robert, s. of Geoffray de Stanlay, by William de Osset.   Surety : Robert de Heyrode.

John de Lepton, by Thomas de Wittelay.   Surety : Richard de Birstall.

John de la More, by William, s. of Junne.   Surety : Richard de Salsa-mara.

John Hod, by Nicholas Hogge.   Surety : William Wildebor.

BAILIFF.—Alice de Skreven, Prioress of Kirkleyes, and Richard, Chaplain of Hertesheved [2s.], agree.   Surety : Thomas de Wittelay.

Henry, s. of Richard del Hide of Rachesdale, sues Robert the Harpour for assault in the town of Eland, calling him false and unfaithful, and felling him to the earth with his bow ; damages, 100s.   Robert says he is not answerable here, because he holds nothing in the fee ; he is therefore discharged.

SOURBY.—Richard de Luddingdene, 6d. for not prosecuting his suit against John Sourmilk.

John, s. of John de Miggelay, 6d. for not prosecuting suit against Julian Wade.

SANDALE.—Thomas, s. of Pelle, and Margery Carpenter (3d.) agree.

HOLNE.—Adam Strekeys gives 18d. to take 1⅔ roods in Alestanlei irom William, s. of Gilbert de Alestanlei.

SANDALE.—Robert Carpenter of Wakefeld [12d.] and John, s. of Ralph Smith [*faber*], agree.

STANLEY.—Richard Poket, 6d. for contempt in court.

ALVERTHORP.—John de Flansowe and William Carpenter of Alverthorp, 2d. each for not coming to answer John Torold.

Johanna, formerly wife of John the Rased, gives 4s. to have the crop of 2 acres of land sown by John the Rased against orders.

SANDALE.—Robert, s. of Pelle, 3d. for not prosecuting suit against John, s. of Margery del Holins.

ALVERTHORP.—An inquisition taken as to the crops of corn and meadow grass in the garden of the Hospital says that the land sown in the said garden is worth 3s., and the meadow 2s.; the grave of Alverthorp is therefore ordered to levy, etc.

Robert Estrild fines 6s. 8d. for the crop of 3¼ acres of villein [*nativa*] land, which Robert sowed against orders.

Thomas, s. of Laurence, is amerced for a false claim against Walter del Hill. He is forgiven at the instance of Master John.

THORNES.—William, s. of Roger, grave of Thornes, 12d. for not coming to the court.

HIPERUM.—Matilda del Clif and Henry, and the other defendants [12d.], agree.

OSSET.—Thomas de Schellay, 6d. for false claim against William the Wyte.

Adam, s. of William, formerly grave of Osset, 12d. for concealing the heriot due on the land of Hugh Pees, who died 2 years ago.

The whole graveship of Osset, with the exception of William de Heton, 6s. 8d. for the same.

THORNES.—The graveship of Thornes, 40d. for not coming to the court.

SANDALE.—Thomas, s. of Roger de Crigelestone, gives 12d. to take 1¼ acres in Crigelestone from Robert, s. of Richard Beausir, for 4 years.

ALVERTHORP.—John Wolmer gives 12d. as a heriot on ½ acre in Alverthorp, after the death of William Wolmer, his father.

WAKEFELD ; new rent.—John, s. of Robert Pollard, gives 6d. to take a piece of unoccupied land in Wakefeld Market, 12 feet by 10 feet, rent 2d.

ALVERTHORP.—The inquisition between Alice, formerly wife of Gerbode, plaintiff, and Robert Gerbode, defendant, as to dower in 11½ acres in Alverthorp, is taken by the oath of Robert de Flansowe, Richard, s. of Philip, Adam Wolf, William de Neuton, John Attebarre, Adam de Flansowe, and Henry Wolf, who say Gerbode surrendered the land to Richard Gerbode, his son, father of defendant, before he married Alice ; she is therefore amerced 3d. for false claim.

BAILIFF.—John Gour gives 2s. for an aid to recover his debts from John Graffard.

ALVERTHORP.—The same John gives 40d. to take a clearing of land in Alverthorp, with the meadow thereto belonging, which he had previously taken from William Hoskel, together with the reversion of the dower therein of Alice, formerly wife of the said John.

OSSET.—Thomas, s. of Hugh Pees, gives 12*d*. as a heriot on 2 acres of land in Osset, after his father's death.

BAILIFF.—Robert the Yonghe, John the Rased, and Henry the Stirter to be attached to answer Ralph de Ecleshill for trespass.

William Cussing to be attached to answer Master William de Rothewell, parson of Normantone church, and John Twyt for trespass.

ALVERTHORP.—Adam de Flansowe and Robert Gerbode [. . .] agree.

BAILIFF.—Alice Graffard to be resummoned to answer Robert Marescall.

William del Okes, Robert de Sandale, clerk, Robert Stere, Robert de la Sale, and William de . . . . . . to be summoned to answer John de Birton.

STANLEY.—Henry Bennyng to be summoned to answer Robert Gunne.

BAILIFF.—Henry de Spotland, indicted at the tourn at Rastrik for sundry thefts, and taken, pays 20*s*. to be under mainprise till the delivery of York Gaol. Surety : Thomas Alayn.

THORNES.—John, s. of Margery, 6*d*.; Philip, s. of Henry, 3*d*.; William, s. of Roger, 6*d*.; and Hugh the Viroun, 2*d*., for escapes.

HOLNE.—Thomas Smith [*faber*], 6*d*.; Agnes, wife of John, s. of Hugh, 3*d*.; Margery, d. of Roger, 4*d*.; and Robert de Stafford, 3*d*. [?], for coals and escapes.

. . . . . .—John Nelot, grave of Wakefeld, concealed an escape.

ALVERTHORP.—Thomas, s. of Stephen, 2*s*. for cutting down oak saplings on villein [*nativa*] land.

Sum total of this Court : 79*s*. 9*d*., and new rent, 2*d*.

i.e.	Hiperum,	12*d*.		Osset,	9*s*.
	Wakefeld,	7*s*. 2*d*., and new rent, 2*d*.			
	Bailiff,	24*s*. . . .		Sourby,	[?] 7*d*.
	Sandale,	2*s*. . . .		Holne,	2*s*. 10*d*.
	Stanley,	6*d*.		Alverthorp,	25*s*. . . .
	Thornes,	5*s*. . . .			

[*mem. 17 dors.*]

Eva Brouneson sues John Rate for trespass.

ALVERTHORP.—John Gerbode sues Richard Wythehoundes for trespass. Surety : Robert Gerbode.

John Rate sues Richard Brouneson for trespass.

STANLEY.—Ralph, s. of Nicholas, sues Richard and John Poket for land. Surety: John atte-Barre.

BAILIFF.—Thomas de Seyvile and Hugh de Tothill severally sue Master Philip the Waleys on an agreement. Sureties: William de Dewesbury and Henry de Gontoun.

Alice de Ecardby sues John de Heton for trespass ; also John de Heton and Amabilla, his wife, and John Graffard, for the same ; and appoints Henry de Wakefeld her attorney.

Richard Milner sues Robert Peger for debt. Surety: John Sibbeson.

William, s. of Nicholas, and John de Newcastle severally sue John de Heton for trespass. Surety: Thomas Alayn.

COURT held at Wakefeld on Friday after the Feast of the Exaltation of the Holy Cross [Sept. 14], 9 Edw. II.

ESSOINS.—Robert de Wyverumpthorp, by John Cay. Surety: Thomas de Wyttelay.

Hugh the Nodder, attorney of Dame Margaret de Neyvile, by Robert Marescall. Surety: Thomas de Seyvile.

John de Leptone by Robert de Horburi. Surety: William Marjoriman.

Thomas de Thorntone, by Thomas de Wyttelay. Surety: Richard de Birstall.

Richard de Crosseland, by William Marjoriman. Surety: Robert de Heyrode.

BAILIFF.—Matilda de Newmarket, 2s. for not prosecuting her suits against John, s. of Robert Mercer of Wakfeld, and Gregory Mercer.

HOLNE.—Matilda, d. of Nicholas de Litlewod, gives 12d. as a fine on one acre of land, which she enclosed after the death of Peter Pede.

Henry Wade gives 8s. for license to take 12½ acres in Cartworth from Richard de Cartworth, and 4s. to take 5¾ acres there from Adam de Dalton and John, his son.

Simon de Monte, 6s. 8d. to take 10 acres in Heppeworth from Thomas Smith [faber] of Scheplay.

Agnes, formerly wife of William, s. of Mary, 2s. for license to marry.

ALVERTHORP.—Thomas the Roller, 2s. to take 4½ acres in the graveship of Alverthorp from John Cussing, for 6 years.

HORBURI.—John, s. of Thomas Smith [*faber*] of Horburi, 4s. to take ½ bovate of land in Horburi from Robert de Scharneston.

ALVERTHORP.—Thomas, s. of Henry the Nonne, and John, his brother, 12d. to take 5 roods from Henry the Nonne in the graveship of Alverthorp.

OSSET.—Alice Wolrik's land to be taken into the lord's hand because she is dead.

STANLEY.—Robert Gonne pays 2s. to take 2⅜ acres in Stanley from John Pollard, junior.

THORNES.—Robert Peger acknowledges he owes Richard Milner ½ quarter of corn and a quarter of oats, and fines 6d.

BAILIFF.—Robert Gunne sues Philip del Hill and Adam the Hewer for debt. Surety: Thomas de Wyttelay.

WAKEFELD.—Henry de Gontoun gives 6d. for license to enlarge a stall belonging to him in Wakefeld Market, by 26 feet towards the West, and 18 feet towards the South, and 13 feet to the North; rent 1½d.

[*A short list of amercements in three columns, and the totals, are so much rubbed that I cannot decipher them with any certainty. The total for the Court appears to be 38s.*]

———————

[*Here begins the Sheffield MS. See Introduction.*]

COURT at Halifax on Tuesday before the Feast of St. Margaret the Virgin [July 20], in the year, etc. [1286].

SOUREBY.—It is found by the inquisition of neighbours that John Styhog unjustly raised the hue on Richard the Tynker, and that the same John unjustly beat Hanne the Walker against the peace. Therefore he shall make satisfaction to him, and he is amerced. . . . . . . He paid the fine of —. Pledges: . . . . . .

Master Peter, proctor of Halifax, alleged on behalf of the men of the church of the same place that they are not bound to lead thieves to York. Therefore, that case is respited until the coming of the Earl.

Thomas Shepherd [*bercarius*] of Haldeworth gives 6d. for license to take 4 acres of land from Roger, son of Peter, to himself and his heirs for ever, doing therefor, etc. Pledge: Hanne the grave.

William del Bothes gives 4d. for having aid to recover 10s. 6d. from William of Hovendene, and 2s. from Ralph of the same. Pledge : Henry the grave. They came and acknowledged the said debt, and have time for payment until the Feast of St. Oswald. Pledge : Ralph of Hovendene and William, son of Amabel of the same.

William de Saltonstall gives 12d. for license to take ½ acre of land in Soureby from William, son of Symon, to him and his heirs for ever.

William the Geldehyrd, apprehended for hunting a doe, found these pledges to answer for him, viz.: Elias Milner, William of . . . . . . Litheseles, Henry, s. of Elias of the same, William de Moor [de Mora], and Henry, s. of William.

Richard, s. of Adam de Waddesworthe, gives 12s. 2d. for the relief of the land of Adam, his father, which he held of Sir [dom] Richard de Thornhill.

Roger de Houwrth [Hawarth] gives 12d. for the escape of 4 cattle in Sakeldene. Pledge : Richard de Waddeswrth.

BAILIFF.—Thomas de Langefeud gives half a mark for having aid to recover 20s. from John Talvis, and he came and admitted [the debt], and found as his pledges to satisfy him [the plaintiff] : Roger, s. of William Tanner, and William, s. of John. The same Thomas gives 12d. for having aid to recover 3s. 6d. from Adam; s. of John, and he came and admitted [the debt]. Pledges : William and Richard, his brother.

Sum of this Court : 26s. 4d.

TOURN there the same day.

THE TWELVE JURORS OF SOUREBY.—Thomas de Langefeud, Thomas de Coppeley, Peter Swerd, Richard de Stansefeud, Adam de Miggeley, ... de Rastrik, Richard del Dene, Richard de Waddeswrth, John de Wylleys, William de Stodlay, Hugh, s. of Alan, Thomas de Connale, who say on their oath that Richard de Heytfeud drew blood from Elena, d. of Richard Long, and because the plaint thereof is in court, therefore, nothing is to be done here.

Also they say that William de Ovendene raised hue unjustly on the servant of the Lady [Domina] of Thornhill. Therefore, he is amerced. He paid fine of 12d. Pledges : Ralph de Ovendene and William, s. of Amabel.

Peter Swerd unrightfully stopped up a certain footpath between Stansfeud and Mankanholes. The obstruction is to be cast down, and he himself is amerced. He paid a fine of 12d. Pledge : Hugh del Lowe.

Thomas, s. of John de Grenewode, cut the purse of William de Miggeley [?] by night, and took therefrom . . . 16d. Let him be taken when he can be found.

Richard de Crosseley drew blood from Richard the Tynker and his wife. Let him make satisfaction to them, and he himself is amerced.

Richard the Tynker drew blood from the same Richard de Crosseley. Therefore, he is amerced. He is pardoned because . . . . . . he defends himself.

John Styhog stole two oxen from Roger Foulmoth, and he was the companion of Thomas de Hyllingwrth, who was hanged at York. He put himself [cepit se] upon the country, and so was sent to York prison.

William, s. of Ivo de Werloley, took two bows from stranger men who were guests at the house of William de Miggeley, but they [the jurors] know not by what warrant. He is amerced. He paid a fine of 12d. Pledge : Ivo de Werloley.

John Styghog raised the hue unjustly on Richard the Tynker. Because the case is in court it is not dealt with here.

Avicia, the wife of Thomas de Westwode, is amerced because she did not send for the ale tasters [custodes cervisie], 6d.

The wife of Nicholas de Werloley for the same, 6d.

Cecilia de Halgate for the same is pardoned.

The wife of Thomas the Spenser for the same, 6d.

The wife of John the grave for the same is pardoned, because she is favourable [sic] [favorabilis] to the Earl's bailiffs.

Agnes de Assewelle for the same, 6d.

The wife of Ralph de Ovendene for the same, 6d.

Matilda, wife of the Fuller, for the same, 6d.

The wife of Robert of Loue [Lowe] for the same, 6d.

Peter Swerd unjustly ejected Alice del Croft from her land in Mancanholes, and cast down her house. Let him make satisfaction to her for damages, [assessed at] 10s. 6d. He is amerced. Paid a fine of 12d. Pledges : Richard de Sandiforth and Henry del Salie [? Sale].

Sum of this Tourn : 9s.

COURT at the Bridge of Rastrik, which is a member of the Court of Wakefeud, on Thursday next before the Feast of St. Margaret the Virgin [July 20], in the year and time aforesaid.

HYPERUM.—Thomas, s. of William de Sypêdene, gives 3s. for the relief of the land of his father, viz. 14 acres of free land and . . . . . . of native land. Pledges : Henry the Grave and Symon Milner, and the aforesaid Henry and Symon shall have the aforesaid land . . . . . for the term of six years on account of the debt for which his [Thomas'] father was bound, and shall do during the [said] term the services and . . . . . .

Dionysia, the wife of John Petronille, gives 6d. for having admittance to her dowry in the aforesaid land. Pledge : Ivo, her brother.

It is ordered to distrain Adam, s. of Henry, because he entered the Earl's fee at Croslande without license.

Henry, s. of Susanna, is charged with being an evildoer and with fighting with the Earl's men. He found these pledges for his keeping the peace, viz.: Richard, s. of John, Adam, s. of John, Adam, s. of Roger, William Bryd, John the Grave, and John Fox.

Alota de Hyperum gives 12d. for having an inquisition concerning 30 acres of land in Hyperum, and the third part which falls to her as dower, which Adam, her son, holds, and they compromise by leave [of the court]. Therefore, he gave to her one acre of land with its crops [vesturis]. Pledge : Henry the Grave.

It is found by the inquisition that Henry de Astey carried away wood belonging to Adam Bryd in Hyperum wood. Therefore, let him make satisfaction. He is amerced. He paid the fine of 12d. Pledge : Henry the Grave.

RASTRIK.—Adam , s. ofHenry Carpenter, gives 6d. for license to take 6 acres of free land in Linth[w]ayt of Dionysia, the wife of Peter de Mallsheved, for the term of six years. Pledge : John the Grave.

BAILIFF.—John de Langeley came and waged the peace to Thomas de Garderobe, because this, on account of threats [that he had made], was imposed on him. Pledges : Hanne, s. of Sosanna, Richard, s. of John, Adam, s. of Roger the Fuller, and Adam, s. of John, for his keeping the peace for ever towards him.

RASTRIK.—It is found by an inquisition of neighbours that Richard de Tothill was the companion of Roger de Bosco to plough jointly with his plough, and at the time of ploughing cast him off,

K

so that his land lies untilled. Therefore, let him make satisfaction to him for the damages, that are taxed at 10s. He himself is amerced. He paid a fine of 12d. Pledges : Matthew de Bosco and John de Botherode, and he has a day [respite] until the feast of St. Michael.

William, s. of Roger de Bosco, gives 6d. for license to compromise with Alexander de Wodehouses concerning a plea of trespass. Pledge : Robert de Horton.

HYPERUM.—Richard, s. of Jordan de Northoverum, gives 4s. for the relief of the land of Jordan, his father. Pledge : Henry the Grave.

It is found by the inquisition that Gilbert de Bothes appointed Roger del Clyff his pledge in regard to the Proctor of Halifax for [the sum of] 10d., which he paid in default of the same Gilbert Let him make satisfaction to him. He is amerced. He paid a fine of 2s. Pledge : Henry the Grave.

RASTRIK.—Thomas, s. of Alota de Steynland, gives 6d. for having aid to recover 10d. from Henry Smith [faber]. They have a " love-day," and the said Thomas gives 6d. for license to compromise with Henry. Pledges : Henry Smith and William of
. . . . . .

Richard del Rode surrendered to Emma, d. of Walter de Rastrik, her dower out of five acres of land . . . . . and Richard de Tothylle and Alcok de Wodehouses surrendered to the same Emma her dower out of eight acres of land. She gives for admittance 6d. Pledge : William, s. of Roger. They are amerced, and pay a fine of 12d. Pledge : one for the other.

HYPERUM.—Henry de Schypedene gives 6d. for having an inquisition touching half an acre of land in Northoverum, which Hanne, s. of God . . . . . . He defends [his suit], and an inquisition comes thereon and says that Hanne has right in his demand. Therefore, let him hold [the land] in peace. Henry, for false plaint, is amerced. He pays a fine of 6d. Pledge : Henry the Grave.

The land of John, s. of Richard de Northoverum, is in the lord's hand, because he is dead.

RASTRIK.—John, s. of Adam de Querneby, appeared against Adam de Barkisland, and says that he is bound to him in one calf or in 14d. And he is thereof convicted. Therefore, let him make satisfaction to him. He is amerced. Pays a fine of 6d. Pledge : Thomas de Gledehylle.

HYPERUM.—Thomas de Hyltone found these pledges for his waging his law [*quod erit legem* [sic] *patiens*], viz.: William de Hyperum, Robert, s. of Susan, and Adam, s. of John.

John Milner gives 6d. for license to take one acre of land in Hyperum of Roger, his son, to himself and his heirs for ever, doing therefor, etc. Surety : Roger, his son.

Roger, s. of John Milner, gives 6d. for license to take one acre in Hyperum of John, his father, to himself and his heirs for ever, doing therefor, etc. Surety : John, his father.

Gilbert de Astey gives 2s. for license to take one acre of land in Hyperum of John de Northclyf to himself and his heirs for ever, doing therefor, etc. Surety : John the Barne.

Malina, the wife of John de Horton, complains of Henry, s. of Susanna, and his wife concerning a plea of trespass. Pledge for the prosecution [of the case] : John de Horton.

BAILIFF.—Henry de Rissewrthe gives 4s. for to be in peace until the coming of the Earl into these parts in regard to the demand made upon him concerning land and pastures bought of Thomas de Thornetone and William de Martone without the lord's leave. Sum of this Court : 24s. 6d.

TOURN there the same day.

THE 12 JURORS. HYPERUM.—Robert de Scolles, John the Barne, Philip de Ferseley, Adam de Lokwode, Adam de Hourum, Gilbert, s. of Adam de Dalton, John de Rodes, Thomas, s. of John de Fekesby, Roger de Linneley, Jordan de Westwode, William de Bradley, and Henry de Heya, who say on their oath that Ralph de Bayrestow made a certain enclosure [*purprestura*] within the bounds of Northourum. He is amerced 12d., and let it be cast down immediately.

John, s. of Magge de Linneley, drew blood from Thomas Edward. He is amerced. Fined nothing here, because he hath no sense [?] [*insensibilis*].

John Smith [*faber*] stole two thraves of oats from his own tithe, that was due from him as tithe. Let him be taken and sent to York.

John de Querneby drew [blood] from Robert, his son, with a cross bow [*balista*]. Let him be distrained to answer therefor.

Richard, s. of William de Slagthayt, burgled the house of Thomas de Fekesby. Let him be taken when he can be found.

John, s. of John de Querneby, drew blood from John, s. of Paulinus of the same. Let him be distrained to answer therefor— 6d.

An ewe with a lamb, the property of Herbert Capel, are in the keeping of Malina de Bosco, whereof she shall answer, and therefore . . . . . .

William, s. of Roger de Bosco, drew blood from Beatrix, the wife of Alcok Smith. She is amerced 6d.

Richard, s. of Hugh Lenns, does not do suit at the lord the Earl's mill as he ought to do. He is distrained 12d.

Also William Willecop gave one quarter of oats in order to receive two quarters after the autumn harvest. Let him be distrained 12d.

Malina, the wife of Thomas Fox, brewed bad beer. Therefore, she is amerced 6d.

Also Malina, wife of Thomas Tyngel, for the same, 6d.

Henry de Barkesland built a certain house, one half of which stands on the highway. Therefore, let him be distrained to answer therefor.

BAILIFF.—The house of Richard de Camera of Hertisheved was burgled, and because the hue was not carried out as it ought to have been, the township is amerced 6d.

HYPERUM.—Jordan, s. of Juliana de Brok, has hand-mills. They are to be laid aside [*deponantur*], and she is amerced 6d.

Elias del Grene for the same, 6d.

John Prykemare for the same, 6d.

John de Coldeley, because he has not done suit to the lord's mill as he should have done, is amerced 6d.

Malina de Presteley for the same, 6d.

Wymark del Brok for the same, 6d.

Robert Clerk for the same, 6d.

Hugh, his son, for the same, 6d.

Alice, d. of Sygeryethe, for the same, 6d.

Alota de Hyperum for the same, 6d.

William, s. of Bron, for the same, 6d.

The house of Jordan, s. of Symon de Hyperum, was burgled, and his bread carried away, and no hue was raised thereon. The township, therefore, is amerced 2s.

Amabel de Stanclyf was married without the lord's license. She is amerced and fined 12d., and because the township of Northorum refused to present this, it is amerced and fined 2s.

John, s. of Gilbert de Bothes, and Mathew, servant of William, for not coming [to the Tourn] are amerced 6*d*. each.

William, s. of William s. of Alan, John, his brother, and Thomas, s. of Christiana, for the same are amerced 6*d*.

John, s. of William de Staynland, Adam, s. of William de Lynneley, and John, s. of Henry de Colleresley, are amerced for the same 6*d*.

Paulinus de Dalton, Thomas s. of Hassolf the Grave, and Adam, s. of Alice the Flemyng, for the same, 6*d*.

John, Thomas the Flemyng's man, and William Willecop of Dalton, for the same, 3*d*.

Bate, Alcok del Clyf's man, Henry Smith, Alan, s. of Elena, for the same, 6*d*.

Hugh Fuller [*fullo*], Ralph de Heliwelle, and Thomas de Heliwelle, for the same, 6*d*.

William de Heliwelle, Adam de Bradeley, and Hanne del Suthwode, for the same, 6*d*.

Hugh de Ekelesley, Thomas, s. of Hanne, and Peter, s. of Mathew, for the same, 6*d*.

Robert de Bosco, Thomas de Hortone, and Thomas, s. of Tylle, for the same, [?] 6*d*.

Richard, serving man [*garcio*] of Alan, Richard, serving man of Richard, s. of William, and Adam, s. of John s. of Elias, for the same, 6*d*.

RASTRIK.—Thomas the Flemyng and John the Flemyng for not coming [to the Tourn] are amerced 6*d*.

Jordan de Byrkes, John, s. of Alot, and William, John the Flemyng's man, for the same are amerced 6*d*.

Richard, the lord's man, and John de Crosland are pardoned because they are poor.

John de Appelyerd, Richard, s. of Walter, and Adam the Hosar [or Hofar], and William, his son, for the same are amerced 6*d*.

William de Gledehill, Hancok, s. of Moll, and John, s. of Thomas, for the same, 6*d*.

Robert, s. of Sara, John, s. of Richard, and Thomas Edward, for the same, 6*d*.

William Coleman, Thomas, servant of Thomas de Slak, and Adam del Lee, for the same, 6*d*.

Robert, s. of Agnes de Wro, William, s. of Jordan, Henry, servant of William del Nonnes, for the same, 6*d*.

Richard, s. of Reyner, Roger, s. of Alexander, and Adam, Alcok del Fryth's man, 6d.

Adam, s. of Alan del Hylle, Hugh, servant of the same Alan, Roger, serving man of the same Alan, and Hanne, serving man of William de Schambandene, for the same, 6d.

Hugh, s. of William de Bothemley, William, s. of Magge de Hyll, and John, William de Bothemley's man, for the same, 6d.

Robert, s. of John s. of Elias, and Peter, s. of Thomas de Barkesland, for the same, 3d.

Sum of this Tourn : 28s. 2d.

TOURN at Wakefeud, Monday, the Feast of St. Mary Magdalene [July 22], in the year aforesaid.

12 JURORS. WAKEFEUD.—Richard de Bretton, Ralph Litster [*tinctor*], Symon de Schevet, William Russell, Walter de Tofteclyf, Thomas de Mytteley, Baldwin de Seyvill, Michael de Floketone, Peter de Waltone, Robert the Erel, John Wytlof, and William, s. of Robert Tanner, who say on their oath that

Symon de Dulber has not come [to the Tourn]. He is therefore amerced 12d.

Richard, s. of Jonne [*sic*], for the same, amerced 6d.

BAILIFF.—Philip Milner [*molendinarius*], William, s. of Ybot, and William, s. of Mitte, for the same, 6d.

Christiana Wade receives strangers at night contrary to the Statute, and is an evildoer. The town of Wakefeud was forbidden her on account of her evil doings. She has stolen malt [*brasium*] to feed her pigs with to the value of 3d. Therefore, let her be taken.

Peter Tyrsi has put his sons to book-learning [*posuit ad librum*], and has married his daughters, but they [*i.e.* the jurors] know not if he had license to do so or not. Let it be enquired into.

The millers in Wakefeud mill take the flour that remains over [*superfluam farinam*], and if flour is not given them they retain the flour entirely until what they will to have is given them. All the millers, also, take the flour of one wynd of corn, and all the country seeks a remedy for this.

BAILIFF.—Adam, s. of Henry s. of the vicar, has committed a theft from the house of Richard de Tonley, value 3d., and has gone away. Therefore, let him be taken.

Robert Gonne is a villein [*nativus*] of the Earl, and holds free land in Northmantone. Let him be distrained.

Robert the Milner of Ekeleshyll received John de Dalton, who has been beheaded [*decapitatus*]. Matilda de Gressebrok did the like. Both are to be taken.

Elias Chaplain has burgled a house in Clayton, Thomas de Wode was his companion, and Beatrice Rabace was consenting. They are to be taken.

Thomas, the serving man of Sir Roger Chaplain, wounded Adam, s. of Adam de Erdeslowe, with a certain arrow, and the said Sir Roger was with him in the aforesaid deed. Let him be distrained when he can be found in the Earl's fee.

Henry Calf drew blood from Walter de Wodesem, and because the plaint is in the court there is nothing here.

Walter Hare has not come, 6*d.*

OSSETE.—Adam, s. of Christiana, demised one house and garden in Stanlay to William the Dyker without license for the term of eight years. Both are amerced, but [the amercement] is condoned for a short term.

BAILIFF.—Symon, s. of David de Donnynglowe, wounded William, s. of William Schyld, with a . . . . . . [*cenypulo ?*]. Amerced 12*d.*

The Preceptor of Neusom took the cattle of Walter de Tofteclyf within the liberty, and drove them into the Wapentake of Schyreyk. Let him be distrained when anything distrainable [*districtio*] is found upon him in the Earl's fee.

Agnes, wife of Hugh de Alverthorpe, and Quenylda, her d., stole 1 wynd of malt, value 9*d.* She is to be taken.

Sum total of this Tourn : 3s. 6d.

COURT at Byrtone, Thursday, the Feast of St. James
[July 25], in the year aforesaid.

HOLNE.—John, s. of Hugh de Littelwode, gives 2*s.* for leave to agree with William, s. of Mocok, on a plea of battery [*verberandi*]. Pledge : Matthew de Holne. 2*s.*

Marcota and Margery, daus. of Adam de Almanbiry, give 12*d.* for leave to take ½ acre of land of Adam de Butterley, doing, etc. Pledge : Richard Grave.

Richard, s. of Hewe de Butterley, gives 12*d.* for leave to take ½ acre of land of Adam de Butterley. Pledge : Richard Grave.

Thomas Bron gives 12*d.* for the holding of an inquisition as to whether Thomas, s. of Richard de Horn, be of full age or not, and whether he can sell land or not. The inquisition of the neighbours comes thereupon, and says that the aforesaid Thomas, s. of Richard, is of full age for selling land, and he comes and surrenders to the aforesaid Thomas Bron a half oxgang of land in Fogelstone to him and his heirs for ever, etc., and he gives for admittance 12*d*. Pledge : Richard Grave.

William, s. of Mocck de Holne, gives 2*s*. for leave to take one acre of land in Holne of John de Holne, which he bought of Elias de Holne, to him, etc., doing the services, etc. Pledge : Matthew Grave.

Avicia, d. of Elias de Holne, gives 6*d*. for leave to take a certain piece of land, containing 60 feet in length and 20 feet in breadth, of Thomas, s. of Matthew, to him, etc., doing the services, etc. Pledge : Richard Grave.

Thomas Bron gives 4*s*. for leave to take 6 acres of land of Agnes, his mother, to him, etc., doing, etc. Pledge : Richard Grave.

Thomas Fernoule gives 2*s*. for leave to take one acre of land of Thomas Bron in Holne, to him, etc., doing, etc. Pledge : R. Grave.

Roger, s. of Adam, gives 2*s*. for leave to take 5 acres of land in Holne of Adam, s. of Robert Yol, for the term of twelve years, doing, etc., together with the dowry of Christiana, his mother. Pledge : William Yol.

William Yol is convicted [*attinctus*] of having beaten and wounded William, s. of Hugh de Littelwode. Let him make satisfaction to him, and he is amerced, and paid a fine of 2*s*. Pledges : Gilbert de Alstanley and William de Thong.

William, s. of Hugh de Littelwode, for the same [offence] against William Yol, is amerced and fined. Pledges : Richard and Gamel de Alstanley.

Also William, s. of Hugh, for the same against John, s. of Agnes, is amerced, and fined 6*s*. 8*d*. Pledges : Richard and Gamel de Alstanley.

John, s. of Hugh de Littelwode, for the same against John, s. of Agnes, is amerced, and pays a fine of 8*s*. Pledges : John de Scholes and William de Littelwode.

Nicholas, s. of Hugh de Littelwode, for the same against the same John, s. of Agnes, is amerced, and paid a fine of 40*d*. Pledge : Thomas de Hallomschyre.

Adam, s. of Hugh Smith [*faber*], came and proved a bullock to be his own, and he found John, s. of Quenylda, and Robert de Mirfeud as his pledges, to answer therefor within a year and a day, and gives for the custody [keeping of the bullock] 3*d*.

Jordan Cheward, for the escape of four horses, is amerced, and paid a fine of 12*d*. Pledge : Gamel.

John de Heton, for an unlawful road [*via*], 6*d*.

·The townships of Scholes and Heppewrthe are amerced 2*s*. for mowing the grass on the common more than is the custom.

Sum of this Court : 40s. 3d.

TOURN there the same day.

JURORS.—Robert del Stokkes, Richard de Thornteley, John de Bramwythe, Richard de Rodes, Henry de Schelley, Adam de Wlwro, Richard de Brokholes, William de Heley, Robert de Mirfeud, Richard del Grene, Thomas de Hallomschyre, and Alan de Wlvedale,· say, etc., that

Robert Stirk had in Carthewrthe mill one dish [*discus*] which ought to be of 17 vessells, and was really of 13½, the said dish being false, to the annoyance [*tedium*] of the whole country, and that he had that dish aforesaid in the mill for eleven weeks. So let him be distrained.

Also that the archers [*archetenentes*] of the Earl of Chester came into Holnefrythes, and would have taken the Earl's flour. The country became aware of the circumstance, and made a rescue from them.

. THORNES.—Elias the Grete sues Margaret, wife of John With-the-Hounds [*cum canibus*], on a charge of calling him a thief. Pledge for prosecuting : Robert, his father.

Robert the Grete sues the same Margaret on the same plea. Pledge of prosecuting : Elias, his son.

Richard Gerbot sues William, s. of Thomas, on a plea of trespass. Pledge for prosecuting : Thomas Heger.

STANLEY.—Elena Lewyar sues Symon, s. of Bateman, on a plea of battery [*verberacio*]. Pledge for prosecuting : Henry Gerrok.

BAILIFF.—Walter de Wodesem sues Henry Calf on a plea of battery. Pledge for prosecuting : . . . . . .

COURT at Wakefeud, Friday, the morrow of St. James the Apostle, year and time aforesaid.

ESSOINS.—Thomas de Schefeud essoins for the first time against William, s. of Roger de Podesey, in a plea of trespass, by John de

Miggeley.   Pledge : William de Castilforthe, and because he appeared a day is given.

BAILIFF.—The suit between Richard Hog and Henry the Schampiun in a plea of trespass is respited until the next court or until the steward view the trespass.

Robert the Greve appeared against Mariota, the wife of German the Mercer, Philip Wlf, John de Ferry, and John Moris, and says that they, on Sunday next after the feast of St. Peter last past, in this year, came and took a red cow of his in a certain place that is called the Brokmilne dam, and drove that cow to the house of German the Mercer, and there detained it from that day until Wednesday next following, to his damage and shame [*dedecus*] to the extent of 2*s.*, against the peace of the lord, etc.   Thereon he brought his suit.   German came and avowed that the taking [of the cow] was good and not unmerited, and says that the aforesaid distraint was made for 7*s.* 6*d.* that the said Robert owed to the said German.   And Robert comes and finds these pledges for doing what justice requires in regard to the said debt, viz.: William de Castilforthe and Richard de Bateley.

THORNES.—Richard, s. of Emma, gives 6*d.* for licence of agreeing with Philip, s. of Alan, in answering Richard concerning a plea of trespass.   Pledge : John, s. of Alan.

SOURBY.—Richard de Haytfeud essoigns for the first time against Elena, d. of Richard de Soureby, in a plea of trespass, by Richard de Bateley.   Pledge : John Hog, and because she appeared a day is given.

BAILIFF ; manucaptors.—Andrew Cutwodecote, taken and imprisoned on suspicion, finds these manucaptors for making his law : viz.: Hugh de Elaund, Robert de Stanelay and Adam de Done, and he is delivered [from gaol].

The suit between John Fox and John the Heuar is respited until the next court in form as before.

HYPERUM.—The suit between Malina, wife of John de Hortone, and Henry, s. of Susanna, and his wife, is respited until the next court.

BA LIFF.—The suit between Walter de Wodesem and Henry Calf in a plea of trespass is respited until the next court.   Pledge : William Wytbelt.

ATTORNEY.—The Lady Margaret de Neville produced the writ of our Lord the King empowering her to appoint an attorney to do suit of that court for her, and she put in her place Peter de Waltone, and he was admitted [to act for her].

[*The Writ is attached to the Roll.*]

Edward, by the grace of God King of England, Lord of Ireland, and Duke of Acquitaine, to the Bailiffs of John de Warren, Earl of Surrey, greeting. Whereas by the Common Council of our realm it is provided that any freman who owes suit to the court of his lord may freely appoint his attorney to make suit for him, We enjoin you that you receive without hindrance on this occasion of our special grace the attorney whom Margaret, who was the wife of Geoffrey de Neville, shall wish by her letters patent to act as attorney in her place in doing suit at the court of your aforesaid lord of Wakefelde, in place of the said Margaret.

Witness Myself at Wynton, 11th day of September, in the thirteenth year of our reign.

[*On the back of the writ is the endorsement, " per Henricum de Kende."*]

STANLEY.—Symon, s. of Bateman, gives 6*d.* for license of agreeing with Elena Lewyn in a plea of trespass. Pledge : Robert Grave.

Elias Brodhege came and proved one red foal [*pultream*] to be his own, and found these pledges to answer therefor within a year and a day, or in regard to the value. Pledges : Richard de Bateley and . . . . . . It is valued at 2*s.*

BAILIFF ; manucaptors.—Robert the Milner of Ekeleshylle, taken and imprisoned by the indictment of 12 [jurors] of the tourn, finds these manucaptors to have him at the Gaol Delivery at York, viz.: William de Barneby, William de Birtone, Richard Clerk, Richard de Barneby, Thomas de Schefeud, and William de Dewsbiry, clerk, and he is handed over to the township, together with his goods, viz., 2 cows and 1 horse, that they may answer [for him].

SOWREBY.—John de Miggeley, for the escape of 3 horses twice, is amerced 6*d.*

William de Saltonstale, for the same in the case of 1 mare, 6*d.*

Seyr de Soureby, for 1 mare, 6*d.*

The same Seyr, because he detained a dog contrary to prohibition, with which he guarded his corn, 12*d.*

John Atte-townend, for the escape of 1 horse, 6*d.*

Alcok A' Wood [*de bosco*], for escape of 1 mare, 6*d.*

Thomas Fuller or Walker [*fullo*] of Werloley, for a certain oak tree felled, 12*d.*

Henry Lageman, for the escape of 6 beasts at the Baytinges, 12*d.*

William del Grene of Soland, for the escape of 9 beasts, 2s.

William de Wodethorpe, for escape of 2 horses, 12d.

John, s. of Symon, for escape of 1 horse, 6d.

OSSETE.—Richard Reaper [messor] of Ossete, for vert, 6d.

William de Waltone, for the same, 6d.

Hugh Cook of Horbiry, for withies, 6d.

Jordan Milner of the same, for the same, 6d.

WAKEFEUD.—Thomas Derneluve, for 2 pounds of dry wood [sicce], 6d.

BAILIFF.—Thomas the Wode was indicted at the Sheriff's Tourn, and absconded [retraxit se], and a cow was found at his house in Erdeslowe, which was delivered to William, s. of Thomas of the same, and to the township of the same [i.e. Erdeslowe] to answer therefor, and it is valued at half a mark.

WAKEFEUD.—Megge, wife of Robert the Roller, sues Robert Damsome in a plea of trespass. Pledge of prosecuting: John Kyde.

STANLEY.—William the Dyker gives 6d. for leave to take a house and a garden in Stanley of Adam, s. of Christiana, for the term of eight years, doing therefor, etc. Pledge: Robert Grave.

THORNES.—It is found by an inquisition of neighbours that William, s. of Thomas, carried away the hay of Richard Gerbot from a certain meadow belonging to the half oxgang of land that he previously had bought of the same William. Therefore, he is amerced, and paid a fine of 6d. Pledge: Thomas, his father.

The suit between Richard the Grete and Elias, his son, plaintiffs, and Margery, wife of John With-the-hounds, in a plea of trespass, is respited until the next court.

OSSETE.—The suit between Richard de Ossete, grave, and Henry the Schampiun is respited, etc.

BAILIFF.—The Abbot of Beghland gives half a mark for respite of the suit of Benteley [sic] that is pending until one month next after the feast of St. Michael. Pledge: Henry de Byri.

ALVERTHORPE.—Richard, s. of Philip de Alverthorpe, gives 12d. for an inquisition concerning 1½ acres of land with a certain meadow in the Morcroft and in the Brokmylndam, in the graveship of Alverthorpe, whereof German the Mercer holds half an acre, German, s. of Philip the Mercer, half an acre and a meadow, and German Swerd holds half an acre. Pledge: Adam Gerbot, and let the inquisition come at the next court, and the aforesaid persons be summoned.

THORNES.—Walter Ape sues Richard, s. of Gerbot, in a plea of trespass. Pledge of prosecuting the suit : Adam Smith [*faber*]. On being summoned they came by license to an agreement, and the amercement is condoned.

Sum of this Court : 21s. 2d.

COURT there, Friday, on the morrow of the Assumption of Blessed Mary [Aug. 15], in the year aforesaid.

ESSOINS.—Henry Campiun essoigned for the first time for suit, by Robert Pes. Pledge : Elias the Grave.

Thomas de Thornetone essoigned for first time, by Thomas de Wytteley. Pledge : John the Flemyng.

John de Querneby [did the like], by Adam de Daltone. Pledge : John the Flemyng.

Peter de Waltone, attorney of Lady Margaret de Neville, essoigned for the first time, by William Wytbelt. Pledge : Baldwin de Seyville.

William de Bately, attorney of Sir John de Horbiry, did likewise. Pledges : Geffray de Buterwrthe and Baldwin de Seyville.

Thomas de Schefeud essoigned for the second time against William, s. of Roger de Podesay, in a plea of trespass, by John Kay. Pledge : Richard the Clerk, and because he appeared a day is given him.

BAILIFF.—It is ordered to resummon Robert del Grene to answer to German the Mercer in a plea of debt.

Richard de Heytfeud essoigned for the second time against Elena, the d. of Richard de Soureby, in a plea of trespass, by German, s. of Philip. Pledge : John Kay, and because he appeared a day is given him.

HOLNE.—Adam de Beumond, for the escape of 2 beasts in Holne-frythe, 6d. Pledge : the Grave.

BAILIFF.—John Fox appeared against John the Hewar, as previously, *re* a demand of 20s.; as he laid his charge previously, and Richard the Clerk, Peter Terfy, and Henry, s. of Robert, say as their finding that the aforesaid John Fox sold to the same John the residue of the wood of Sepeley for 9 marks, whereof he paid 8 marks, and one mark is in arrears. It is, therefore, decided that he satisfy him in regard to the aforesaid mark, and that the said John Fox should claim in regard to the 20s. Therefore he is amerced, and paid a fine of 6d. Pledge : Hyk the Bailiff [*serviens*].

And because the said John the Hewart [*sic*] is convicted, therefore he is amerced, and paid a fine of 11*d*. Pledge [*blank*].

ALVERTHORPE.—Adam de Neutone sues Henry de Swynlingtone in a plea of land. Pledge : John Haskel. Let him be summoned.

HYPERUM.—Malina, wife of John de Hortone, essoigned for the first time against Henry, s. of Susanna, in a plea of trespass, by Henry the Grave. Pledge : Richard de Ossete, and as he appeared a day is given him.

BAILIFF.—Walter de Wodesem appeared against Henry Calf, and says that he, on Sunday next after the feast of the Apostles Peter and Paul last past, met him at Croftune brook, and beat him badly on the back and shoulders with a bow made of holly, to his damage and dishonour [appraised at] half a mark, and thereupon he entered suit. And he [the defendant] came and defends the force, etc., and all that he [the plaintiff] imputed against him. Therefore, let him go to the law. Pledge : the Grave of Daltone.

STANLEY.—Magge, wife of Robert the Roller, appeared against Robert Damsone, and says that he demised to her a meadow in Stanley for four crops [to be taken therefrom], whereof two crops are in arrear, and he says that really she took it for three crops, which she has had, and thereupon they put themselves on the verdict of Ralph, s. of Nicholas, and of John Tryk, who say that the aforesaid Robert Damsone demised the aforesaid meadow to the same Magge for three crops, which she entirely carried away. Therefore, she is amerced for making her plea, and paid a fine of 6*d*. Pledge : John Kay.

THORNES.—The suit between Robert the Grete and Elias, his son, plaintiffs, against Margery, wife of John With-the-hounds, is further respited.

STANLEY.—Nicholas de Wodehalle, for the escape of 4 cows into the herbage of Wodehalle, 12*d*. Pledge : Gerbot de Alverthorpe.

WODEHALLE.—Robert Gos, for the same in the case of 4 beasts, 4*d*. Pledge : Thomas, s. of Richard the Smith [*fabri*].

Robert de Bateley, for the escape of 6 beasts, 6*d*., and for 8, 8*d*.

Robert de Wyrumthorpe, for 6 beasts, 6*d*.

Robert the Turner, 1 beast, 1*d*.

Mariota, d. of Stephen, 2 beasts, 2*d*. Pledge : Robert de Bately.

Nicholas de Wodehalle, for the escape of 8 sheep, 6*d*.

John Fox, for the same many times, 2 horses, 6*d*. Pledge : Peter Terfi.

Robert de Batelay, for the same, 10 beasts twice, 10*d.*

Robert Gos, for the same, 1 beast, 3*d.*

Henry, s. of Robert, for the escape of 1 horse, 1*d.* Pledge : Thomas, s. of Ode.

Adam Tagge, for the same, 4 horses, 4*d.*

William Hogge, for the same, 7 beasts, 7*d.*

Robert Gos, for the same, 1 horse, 3*d.* Pledge : William Hogge.

Philip, s. of Bille, for the same, 5 sheep, 3*d.*

Walter, s. of German, for the same, 1 horse, 1*d.*

Henry the Nonne, for the same, 1 horse, 1*d.*

Nicholas de Wodehalle, for the same, 4 beasts, 12*d.* Pledge : Thomas, s. of Ode.

[*There is a note made by the clerk that all the persons named, as far as John Fox inclusive, " were attached in the year aforesaid," and those that follow " are attached in this present year."*]

HOLNE.—It was presented at the last Tourn at Birton that Robert Styrk, milner, had in Carthewrthe mill a false dish wherewith he took the multure of the Earl for 11 weeks to the damage of the whole country, until it was taken down [*deponabatur*] by Adam Cosin, who delivered to him another dish. The said dishes have been taken and measured, and the aforesaid dish of which the presentment was made has been found good, and the other, that was delivered as good by the said Adam Cosyn, false. And the inquisition and that the said Adam made this presentment through hate and odium. Therefore, he is amerced, and paid 1 mark as fine. Pledges : Richard de Scholes and Nicholas the Grave.

HYPERUM.—Roger del Clyf, because he refused to come when enjoined by the grave to aid in carrying the Earl's wine to Soureby, is amerced 6*d.*

William, s. of Peter, and Richard, s. of Henry, for the same, 6*d.*

Henry the Grave, because he refused to tarry with the wine, is amerced 6*d.*

Richard a' Wood [*de bosco*], John de Sonderland, William, s. of Oto, Richard, s. of Jordan, [all] amerced 6*d.* for same misdeameanour.

STANLEY.—Adam Tagge was summoned by the Grave of Stanley to come before the Steward to find pledges for his land ploughed in the wood [*lucratam sub bosco*]. He does not come, and is, therefore, amerced 6*d.*

Robert, his brother [?], and John Walhot, and Philip Bille, are also amerced 6d. for the same. Henry Stert, for the same, is amerced 3d. Robert, s. of Ralph Ters, is pardoned for the same. Henry Shorthose is amerced 12d., and John, s. of Jose, Richard de Lokwode, Martin Long, John Hogkebeger, and Robert Turner, 6d. each for same offence.

ALVERTHORPE.—Ralph de Ouchethorpe, Walter the Grave, Henry the Nonne, and Adam de Neutone, for the same above offence, are amerced 6d.

BAILIFF.—John Tobbing of Waltone sues Peter the Grave, Robert Attewell [ad fontem], Henry the Constable, and Walter de Wodehosem, on a plea of battery and blood. Pledges of prosecuting : Thomas At-Kirk [ad ecclesiam] and William Assolf. Therefore, let them be attached.

ALVERTHORPE.—The suit between Richard, s. of Philip de Alverthorpe, plaintiff, and German the Mercer, s. of Philip the Mercer, and German, s. of Richard Swerd, is respited until the parties come into the country. ————

[Wakefield].   COURT there the Friday next before the Nativity
          of Blessed Mary [8 Sept.], in the year, etc.

ESSOINS.—William de Bateley, attorney of Sir John de Horbiry, essoined from suit for the second time, by Adam de Mirefeud. Pledge : John the Flemyng.

SOUREBY.—Elena, d. of Richard de Soureby, appeared against Richard de Heytfeud, and says that he evilly beat her, but she did not bring an action [nullam arrainavit sectam] against him. Therefore it is decided that he go quit without a day, because he prayed for judgment [then and there ?], and she is amerced. The fine is condoned. Pledge : [blank].

ESSOINS.—Henry the Schampun essoined from suit for the second time, by Robert Pes. Pledge : Baldwin de Seyville.

BAILIFF.—It is ordered to distrain Robert del Grene to answer to German the Mercer in a plea of debt.

Thomas de Thornetone, who was essoined at the last court, came and placed himself in mercy. The fine is condoned that was due for the relaxation of the warranty of the said essoin.

Walter de Wodesem essoins for the first time in regard to the law that Henry Calf waged to him at the last court, by William Pymerige. Pledge : Peter de Waltone the grave, and because the aforesaid Walter neither came nor essoined, therefore, he and his pledges are amerced. He paid a fine of 6*d.*, and Walter is to recover his damages. Pledge : Malger de Wodesem.

Henry the Constable essoined for the first time against John Tobbing in a plea of trespass, by William, s. of Symon. Pledge : Peter de Waltone, and because he appeared a day is given.

Robert Atte-well essoined for the first time against John Tobbing in a plea of trespass, by John de Waltone. Pledge : Peter de Stansfeud, and because he appeared a day is given.

John Tobbyng appeared against Peter de Waltone the Grave, and says that he on Sunday on the feast of St. Giles last, assaulted him on the King's highway on the western side of the town of Scharnestone, together with Henry the Constable, Walter de Wodosem, and Robert Atte-well, and by [his] procuration and counsel he was beaten by the said Henry [*sic*] to the damages of 40*s.*, and thereupon he brought his suit. And he [the defendant] comes and defends the force, etc., and all that was laid against him. Let him go to the law. Pledge : Peter de Walton.

It is ordered to attach Walter de Wodosem to answer to John Tobbyng in a plea of trespass.

William, s. of Roger de Podesay, gives 2*s.* for license to compromise with Thomas de Schefeud in a plea of trespass. Pledge : Thomas de Thornetone. Provided that if the said William shall be able to prove against the said Thomas by the view of lawful men that he broke the agreement concerning 30 oaks, he shall make the restitution of them by the view of legal men.

SANDALE.—Alice, the d. of Adam del Stones, gives 2*s.* for license to take half an [acre ?] with buildings in the Neubiggeing of Adam, her father, to him and his heirs, etc., for ever, doing, etc. Pledge : William de Pleggewyke. She is [in consideration of this grant] to find all things necessary for her said father's food and clothing all the days of his life ; otherwise all the land shall revert to him.

BAILIFF.—John de Querneby and John de Mora made default. Let them be distrained.

ALVERTHORPE.—In the suit between Adam de Neutone and Henry de Swynlingtone, the parties have a love-day until the next court.

HYPERUM.—The suit between Malina, wife of John de Hortone, and Hanne, the s. of Susanna, is respited until the next court.

THORNES.—The suit between Robert the Grete and Elias, his son, and the wife of John With-the-hounds is respited until the next court.

L

OSSETE.—The suit between Richard Hog and Henry the Schampiun is further respited as before.

ALVERTHORPE.—Richard, s. of Gerbot, gives 2s. for license to take ½ a rood of land in the waste of Alverthorpe of Alexander Lucas, then Steward, paying thereout to the lord 1 halfpenny a year at the feast of St. Michael.

HOLNE.—The inquisition taken by the Steward as to who placed a false dish in Carthewrthe mill, comes by Richard de Grene, Gamel de Altstanley, Nicholas de Heppewrthe, William de Heppewrthe, Thomas de Hallomschyre, Alan de Wlvedale, Adam de Wlyvedale, Walter de Wlvedale, Thomas, son-in-law of Alcok, Richard the Carpenter, Adam Daniel, and Thomas de Slaghthayt, who say, etc., that Robert Styrk the Milner took down from the said miln a true [*rectum*] dish and placed a false one [there]. Therefore, he is amerced, and he paid a fine of 4s. Pledge: [*blank*].

SOUREBY.—Adam del Bothem, for the escape of 3 beasts in Mithomrode, 6d. Pledge: Robert the Grave.

John Attonehend, for the same, 11 beasts, 6d. Pledge: John, s. of Peter.

Elias de Waddeswrthe, for the same, 2 beasts, 12d. Pledge: Elias the Forester.

The same Elias, for the same, 1 beast in the Frythe, 6d. Pledge: Elias the Forester.

Alice de Wyttcley, for the escape of 2 beasts, 6d. Pledge: Richard Hodde.

Ivo de Werloley, for the same, 12 sheep, 6d. Pledge: John, s. of William.

John, s. of William, for the same, 4 sheep, 6d. Pledge: Ivo de Werloley.

Ivo de Soland, for the escape of 1 beast, 3d. Pledge: Thomas de Asses.

Thomas de Asses, for 1 beast, 6d. Pledge: Ivo de Soland.

Hanne de Lytheseles, 1 beast, 6d. Pledge: Thomas de Asses.

Alan a' Wood [*de bosco*] of Rastrik, for 1 beast, 6d. Pledge: William, s. of Alcok.

John, s. of Elias de Barkesland, 1 beast, 6d. Pledge: John, s. of William.

John, s. of William, 1 beast, 6d. Pledge: John, s. of Elias.

Adam, s. of Andrew, 1 beast, 6d. Pledge: Geppe, s. of Adam.

Geppe, s. of Adam, for 1 beast, 6d. Pledge: Adam, s. of Andrew.

HOLNE.—Thomas, s. of Robert de Carlecotes, for the escape of 7 beasts, 2s. Pledge : Henry Fokelstone.

Robert the Harpour, because he mowed grass in the pasture, 12d. Pledge : the Grave.

STANLEY.—Robert Typet, for a cartload of dry wood, 6d. Pledge : Adam, his father.

ALVERTHORPE.—Richard, s. of Bron, for vert, 6d. Pledge : Philip Torald.

Walter, s. of German, for the same, 6d. Pledge : Ralph de Ouchethorpe.

Ralph de Ouchethorpe, for the same, 6d. Pledge : Walter, s. of German.

BAILIFF.—John de Kyrkeby sues William, s. of Peter de Floke-tone, on a plea of taking cattle. Pledge of prosecution : William Hyngres.

Thomas, s. of Robert Aleyn, sues Henry the Schampiun on a plea of trespass. Pledge of prosecution : William de Metheley.

RASTRIK.—Thomas the Milner sues John Fox on a plea of battery and blood. Pledge of prosecution : John de Querneby.

SOUREBY.—William, s. of John de Stansfeud, sues Richard del Estwode on a plea of taking cattle. Pledge of prosecution : Reginald Tannar.

The land of Seyr de Soureby is in the hands of the lord, because he is dead.

OSSETE.—Nalle de Ossete, wife of John Certe, sues Richard Hyrming and Elias the Schampiun on a plea of trespass. They are attached. Pledge of prosecution : Richard.

COURT there on Friday next before the feast of St. Michael [Sept. 29], in the year and time aforesaid.

BAILIFF.—Henry the Constable essoined for the second time against John Tobbyng on a plea of trespass, by Symon, s. of Henry, and Bate, s. of Hugh, and because he appeared a day is given.

John Tobbing appeared against Robert Atte-well, and says that he on Sunday on the Feast of St. Giles last past assaulted him in the King's highway on the western side of the town of Scharnestone with malicious words, and then with a hazel stick struck him on the head and shoulders, to his damage and dishonour of the value of 40s. And, thereupon, he [the plaintiff] entered his suit. And he [the defendant] comes and defends the force, etc., and all that was charged against him. Therefore, he is to go to the law. Pledge : John Malefox [?] de Waltone.

It is ordered to distrain further Robert del Grene to answer German the Mercer on a plea of debt.

It is ordered to make a better distress on Walter de Wodosem to answer John Tobbing on a plea of battery.

Peter de Waltone the Grave came and made his law as he ought against John Tobbing, as he was charged to do at the last court. Therefore, let the said Peter go quit without a day and the said John be amerced. He made a fine of 12*d*. Pledge : Thomas de Erd..

HYPERUM.—Malina, the wife of John de Hortone, gives 6*d*. for leave to compromise with Hanne, s. of Susanna, in a plea of trespass. Pledge : Henry the Grave.

ALVERTHORPE.—It is ordered to distrain Henry de Swynlingtone to answer Adam de Neutone in a plea of trespass at the next court.

BAILIFF.—John de Querneby made default at the last court, and found John the Flemang as pledge to make satisfaction for it at the coming of the Steward. He is released by the Steward.

John de Mora made similar default, and found Thomas de Thornetone as pledge to make satisfaction at the coming of the Steward. He is released by the Steward.

John de Kyrkeby gives 6*d*. for leave to compromise with William, s. of Peter of Floketone, in a plea of taking cattle. Pledge : William Hyngres.

Thomas, s. of Robert Alayn, and Henry the Schampiun, have a love-day until the next court.

Thomas Milner sues John Fox, and says that he has wounded him, and thereupon comes the said John and gives 6*d*. for leave to compromise with the said Thomas. He will give him 2*s*. at the next court, and 2*s*. at the Feast of All Saints. Pledges : John the Grave of Rastrik and Richard de Bateley.

SOUREBY.—Geoffrey, s. of Seyr de Soureby, gives 4*s*. for the relief of the land and houses of his father, doing, etc. Pledge : Elias the Grave.

HOLNE.—Robert the Tynker imprisoned on suspicion of theft, found these manucaptors to have his body at the next court, viz.: Thomas de Hallomschyre, Jordan Milner, Gamel de Alstanley, and Robert Lorimer.

Gamel de Alstanley, because he entertained the said Robert the Tynker in the face of a prohibition, is amerced, and paid a fine of 12*d*. Pledge : Thomas de Allomschire.

STANLEY.—Nicholas de Wodehalle gives 6*d*. for the holding of an inquisition as to who grazed the grass of the Earl at Wodehalle, and [to prove] that his beasts were not taken there. So let the inquisition come at the next court.

BAILIFF.—Robert de Donecastre sues William, s. of Ralph Smith, on a plea of battery and blood. Pledge of prosecution : Henry Waryn. Therefore, he is attached.

Henry Waryn sues John Patrik on a plea of taking cattle. Pledge of prosecution : Thomas de Donefeld. Therefore, etc.

RASTRIK.—Adam de Gledehylle sues Alan, s. of Ellen, on a plea of a house [*de placito unius domus*]. Pledge of prosecution : John the Barne.

STANLEY.—Enoc Ro sues Richard, s. of Locok, on a plea of battery. Pledge of prosecution : Philip the Syur.

APPENDIX I.

THE COMPUTUS OF 1305.

Under " Wakefield with its Soke," we have the rents received for the tenants there for each of the three rent days in the year, viz. Michaelmas, Lady Day, and Easter. The rents for the year were:—

	£	s.	d.
Free Tenants - - - - - - -	22	10	0
Neifs - - - - - - - -	106	18	3
Rents of divers tenants at Horbury - -	4	0	0
From Nicholas de Worteley for the lord's mill-pond at Horbury, to be placed on the earl's land. Payable at Martinmas - - -	1	0	0
Acquittance of the neifs in the Soke of Wakefield	5	6	8
Custom of swine - - - - - -	2	10	0
Six score hens, rent of, at Alverthorpe - -	—		

Demesne Lands.

	£	s.	d.
Rents of demesne lands of the Earl at Sandal let to farm - - - - - -	0	18	9¼
Do., at Horbury - - - - - -	1	6	8
Do., of 12 acres at Wakefield - - - -	1	10	0
Do., of a certain pasture there - - -	0	7	10

Town and Mills.

	£	s.	d.
Farm of the Town and Mills of Wakefield, and of 2 mills at Sandal - - - - -	46	14	4
Farm of fulling mill there - - - -	1	10	0
,, Cartworth mill - - - - -	5	0	0
,, Soyland mill - - - - -	1	0	0
,, Rastrick mill - - - - -	5	6	8

Pannage.

	£	s.	d.
Pannage of swine there this year - - -	1	15	9

Timber.

	£	s.	d.
Timber blown down by the wind there - -	18	0	0
Pleas and Perquisites of the Courts there between Michaelmas and Easter - -	12	6	8

[Sundries.]

£6 13s. 4d. from William of Wakefield in part
    payment of £56 issuing from 80 acres of
    underwood at Wakefield sold to the said
    William by Master Richard de Haveringes.

The total receipts for 'Wakefield and its soke are reckoned up
to £173 1s. 8¾d.

We then have these disbursements:

Wages of Foresters.

Wages of Thomas de Sandal, Constable of Sandal Castle,
and Head Forester of Wakefield, Sowerbyshire, and Holmfirth,
£5 17s. 10d., from Michaelmas to Easter, 202 days, receiving 7d.
a day, whereas there used to be 3 keepers who took for their wages
11d. a day.

Wages of 9 foresters and one " paler " [*palicarii*] under the
same Thomas in the same keepership [*custodia*] during the aforesaid
time, viz. William de Bosco [and] Thomas de Aula, foresters in
Sowerbyshire, William de Heitfeld, forester in Holmfirth, Adam le
Hunte [and] John son of Adam le Hunte, foresters in the New Park
of Wakefield; Hugh de Balne & Robert del Lightes, foresters in
the Out Wood [*bosco forinseco*] there, John de Reygate, forester in
the Old Park there; Robert son of Nelle, forester in Thurstanhawe;
and Robert de Wrengate, keeper of the palisade there, £8 8s. 4¼d.,
each of them receiving 1d. a day.   Sum: £14 6s. 2d. without livery
[*roba*].

Paid to John de Dancastre, Steward of the lands and tenements
that belonged to John de Warren, Earl of Surrey, in the County
of York, which John [de Dancastre] was associated with Master
Richard de Haveringes in the custody of the said lands, etc., 10
marks as his moiety.   Sum: £6 13s. 4d.

APPENDIX II.

THE SHEFFIELD MS.

View of the Computus of John de Amyas, farmer of the Town, Market, and Mills of Wakefeld and of the Soke of the same, from the Feast of the Annunciation of Blessed Mary in the 9th year of the reign of King Edward [1316] until the Feast of St. Michael next following in the 10th year.

Receipts.—The same answers for £48 17s. 9½d. of arrears of the preceding View; for £62 from the farm of Wakefeud in rents, farms, tolls, and other issues, [also] from the perquisites of the Burgesses' Court, and of the fair [*fori*] within and without the town, together with the fulling mill and two mills in Wakefeld, of the mill of Thurstanhawe, the mill of Horbury, and the mill of Cartworthe farmed of the lord for a term of four years . . . . . .

Sum of the whole Receipts together with the arrears, £110 17s. 9½d.

Expenses. — Of these, there has been delivered [paid] to Sir Matthew the chaplain, the Earl's Receiver, [as] by one letter patent of the same Sir Matthew remaining with the said John, £48 17s. 9½d. Also delivered to the same Sir Matthew [as] by one letter patent remaining with the said John, £52. Sum, £100 17s. 9½d.

Item, for two millstones bought for the mill of Thurstenhaghe, 8d. For making the wheels of the two Wakefeld mills, 6s. 8d. Also for two millstones on the . . . of Wakefeld, 8s. Also in regard to two millstones for the Wakefeld mills for the moiety of their cost, 4s., and the other moiety of the cost the customary [tenants] of the Soke have, according to custom, paid. For repairing the walls of the same mill, 2s. For an allowance made to the said John for the farm of Cartworthe mill by the same [John], taken and delivered unto him to farm by the Steward from the term of St. Michael, £8 14s. 4d. Sum, £10 2s. 0d.

Sums of all the expenses and payments, £110 0s. 9½d., and so there is owing to the said John the farmer, 2s., which will be paid to him as an allowance in the Computus made in the following year.

Cartworth Mill, 9 Edw. II.

From the " Computus of Adam Strakeys, grave of Holne, for the 9th year of the reign of King Edward [II], from the feast of the Annunciation of the Blessed Virgin Mary to the feast of St. Michael next following in the same year."

Expenses. — For two millwheels bought for Cartworth mill, 5s. For one wheel made for the said mill out of the lord's timber, 2s. 1d.   For two new chests [*archis*] bought for the new mill . . .

For one iron spindle [*fusillus*] repairing for Cartworth mill, 2s.

For one wooden ring for the millstone of the same mill, 4d.

For making a new " hirst " [1] for receiving the flour outside the millstones, with nails for the same, 3s. 1d.

---

[1] Miln-hirst is the place on which the *cribs* or crubs (as they call them) lie, within which the millstone *hirsts* or *hirsills*. Jameson, *Scottish Dictionary*.

NOTES.

Page 1, line 27. John, son of Sir John, Earl of Warren, inducted to the church of Dewsbury, July 18, 1293.

Page 2, line 19. Henry de Percy, son of Henry de Percy and of Eleanor his wife, daughter of John, Earl of Warren and Surrey. He purchased Alnwick Castle, died 1315, and was buried in Fountains Abbey. See *Extinct and Dormant Peerages*, by J. W. Clay, p. 161.

Page 4, line 3. Widow of Geoffrey FitzRobert, Lord of Raby, etc. She was daughter of Sir John Longvillers. She held three carucates of land at Cleckheaton. See Kirkby's *Inquest*, and *Wakefield Court Rolls*, vol. i, p. 184.

Page 11, line 35. Hence "posnet" (?).

Page 14, line 3. See Appendix II, and vol. ii, p. 117.

Page 18, line 17. See vol. i, p. 283.

Page 20, line 31. See particulars of the lease, vol. ii, p. 117, and Appendix II.

Page 21, line 39. See pp. 25 and 42.

Page 25, line 25. See p. 1.

Page 26, line 2. See pp. 21 and 42.

Page 39, line 12. "Serviens" is here translated bailiff, "ballivus."

Page 39, line 22. ? A broad dole, *i.e.* broad strip of meadow.

Page 42, line 28. See pp. 21, 25, 42.

Page 46, line 14. "Marrue" should probably be "Marwe."

Page 52, line 27. *Sic, cf.* p. 26.

Page 55, line 38. See vol. ii, p. 201, also Introduction to vol. ii, p. vi.

Page 56, line 15. Though generally members of this family at this time are described as "de Seyvile," sometimes we find "le Seyvile."

Page 61, line 30. Eatage.

Page 62, line 5. See p. 59.

Page 66, line 22. See vol. ii, p. vi.

Page 67, line 31. See Appendix II.

Page 82, line 29. *i.e.* That they might have mainprise instead of being imprisoned, the pledges for their appearance at York being the six persons named.

Page 83, line 4. "Bullace, a small black and tartish plum." *Halliwell*. "Bolaces and blackeberies that on breres growen." *Will. of Palerne*, ed. Skeat, 1909.

Page 91, line 38. See Introduction, vol. ii, p. xx.

Page 98, line 20. See Introduction, vol. ii, p. xx.

Page 111, line 38. Ingelard Turbard, first Vicar of Halifax, inducted 1274, died 1315.

Page 113, line 3. See p. 111.

Page 113, line 29. See p. 108.

Page 120, line 15. Sir Richard de Hilagh, instituted 1309.

Page 140, line 16. See p. 111. He died May 28, 1315. *Watson.*

Page 154, line 15. See *Kirklees Priory*, by S. J. Chadwick, F.S.A., *Yorkshire Archæological Journal*, vol. xvi, p. 321.

Page 158, line 29. Proctor of the monks of St. Pancras, at Lewes, who held the rectorial manor of Halifax.

Page 166, line 33. A "windle" equals a bushel. *Halliwell.*

Page 172, line 31. ? Byland.

Page 175, line 27. See page 169.

Page 178, line 15. See pp. 169, 175.

INDEX OF PERSONS AND PLACES.

M

151, 177, 180; Matthew de, 12; Philip de, 4, 31, 130; Robert de, 1, 18; Thomas de, 78; William,130
Morcroft, Morecroftes, le Morecroftes, ˜21, 38, 41, 141, 172
More, Adam del, 77; John atte *or* de la, 38, 56, 82, 96, 124, 148, 154; Philip de la, 101; William de, 159
Moris, John, 170
Morlay, Morley, 52, 133, 134; John de, 52; William *or* William de, 120, 132
Moseley Hay, 84
Mous, Mouse, John, 95; Magota, 33
Moyce, Margery, 71
Murre, Morre, Custance, 133, 134, 137
Mythumrode, Mithomrode, 110, 178

Nabbe, Robert s. of, 39
Nalk, Nalkes, 105, 141; John s. of, 93, 150
Nalle, Nelle, Adam s. of, 100; Alice d. of, 29; Henry s. of, 7; Hugh s. of, 44; Ivo s. of, 30; John s. of, 125; Richard s. of, 133, 150; Thomas s. of, 131
Nautherde, Nauthird, Henry the, 30, 55, 84, 94, 102, 103
Nelot, Nelotes, Nelottes, John, 33, 89, 103, 139, 156; Margery, 144; Robert, 36; William, 10, 40, 55, 57, 94, 99, 102, 107, 126, 137, 144
Nettelton, Nettilton, John de, 78, 120; Lovecokes de, 47
Neubigging, the, Neubigginges, le, Newbigging, Newebigging, Newebygging, Newebyggyng, Nubigging, 60, 83, 140, 177; Agnes, 145, 149; Geoffrey del, 145, 149; Peter del, 105; Robert del, 69, 89, 96; Sybil del, 22
Neuson, Preceptor of, 167
Neuton, Neutone, Neweton, Newton, 3, 26, 84, 88, 102, 111, 128, 152; Adam de, 174, 176, 177, 180; Field *or* Fields, 27, 88; Ralph de, 115, 130, 133; Robert, 115, 130, 133; Walter de, 17, 21; William de, 17, 21, 88, 155
Neutonclyf, 36
Nevil, Nevile, Nevill, Neville, Nevylle, Neyvile, Dame Margaret de *or* Lady Margaret de *or* Margaret de, 1, 4, 23, 28, 36, 38, 49, 59, 64, 66, 86, 96, 108, 133, 140, 143, 151, 157, 170, 171, 173; Geoffrey de, 171
Newcastle, John de, 157
Newmarket, Matilda de, 147, 157
New Park, 42, 83
Nicholas, Adam s. of, 13, 113; John

s. of, 100, 108; Matilda d. of, 142, 151; Ralph s. of, 61, 64, 157, 174; Richard s. of, 80; Robert s. of, 81; the Grave, 175; William s. of, 33, 157
Nodder, Noddere, Nordar, Henry the, 59; Hugh the, 4, 23, 28, 36, 38, 49, 64, 66, 86, 96, 108, 133, 140, 143, 151, 157,
Nodger, Nicholas, 5, 22, 26, 58, 84, 103; Robert, 103
Nondy, Nundy, Alice, 93, 102; Thomas, 93, 102
Nonne, Nonnes, Nonnys, Nunne, Henry *or* Henry the, 19, 23, 27, 31, 32, 126, 128, 132, 137, 139, 141, 152, 158, 175, 176; John s. of Henry the, 128, 158; Robert de, 142; Thomas s. of Henry the, 158; William del, 165
Normanton, Normantone, Northmantone, 125, 127, 128, 132, 166; John de, 143; Parson of, 156
Normaund, Normaunt, Edmund the, 14, 18, 23, 28, 31, 38, 41, 49, 50, 53, 56; John, 50
Northclif, Northclifes, Northclyf, Northclyffes, Alice de, 76; Henry de, 41, 67, 76, 109, 142; John de, 76, 163; Roger de, 76; Thomas de, 98
Northend, Northenes, John de, 65; Thomas del, 61
Northewod, Northwod, Northwode, John de, 34, 37, 63, 70, 83, 88
Northland, 65, 72, 73, 75, 87, 141, 148; Adam, 72; Christiana de, 75; Hanne de, 116; Henry, 121; Hugh de, 22; John de, 73, 74; Nalle *or* Nalle de, 121, 129; Richard, 75; Thomas de, 1; William de, 72, 116, 129
Northorum, Northourum, Northourn, 9, 19, 24, 29, 46, 76, 117, 119, 120, 136, 163, 164; Alice de, 10, 76; Christiana de, 18, 46; Hugh de, 150; John, 46, 162; Jordan de, 46, 131, 135, 136, 137, 162; Matilda de, 10; Richard, 46, 76, 131, 135, 136, 137, 162; Robert de, 18, 46; Walter de, 15, 46, 76; William de, 20
Northourumclyf, 20
Norton, William de, 1
Noteschage, Notschagh, John de, 70, 74
Notton, William de, 17, 20, 92

Odam, Walter *or* Walter de, 23, 37, 84, 138

Ode, Thomas s. of, 175
Okerrodes, Adam de, 63
Okes, Oke, Okys, del, 10; Adam del,
22; Robert atte *or* del, 52, 112;
William del, 1, 14, 18, 20, 28, 49,
56, 61, 64, 66, 82, 86, 91, 97, 99,
100, 108, 109, 133, 136, 146, 148,
151, 156
Oldefeld, Oldfeld, Roger del, 80, 122,
123
Olderode, Oldrode, 50; Adam de, 75,
150
Oldman, Thomas, 67
Old Park, 16, 21, 102
Olyve, William, 106
Osset, Ossete, Ossett, Ossettes, 3, 4,
10, 14, 15, 17, 18, 21, 23, 26, 27,
28, 29, 30, 31, 32, 34, 35, 36, 37,
38, 39, 40, 42, 43, 51, 52, 55, 56,
59, 60, 61, 63, 65, 66, 67, 68, 71, 85,
88, 89, 90, 92, 94, 96, 98, 101, 103,
106, 107, 109, 111, 112, 114, 115,
127, 129, 130, 132, 135, 136, 137,
138, 139, 141, 143, 145, 147, 151,
153, 155, 156, 158, 167, 172, 178,
179; Adam serving-man to Robert
de, 17; Agnes de, 51; Bate de, 51;
Eva de, 83; Grave of, 112, 114;
John de, 41, 83, 90, 97, 109, 112;
Matthew de, 43, 90, 92, 98, 101;
Nalle de, 179; Richard de, 41, 51,
83, 90, 97, 109, 111, 172, 174;
Robert de, 17; Swayn de, 4, 83,
129; William de, 86, 154
Otes, Thomas, 55; William son-in-
law of, 65
Oto, Alice, 22; Cecilia, 22; William
s. of, 175
Otteley, Richard de, 22
Ouchethorp, Ouchethorpe (Ouche-
phorp (*sic*)), 15, 42, 62; Eva, 86;
Ralph de, 176, 179; William de, 86
Ourum, Ourom, 65; Richard de, 118;
Robert de, 61
Ovenden, Ovendene, Alexander de,
65; Big Hugh of, 57; Hugh de, 57;
John, 57; Ralph de, 159, 160;
Symon de, 65; William de, 65
Overdene, Grave of, 24
Overhall, Alice, 124; Michael de, 124;
William del, 102, 128
Overthwong, Overthwonges, 29, 80
Overton, Nicholas, 92; Roger de, 92
Oxnop, Adam de, 133

Page, John, 4, 37, 106, 131, 134
Painelhoton, Paynelhoton, 40, 49, 53
Painter, Payntour, Peyntour, Adam
or Adam the, 6, 16, 137, 141;
William the, 115, 131

Paldene, Adam de, 22; Henry de, 87
Panteria, Henry de, 58
Parson of Wakefeld, 125
Parsonsflat, the, 149
Pasmer, Passemer, Passmer, John,
131; Richard, 4, 31, 40, 42, 66, 83
Patrick, Patrickes, Patrik, Patrike,
Patrykes, John, 1, 5, 17, 18, 20,
23, 25, 28, 31, 38, 49, 50, 51, 66,
68, 69, 82, 85, 86, 91, 96, 97, 99,
100, 108, 124, 136, 143, 147, 151,
181; Robert, 1, 68, 82
Paulinus, John s. of, 164
Pawe, Adam, 51
Paytur, Symon the, 93
Pedder, Richard the, 121
Pede, Peede, 12, 79, 142, 151, 157
Pees, Pes, Hugh, 153, 155, 156;
John, 58; Robert, 35, 38, 39, 41,
51, 52, 59, 83, 87, 91, 106, 139,
147, 173, 176; Thomas, 15, 19, 21,
35, 41, 51, 58, 64, 101, 106, 156
Peger, Pegher, Agnes, 85; Alice, 58;
Amabilla, 63, 64, 66; John, 3, 4,
5, 16, 33, 37, 99; Magota, 93; Mar-
gery, 99, 126; Richard, 32, 42, 53,
103; Robert, 16, 24, 63, 64, 92, 99,
112, 115, 157, 158; Roger, 66;
William, 58, 90, 93, 102, 134
Pek, Robert, 65
Pelle, Robert s. of, 69, 106, 132, 134,
150, 152, 154; Thomas s. of, 89,
92, 98, 102, 103, 128, 145, 150,
151, 154
Penne, Peny, Adam s. of, 58; John,
153; Robert, 153
Percy, Dom. Henry de, 2
Pesci, Pescy, Robert, 23, 102, 114
Peter, Adam s. of, 60, 131; Elias *or*
Elyas s. of, 4, 33, 99, 101, 103;
Henry s. of, 46; Master, 162;
Richard s. of, 138; Roger s. of, 158;
William s. of, 46, 70, 110, 175
Peti, William, 138
Petit, William, 107
Petronilla, Petronille, Dionysia, 161;
John, 161; Robert s. of, 31, 39
Peukes, John, 57
Philip, Elyas s. of, 73; German s. of,
173; Hugh s. of, 144; John s. of,
90, 103, 144; Richard s. of, 28, 31,
32, 42, 155; Thomas, 28, 94
Pichak, Pichake, William, 63, 85
Pikenote, William, 137
Pikescolle, Pickerstulle, Pykescull,
Philip, 86, 139, 141
Pikeston, Pykeston, John, 8, 44, 72,
73, 116, 144
Pimerich, Pimeriche, Pymerich, Py-
merige, Agnes, 29, 31; John, 29,

Sagher, Segar, William the, 81, 124
St. Ambrose, 38
St. Boniface, 140
St. Dionysius, 3
St. Dunstan, 43, 46, 48, 49
St. Edmund, 18
St. Faith, 1
St. George, 41
St. Giles, 177, 179
St. Gregory, 36, 42
St. Hilary, 25
St. James, 146, 167, 169
St. John Bap., 64, 143, 154
St. Laurence, 61
St. Luke, 6, 8, 10, 72, 76, 79, 82
St. Margaret, 59, 158, 161
St. Martin, 86
St. Mary Magdalene, 166
St. Matthew, 66
St. Matthias, 108
St. Michael, 172, 178, 179
St. Nicholas, 91
St. Oswald, 151, 159
St. Paul, 104
St. Peter, 69, 170
St. Peter in Cathedra, 31
St. Swithin, Swythin, John de, 4, 22, 84
St. Thomas, 23, 96
St. Tiburtius, 133
St. Valerian, 133
St. Wilfrid, 5
SS. Peter and Paul, 56, 174
SS. Simon and Jude, 14
Sakeldene, 159
Sale, Salie, Henry del, 160; Robert de la, 156; Thomas de la, 82
Salman, John, 27, 33
Salsa-mara, Richard de, 23, 25, 28, 36, 38, 53, 59, 66, 68, 82, 85, 97, 109, 124, 133, 136, 140, 143, 148, 154
Salter, Adam, 78
Saltonstal, Saltonstall, 44, 57, 72, 73, 132, 141, 148; Dairy, 132; Elias de, 1, 6; Eva, 45; Henry de, 7, 8, 17, 45, 50, 72, 74, 75, 112, 117, 119, 131, 140, 142, 147; Ivo de, 1, 6, 30, 75, 109, 110; John, 44; Richard de, 8, 13, 18, 22, 30, 45, 61, 72, 73, 109, 116, 133, 148; Robert de, 1, 6, 7, 8, 44, 70, 72, 90, 97, 105, 116, 128, 129, 131, 136; Thomas de, 57, 132, 133; William de, 8, 18, 39, 110, 117, 159, 171
Sandal Castle, 21
Sandal, Sandale, 2, 4, 5, 14, 17, 19, 20, 21, 22, 23, 28, 30, 31, 34, 35, 39, 40, 41, 54, 56, 58, 59, 60, 61, 67, 68, 69, 71, 83, 85, 86, 88, 90, 91, 92, 96, 97, 98, 99, 100, 102, 103,

104, 105, 106, 107, 110, 111, 112, 113, 115, 124, 125, 126, 127, 128, 129, 130, 131, 132, 134, 135, 137, 138, 139, 140, 141, 143, 145, 146, 147, 148, 150, 151, 152, 153, 154, 155, 156, 177; Geoffrey de, 130; Gilbert de, 89; Grave of, 31; Henry de, 140; John, 130; Robert de, 123, 131, 132; Thomas, 131, 132; William de, 2, 16, 19, 27, 34, 40, 55, 123, 126, 132
Sandiforth, Richard de, 160
Sara, Sarah, Adam s. of, 78; Robert s. of, 142, 165
Satilworth, 72; see also Sadelworth
Saucemer, Saucemier, Sausemer, Saussemer, Saussemere, Richard or Richard the, 14, 19, 38, 41, 104, 108, 131; Thomas, 65; William, 131
Sawyer, Henry the, 11; Philip the, 23, 153
Saynt, Agnes d. of, 40
Scammendene, Skamendene, 105
Scapman, Hugh, 33
Scauberkes, Robert the, 105
Scelveley, Schelveley, Christiana de, 13; Matthew de, 41
Schacer, Emmote the, 33; Philip, 33
Schage, Schaghe, Adam del, 8, 45, 60, 70, 74; Henry del, 133
Schagh, Adam del, 116; John del, 78; William del, 78
Schagheley, 129
Schakelokes, Adam, 125
Schambandene, William de, 166
Schampiun, Campiun, Elias the, 179; Henry the, 170, 172, 173, 176, 178, 179, 180
Scharneston, Scharnestone, 177, 179; John de, 132; Robert de, 158
Scharp, John, 146; William, 67, 98, 142
Schaveley, 123
Schaylhora, Gilbert, 67
Schefeld, Scheffeld, Schefeud, Scheffeud, Dom. Thomas de, 102; Ralph de, 97; Thomas de, 2, 169, 171, 173, 177; William de, 48
Schellay, Schelley, 42, 50, 81, 84; Christiana de, 81, 106, 123; Henry de, 80, 87, 101, 109, 123; John, 81; Matthew de, 35; Margaret, 135; Margery, 137, 141; Nicholas de, 81; Mokoc de, 78; Robert de, 130, 153; Roger, 78; Thomas de, 135, 137, 141, 153, 155; William de, 153
Schepe, Henry, 5, 33
Schepehird, see Shepherd
Scheplay, Schepeley, Schipleye, 68, 87, 122, 124, 139, 147, 157; Clerk of, 79; John de, 9, 37, 43, 47, 68,

INDEX OF SUBJECTS.

INDEX TO APPENDICES.

INDEX TO INTRODUCTION.

J. Whitehead & Son, Printers, Leeds and London.

For EU product safety concerns, contact us at Calle de José Abascal, 56–1°,
28003 Madrid, Spain or eugpsr@cambridge.org.

www.ingramcontent.com/pod-product-compliance
Ingram Content Group UK Ltd.
Pitfield, Milton Keynes, MK11 3LW, UK
UKHW010040140625
459647UK00012BA/1506